Real-Time Big Data Analytics

Design, process, and analyze large sets of complex data in real time

Sumit Gupta

Shilpi Saxena

BIRMINGHAM - MUMBAI

Real-Time Big Data Analytics

First published: February 2016

Production reference: 1230216

Published by Packt Publishing Ltd.
Livery Place
35 Livery Street
Birmingham B3 2PB, UK.

ISBN 978-1-78439-140-9

www.packtpub.com

Credits

Authors
Sumit Gupta
Shilpi Saxena

Reviewer
Pethuru Raj

Commissioning Editor
Akram Hussain

Acquisition Editor
Larissa Pinto

Content Development Editor
Shweta Pant

Technical Editors
Taabish Khan
Madhunikita Sunil Chindarkar

Copy Editors
Roshni Banerjee
Yesha Gangani
Rashmi Sawant

Project Coordinator
Kinjal Bari

Proofreader
Safis Editing

Indexer
Tejal Daruwale Soni

Graphics
Kirk D'Penha
Disha Haria

Production Coordinator
Manu Joseph

Cover Work
Manu Joseph

About the Authors

Sumit Gupta is a seasoned professional, innovator, and technology evangelist with over 100 man months of experience in architecting, managing, and delivering enterprise solutions revolving around a variety of business domains, such as hospitality, healthcare, risk management, insurance, and so on. He is passionate about technology and overall he has 15 years of hands-on experience in the software industry and has been using Big Data and cloud technologies over the past 4 to 5 years to solve complex business problems.

Sumit has also authored *Neo4j Essentials* (`https://www.packtpub.com/big-data-and-business-intelligence/neo4j-essentials`), *Building Web Applications with Python and Neo4j* (`https://www.packtpub.com/application-development/building-web-applications-python-and-neo4j`), and *Learning Real-time Processing with Spark Streaming* (`https://www.packtpub.com/big-data-and-business-intelligence/learning-real-time-processing-spark-streaming`), all with Packt Publishing.

I want to acknowledge and express my gratitude to everyone who has supported me in writing this book. I am thankful for their guidance, valuable, constructive, and friendly advice.

Shilpi Saxena is an IT professional and also a technology evangelist. She is an engineer who has had exposure to various domains (machine to machine space, healthcare, telecom, hiring, and manufacturing). She has experience in all the aspects of conception and execution of enterprise solutions. She has been architecting, managing, and delivering solutions in the Big Data space for the last 3 years; she also handles a high-performance and geographically-distributed team of elite engineers.

Shilpi has more than 12 years (3 years in the Big Data space) of experience in the development and execution of various facets of enterprise solutions both in the products and services dimensions of the software industry. An engineer by degree and profession, she has worn varied hats, such as developer, technical leader, product owner, tech manager, and so on, and she has seen all the flavors that the industry has to offer. She has architected and worked through some of the pioneers' production implementations in Big Data on Storm and Impala with autoscaling in AWS.

Shilpi has also authored *Real-time Analytics with Storm and Cassandra* (`https://www.packtpub.com/big-data-and-business-intelligence/learning-real-time-analytics-storm-and-cassandra`) with Packt Publishing.

I would like to thank and appreciate my son, Saket Saxena, for all the energy and effort that he has put into becoming a diligent, disciplined, and a well-managed 10 year old self-studying kid over last 6 months, which actually was a blessing that enabled me to focus and invest time into the writing and shaping of this book. A sincere word of thanks to Impetus and all my mentors who gave me a chance to innovate and learn as a part of a Big Data group.

About the Reviewer

Pethuru Raj has been working as an infrastructure architect in the IBM Global Cloud Center of Excellence (CoE), Bangalore. He finished the CSIR-sponsored PhD degree at Anna University, Chennai and did the UGC-sponsored postdoctoral research in the department of Computer Science and Automation, Indian Institute of Science, Bangalore. He also was granted a couple of international research fellowships (JSPS and JST) to work as a research scientist for 3.5 years in two leading Japanese universities. He worked for Robert Bosch and Wipro Technologies, Bangalore as a software architect. He has published research papers in peer-reviewed journals (IEEE, ACM, Springer-Verlag, Inderscience, and more). His LinkedIn page is at `https://in.linkedin.com/in/peterindia`.

Pethuru has also authored or co-authored the following books:

- *Cloud Enterprise Architecture*, CRC Press, USA, October 2012 (`http://www.crcpress.com/product/isbn/9781466502321`)
- *Next-Generation SOA*, Prentice Hall, USA, 2014 (`http://www.amazon.com/Next-Generation-SOA-Introduction-Service-Orientation/dp/0133859045`)
- *Cloud Infrastructures for Big Data Analytics*, IGI Global, USA, 2014 (`http://www.igi-global.com/book/cloud-infrastructures-big-data-analytics/95028`)
- *Intelligent Cities: Enabling Tools and Technology*, CRC Press, USA, June 2015 (`http://www.crcpress.com/product/isbn/9781482299977`)
- *Learning Docker*, Packt Publishing, UK, July 2015 (`https://www.packtpub.com/virtualization-and-cloud/learning-docker`)
- *High-Performance Big-Data Analytics*, Springer- Verlag, UK, Nov-Dec 2015 (`http://www.springer.com/in/book/9783319207438`)
- *A Simplified TOGAF Guide for Enterprise Architecture (EA) Certifications*, (`www.peterindia.net`)
- *The Internet of Things (IoT): The Use Cases, Platforms, Architectures, Technologies and Databases*, CRC Press, USA, 2016 (to be published)

www.PacktPub.com

eBooks, discount offers, and more

Did you know that Packt offers eBook versions of every book published, with PDF and ePub files available? You can upgrade to the eBook version at www.PacktPub.com and as a print book customer, you are entitled to a discount on the eBook copy. Get in touch with us at customercare@packtpub.com for more details.

At www.PacktPub.com, you can also read a collection of free technical articles, sign up for a range of free newsletters and receive exclusive discounts and offers on Packt books and eBooks.

https://www2.packtpub.com/books/subscription/packtlib

Do you need instant solutions to your IT questions? PacktLib is Packt's online digital book library. Here, you can search, access, and read Packt's entire library of books.

Why subscribe?

- Fully searchable across every book published by Packt
- Copy and paste, print, and bookmark content
- On demand and accessible via a web browser

Table of Contents

Preface

Processing historical data for the past 10-20 years, performing analytics, and finally producing business insights is the most popular use case for today's modern enterprises.

Enterprises have been focusing on developing data warehouses (`https://en.wikipedia.org/wiki/Data_warehouse`) where they want to store the data fetched from every possible data source and leverage various BI tools to provide analytics over the data stored in these data warehouses. But developing data warehouses is a complex, time consuming, and costly process, which requires a considerable investment, both in terms of money and time.

No doubt that the emergence of Hadoop and its ecosystem have provided a new paradigm or architecture to solve large data problems where it provides a low cost and scalable solution which processes terabytes of data in a few hours which earlier could have taken days. But this is only one side of the coin. Hadoop was meant for batch processes while there are bunch of other business use cases that are required to perform analytics and produce business insights in real or near real-time (subseconds SLA). This was called real-time analytics (RTA) or near real-time analytics (NRTA) and sometimes it was also termed as "fast data" where it implied the ability to make near real-time decisions and enable "orders-of-magnitude" improvements in elapsed time to decisions for businesses.

A number of powerful, easy to use open source platforms have emerged to solve these enterprise real-time analytics data use cases. Two of the most notable ones are Apache Storm and Apache Spark, which offer real-time data processing and analytics capabilities to a much wider range of potential users. Both projects are a part of the Apache Software Foundation and while the two tools provide overlapping capabilities, they still have distinctive features and different roles to play.

Interesting isn't it?

Let's move forward and jump into the nitty gritty of real-time Big Data analytics with Apache Storm and Apache Spark. This book provides you with the skills required to quickly design, implement, and deploy your real-time analytics using real-world examples of Big Data use cases.

What this book covers

Chapter 1, Introducing the Big Data Technology Landscape and Analytics Platform, sets the context by providing an overview of the Big Data technology landscape, the various kinds of data processing that are handled on Big Data platforms, and the various types of platforms available for performing analytics. It introduces the paradigm of distributed processing of large data in batch and real-time or near real-time. It also talks about the distributed databases to handle high velocity/frequency reads or writes.

Chapter 2, Getting Acquainted with Storm, introduces the concepts, architecture, and programming with Apache Storm as a real-time or near real-time data processing framework. It talks about the various concepts of Storm, such as spouts, bolts, Storm parallelism, and so on. It also explains the usage of Storm in the world of real-time Big Data analytics with sufficient use cases and examples.

Chapter 3, Processing Data with Storm, is focused on various internals and operations, such as filters, joins, and aggregators exposed by Apache Storm to process the streaming of data in real or near real-time. It showcases the integration of Storm with various input data sources, such as Apache Kafka, sockets, filesystems, and so on, and finally leverages the Storm JDBC framework for persisting the processed data. It also talks about the various enterprise concerns in stream processing, such as reliability, acknowledgement of messages, and so on, in Storm.

Chapter 4, Introduction to Trident and Optimizing Storm Performance, examines the processing of transactional data in real or near real-time. It introduces Trident as a real time processing framework which is used primarily for processing transactional data. It talks about the various constructs for handling transactional use cases using Trident. This chapter also talks about various concepts and parameters available and their applicability for monitoring, optimizing, and performance tuning the Storm framework and its jobs. It touches the internals of Storm such as LMAX, ring buffer, ZeroMQ, and more.

Chapter 5, Getting Acquainted with Kinesis, talks about the real-time data processing technology available on the cloud—the Kinesis service for real-time data processing from Amazon Web Services (AWS). It starts with the explanation of the architecture and components of Kinesis and then illustrates an end-to-end example of real-time alert generation using various client libraries, such as KCL, KPL, and so on.

Chapter 6, Getting Acquainted with Spark, introduces the fundamentals of Apache Spark along with the high-level architecture and the building blocks for a Spark program. It starts with the overview of Spark and talks about the applications and usage of Spark in varied batch and real-time use cases. Further, the chapter talks about high-level architecture and various components of Spark and finally towards the end, the chapter also discusses the installation and configuration of a Spark cluster and execution of the first Spark job.

Chapter 7, Programming with RDDs, provides a code-level walkthrough of Spark RDDs. It talks about various kinds of operations exposed by RDD APIs along with their usage and applicability to perform data transformation and persistence. It also showcases the integration of Spark with NoSQL databases, such as Apache Cassandra.

Chapter 8, SQL Query Engine for Spark - Spark SQL, introduces a SQL style programming interface called Spark SQL for working with Spark. It familiarizes the reader with how to work with varied datasets, such as Parquet or Hive and build queries using DataFrames or raw SQL; it also makes recommendations on best practices.

Chapter 9, Analysis of Streaming Data Using Spark Streaming, introduces another extension of Spark—Spark Streaming for capturing and processing streaming data in real or near real-time. It starts with the architecture of Spark and also briefly talks about the varied APIs and operations exposed by Spark Streaming for data loading, transformations, and persistence. Further, the chapter also talks about the integration of Spark SQL and Spark Streaming for querying data in real time. Finally, towards the end, it also discusses the deployment and monitoring aspects of Spark Streaming jobs.

Chapter 10, Introducing Lambda Architecture, walks the reader through the emerging Lambda Architecture, which provides a hybrid platform for Big Data processing by combining real-time and pre-computed batch data to provide a near real-time view of the data. It leverages Apache Spark and discusses the realization of Lambda Architecture with a real life use case.

What you need for this book

Readers should have programming experience in Java or Scala and some basic knowledge or understanding of any distributed computing platform such as Apache Hadoop.

Who this book is for

If you are a Big Data architect, developer, or a programmer who wants to develop applications or frameworks to implement real-time analytics using open source technologies, then this book is for you. This book is aimed at competent developers who have basic knowledge and understanding of Java or Scala to allow efficient programming of core elements and applications.

If you are reading this book, then you probably are familiar with the nuisances and challenges of large data or Big Data. This book will cover the various tools and technologies available for processing and analyzing streaming data or data arriving at high frequency in real or near real-time. It will cover the paradigm of in-memory distributed computing offered by various tools and technologies such as Apache Storm, Spark, Kinesis, and so on.

Conventions

In this book, you will find a number of text styles that distinguish between different kinds of information. Here are some examples of these styles and an explanation of their meaning.

Code words in text, database table names, folder names, filenames, file extensions, pathnames, dummy URLs, user input, and Twitter handles are shown as follows: "The `PATH` variable should have the path to Python installation on your machine."

A block of code is set as follows:

```
public class Count implements CombinerAggregator<Long> {
   @Override
   public Long init(TridentTuple tuple) {
      return 1L;
   }
```

Any command-line input or output is written as follows:

```
> bin/kafka-console-producer.sh --broker-list localhost:9092 --topic test
```

New terms and **important words** are shown in bold. Words that you see on the screen, for example, in menus or dialog boxes, appear in the text like this: "The landing page on Storm UI first talks about **Cluster Summary**."

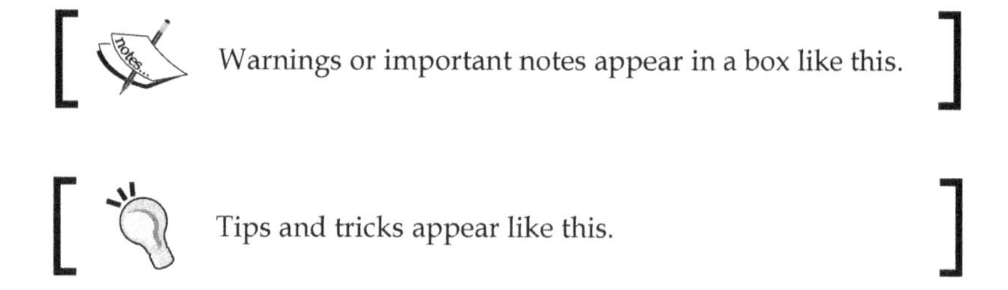

Warnings or important notes appear in a box like this.

Tips and tricks appear like this.

Reader feedback

Feedback from our readers is always welcome. Let us know what you think about this book—what you liked or disliked. Reader feedback is important for us as it helps us develop titles that you will really get the most out of.

To send us general feedback, simply e-mail feedback@packtpub.com, and mention the book's title in the subject of your message.

If there is a topic that you have expertise in and you are interested in either writing or contributing to a book, see our author guide at www.packtpub.com/authors.

Customer support

Now that you are the proud owner of a Packt book, we have a number of things to help you to get the most from your purchase.

Downloading the example code

You can download the example code files for this book from your account at http://www.packtpub.com. If you purchased this book elsewhere, you can visit http://www.packtpub.com/support and register to have the files e-mailed directly to you.

You can download the code files by following these steps:

1. Log in or register to our website using your e-mail address and password.
2. Hover the mouse pointer on the **SUPPORT** tab at the top.
3. Click on **Code Downloads & Errata**.

4. Enter the name of the book in the **Search** box.
5. Select the book for which you're looking to download the code files.
6. Choose from the drop-down menu where you purchased this book from.
7. Click on **Code Download**.

Once the file is downloaded, please make sure that you unzip or extract the folder using the latest version of:

- WinRAR / 7-Zip for Windows
- Zipeg / iZip / UnRarX for Mac
- 7-Zip / PeaZip for Linux

Errata

Although we have taken every care to ensure the accuracy of our content, mistakes do happen. If you find a mistake in one of our books—maybe a mistake in the text or the code—we would be grateful if you could report this to us. By doing so, you can save other readers from frustration and help us improve subsequent versions of this book. If you find any errata, please report them by visiting `http://www.packtpub.com/submit-errata`, selecting your book, clicking on the **Errata Submission Form** link, and entering the details of your errata. Once your errata are verified, your submission will be accepted and the errata will be uploaded to our website or added to any list of existing errata under the Errata section of that title.

To view the previously submitted errata, go to `https://www.packtpub.com/books/content/support` and enter the name of the book in the search field. The required information will appear under the **Errata** section.

Piracy

Piracy of copyrighted material on the Internet is an ongoing problem across all media. At Packt, we take the protection of our copyright and licenses very seriously. If you come across any illegal copies of our works in any form on the Internet, please provide us with the location address or website name immediately so that we can pursue a remedy.

Please contact us at `copyright@packtpub.com` with a link to the suspected pirated material.

We appreciate your help in protecting our authors and our ability to bring you valuable content.

Questions

If you have a problem with any aspect of this book, you can contact us at `questions@packtpub.com`, and we will do our best to address the problem.

1
Introducing the Big Data Technology Landscape and Analytics Platform

The Big Data paradigm has emerged as one of the most powerful in next-generation data storage, management, and analytics. IT powerhouses have actually embraced the change and have accepted that it's here to stay.

What arrived just as Hadoop, a storage and distributed processing platform, has really graduated and evolved. Today, we have whole panorama of various tools and technologies that specialize in various specific verticals of the Big Data space.

In this chapter, you will become acquainted with the technology landscape of Big Data and analytics platforms. We will start by introducing the user to the infrastructure, the processing components, and the advent of Big Data. We will also discuss the needs and use cases for near real-time analysis.

This chapter will cover the following points that will help you to understand the Big Data technology landscape:

- Infrastructure of Big Data
- Components of the Big Data ecosystem
- Analytics architecture
- Distributed batch processing
- Distributed databases (NoSQL)
- Real-time and stream processing

Big Data – a phenomenon

The phrase *Big Data* is not just a new buzzword, it's something that arrived slowly and captured the entire arena. The arrival of Hadoop and its alliance marked the end of the age for the long undefeated reign of traditional databases and warehouses.

Today, we have a humongous amount of data all around us, in each and every sector of society and the economy; talk about any industry, it's sitting and generating loads of data—for instance, manufacturing, automobiles, finance, the energy sector, consumers, transportation, security, IT, and networks. The advent of Big Data as a field/domain/concept/theory/idea has made it possible to store, process, and analyze these large pools of data to get intelligent insight, and perform informed and calculated decisions. These decisions are driving the recommendations, growth, planning, and projections in all segments of the economy and that's why Big Data has taken the world by storm.

If we look at the trends in the IT industry, there was an era when people were moving from manual computation to automated, computerized applications, then we ran into an era of enterprise level applications. This era gave birth to architectural flavors such as SAAS and PaaS. Now, we are into an era where we have a huge amount of data, which can be processed and analyzed in cost-effective ways. The world is moving towards open source to get the benefits of reduced license fees, data storage, and computation costs. It has really made it lucrative and affordable for all sectors and segments to harness the power of data. This is making Big Data synonymous with low cost, scalable, highly available, and reliable solutions that can churn huge amounts of data at incredible speed and generate intelligent insights.

The Big Data dimensional paradigm

To begin with, in simple terms, Big Data helps us deal with the three Vs: volume, velocity, and variety. Recently, two more Vs—veracity and value—were added to it, making it a five-dimensional paradigm:

- **Volume**: This dimension refers to the amount of data. Look around you; huge amounts of data are being generated every second—it may be the e-mail you send, Twitter, Facebook, other social media, or it can just be all the videos, pictures, SMS, call records, or data from various devices and sensors. We have scaled up the data measuring metrics to terabytes, zettabytes and vronobytes—they are all humongous figures. Look at Facebook, it has around 10 billion messages each day; consolidated across all users, we have nearly 5 billion "likes" a day; and around 400 million photographs are uploaded each day. Data statistics, in terms of volume, are startling; all the data generated from the beginning of time to 2008 is kind of equivalent to what we generate in a day today, and I am sure soon it will be an hour. This volume aspect alone is making the traditional database unable to store and process this amount of data in a reasonable and useful time frame, though a Big Data stack can be employed to store, process, and compute amazingly large datasets in a cost-effective, distributed, and reliably efficient manner.
- **Velocity**: This refers to the data generation speed, or the rate at which data is being generated. In today's world, where the volume of data has made a tremendous surge, this aspect is not lagging behind. We have loads of data because we are generating it so fast. Look at social media; things are circulated in seconds and they become viral, and the insight from social media is analyzed in milliseconds by stock traders and that can trigger lot of activity in terms of buying or selling. At target point of sale counters, it takes a few seconds for a credit card swipe and, within that, fraudulent transaction processing, payment, bookkeeping, and acknowledgement are all done. Big Data gives me power to analyze the data at tremendous speed.
- **Variety**: This dimension tackles the fact that the data can be unstructured. In the traditional database world, and even before that, we were used to a very structured form of data that kind of neatly fitted into the tables. But today, more than 80 percent of data is unstructured; for example, photos, video clips, social media updates, data from a variety of sensors, voice recordings, and chat conversations. Big Data lets you store and process this unstructured data in a very structured manner; in fact, it embraces the variety.

- **Veracity**: This is all about validity and the correctness of data. How accurate and usable is the data? Not everything out of millions and zillions of data records is corrected, accurate, and referable. That's what veracity actually is: how trustworthy the data is, and what the quality of data is. Two examples of data with veracity are Facebook and Twitter posts with nonstandard acronyms or typos. Big Data has brought to the table the ability to run analytics on this kind of data. One of the strong reasons for the volume of data is its veracity.
- **Value**: As the name suggests, this is the value the data actually holds. Unarguably, it's the most important V or dimension of Big Data. The only motivation for going towards Big Data for the processing of super-large datasets is to derive some valuable insight from it; in the end, it's all about cost and benefits.

The Big Data ecosystem

For a beginner, the landscape can be utterly confusing. There is vast arena of technologies and equally varied use cases. There is no single go-to solution; every use case has a custom solution and this widespread technology stack and lack of standardization is making Big Data a difficult path to tread for developers. There are a multitude of technologies that exist which can draw meaningful insight out of this magnitude of data.

Let's begin with the basics: the environment for any data analytics application creation should provide for the following:

- Storing data
- Enriching or processing data
- Data analysis and visualization

If we get to specialization, there are specific Big Data tools and technologies available; for instance, ETL tools such as Talend and Pentaho; Pig batch processing, Hive, and MapReduce; real-time processing from Storm, Spark, and so on; and the list goes on. Here's the pictorial representation of the vast Big Data technology landscape, as per Forbes:

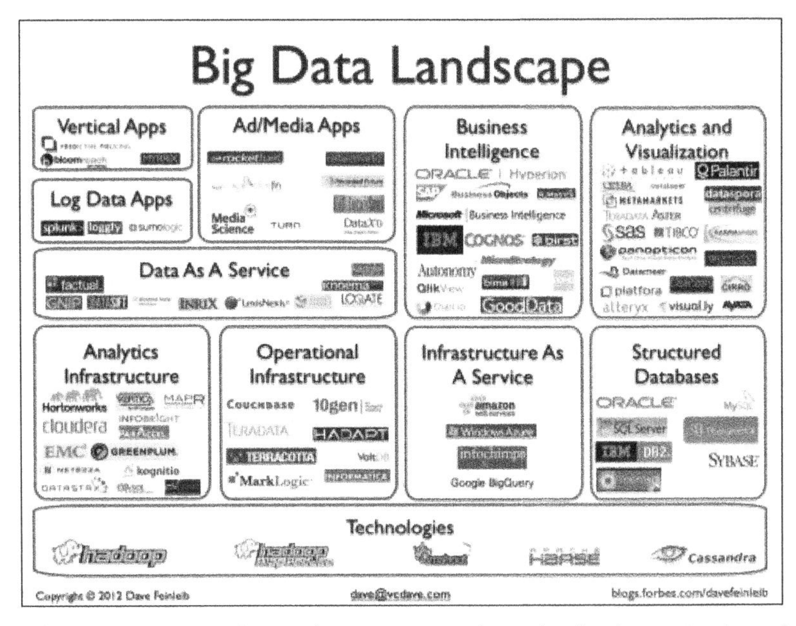

Source: `http://www.forbes.com/sites/davefeinleib/2012/06/19/the-big-data-landscape/`

It clearly depicts the various segments and verticals within the Big Data technology canvas:

- Platforms such as Hadoop and NoSQL
- Analytics such as HDP, CDH, EMC, Greenplum, DataStax, and more
- Infrastructure such as Teradata, VoltDB, MarkLogic, and more
- **Infrastructure as a Service** (**IaaS**) such as AWS, Azure, and more
- Structured databases such as Oracle, SQL server, DB2, and more
- **Data as a Service** (**DaaS**) such as INRIX, LexisNexis, Factual, and more

And, beyond that, we have a score of segments related to specific problem area such as **Business Intelligence** (**BI**), analytics and visualization, advertisement and media, log data and vertical apps, and so on.

The Big Data infrastructure

Technologies providing the capability to store, process, and analyze data are the core of any Big Data stack. The era of tables and records ran for a very long time, after the standard relational data store took over from file-based sequential storage. We were able to harness the storage and compute power very well for enterprises, but eventually the journey ended when we ran into the five Vs.

At the end of its era, we could see our, so far, robust RDBMS struggling to survive in a cost-effective manner as a tool for data storage and processing. The scaling of traditional RDBMS at the compute power expected to process a huge amount of data with low latency came at a very high price. This led to the emergence of new technologies that were low cost, low latency, and highly scalable at low cost, or were open source. Today, we deal with Hadoop clusters with thousands of nodes, hurling and churning thousands of terabytes of data.

The key technologies of the Hadoop ecosystem are as follows:

- **Hadoop**: The yellow elephant that took the data storage and computation arena by surprise. It's designed and developed as a distributed framework for data storage and computation on commodity hardware in a highly reliable and scalable manner. Hadoop works by distributing the data in chunks over all the nodes in the cluster and then processing the data concurrently on all the nodes. Two key moving components in Hadoop are mappers and reducers.
- **NoSQL**: This is an abbreviation for No-SQL, which actually is not the traditional structured query language. It's basically a tool to process a huge volume of multi-structured data; widely known ones are HBase and Cassandra. Unlike traditional database systems, they generally have no single point of failure and are scalable.
- **MPP** (short for **Massively Parallel Processing**) databases: These are computational platforms that are able to process data at a very fast rate. The basic working uses the concept of segmenting the data into chunks across different nodes in the cluster, and then processing the data in parallel. They are similar to Hadoop in terms of data segmentation and concurrent processing at each node. They are different from Hadoop in that they don't execute on low-end commodity machines, but on high-memory, specialized hardware. They have SQL-like interfaces for the interaction and retrieval of data, and they generally end up processing data faster because they use in-memory processing. This means that, unlike Hadoop that operates at disk level, MPP databases load the data into memory and operate upon the collective memory of all nodes in the cluster.

Components of the Big Data ecosystem

The next step on journey to Big Data is to understand the levels and layers of abstraction, and the components around the same. The following figure depicts some common components of Big Data analytical stacks and their integration with each other. The caveat here is that, in most of the cases, HDFS/Hadoop forms the core of most of the Big-Data-centric applications, but that's not a generalized rule of thumb.

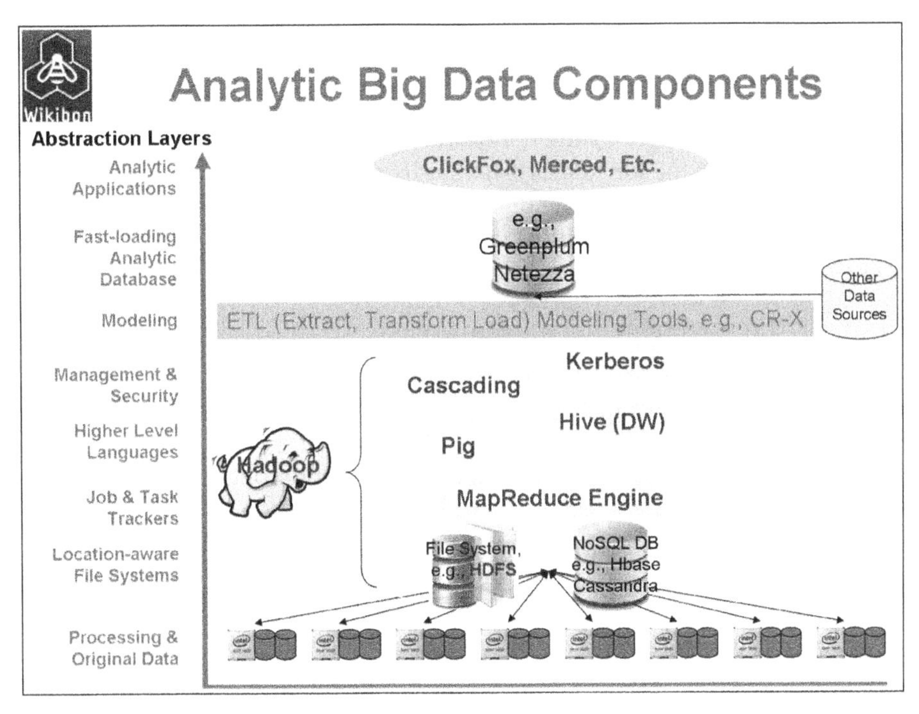

Source: `http://wikibon.org/w/images/0/03/BigDataComponents.JPG`

Talking about Big Data in a generic manner, its components are as follows:

- A storage system can be one of the following:
    - **HDFS** (short for **Hadoop Distributed File System**) is the storage layer that handles the storing of data, as well as the metadata that is required to complete the computation
    - NoSQL stores that can be tabular stores such as HBase or key-value based columnar Cassandra

- A computation or logic layer can be one of the following:
    - **MapReduce**: This is a combination of two separate processes, the mapper and the reducer. The mapper executes first and takes up the raw dataset and transforms it to another key-value data structure. Then, the reducer kicks in, which takes up the map created by the mapper job as an input, and collates and converges it into a smaller dataset.
    - **Pig**: This is another platform that's put on top of Hadoop for processing, and it can be used in conjunction with or as a substitute for MapReduce. It is a high-level language and is widely used for creating processing components to analyze very large datasets. One of the key aspects is that its structure is amendable to various degrees of parallelism. At its core, it has a compiler that translates Pig scripts to MapReduce jobs.

      It is used very widely because:
    - Programming in Pig Latin is easy
    - Optimizing the jobs is efficient and easy
    - It is extendible
- Application logic or interaction can be one of the following:
    - **Hive**: This is a data warehousing layer that's built on top of the Hadoop platform. In simple terms, Hive provides a facility to interact with, process, and analyze HDFS data with Hive queries, which are very much like SQL. This makes the transition from the RDBMS world to Hadoop easier.
    - **Cascading**: This is a framework that exposes a set of data processing APIs and other components that define, share, and execute the data processing over the Hadoop/Big Data stack. It's basically an abstracted API layer over Hadoop. It's widely used for application development because of its ease of development, creation of jobs, and job scheduling.
- Specialized analytics databases, such as:
    - Databases such as Netezza or Greenplum have the capability for scaling out and are known for a very fast data ingestion and refresh, which is a mandatory requirement for analytics models.

The Big Data analytics architecture

Now that we have skimmed through the Big Data technology stack and the components, the next step is to go through the generic architecture for analytical applications.

We will continue the discussion with reference to the following figure:

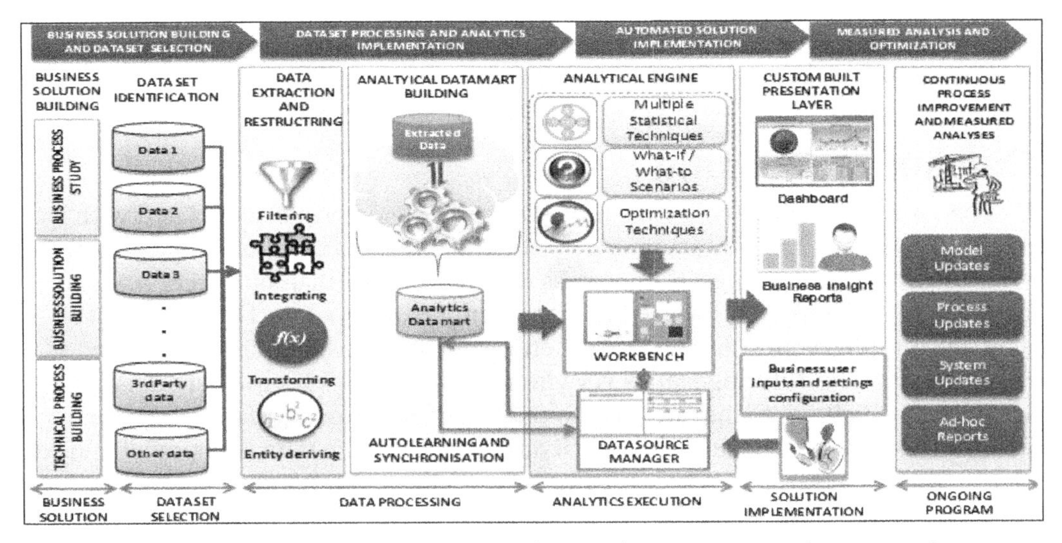

Source: `http://www.statanalytics.com/images/analytics-services-over.jpg`

If you look at the diagram, there are four steps on the workflow of an analytical application, which in turn lead to the design and architecture of the same:

- Business solution building (dataset selection)
- Dataset processing (analytics implementation)
- Automated solution
- Measured analysis and optimization

Now, let's dive deeper into each segment to understand how it works.

Building business solutions

This is the first and most important step for any application. This is the step where the application architects and designers identify and decide upon the data sources that will be providing the input data to the application for analytics. The data could be from a client dataset, a third party, or some kind of static/dimensional data (such as geo coordinates, postal code, and so on).While designing the solution, the input data can be segmented into business-process-related data, business-solution-related data, or data for technical process building. Once the datasets are identified, let's move to the next step.

Dataset processing

By now, we understand the business use case and the dataset(s) associated with it. The next steps are data ingestion and processing. Well, it's not that simple; we may want to make use of an ingestion process and, more often than not, architects end up creating an **ETL** (short for **Extract Transform Load**) pipeline. During the ETL step, the filtering is executed so that we only apply processing to meaningful and relevant data. This **filtering** step is very important. This is where we are attempting to reduce the volume so that we have to only analyze meaningful/valued data, and thus handle the velocity and veracity aspects. Once the data is filtered, the next step could be **integration**, where the filtered data from various sources reaches the landing data mart. The next step is **transformation**. This is where the data is converted to an entity-driven form, for instance, Hive table, JSON, POJO, and so on, and thus marking the completion of the ETL step. This makes the data ingested into the system available for actual processing.

Depending upon the use case and the duration for which a given dataset is to be analyzed, it's loaded into the analytical data mart. For instance, my landing data mart may have a year's worth of credit card transactions, but I just need one day's worth of data for analytics. Then, I would have a year's worth of data in the landing mart, but only one day's worth of data in the analytics mart. This segregation is extremely important because that helps in figuring out where I need real-time compute capability and which data my deep learning application operates upon.

Solution implementation

Now, we will implement various aspects of the solution and integrate them with the appropriate data mart. We can have the following:

- **Analytical Engine**: This executes various batch jobs, statistical queries, or cubes on the landing data mart to arrive at the projections and trends based on certain indexes and variances.

- **Dashboard/Workbench**: This depicts some close to real-time information on to some UX interfaces. These components generally operate on low latency, close to real-time, analytical data marts.
- **Auto learning synchronization mechanism**: Perfect for advanced analytical application, this captures patterns and evolves the data management methodologies. For example, if I am a mobile operator at a tourist place, I might be more cautious about my resource usage during the day and at weekends, but over a period of time I may learn that during vacations I see a surge in roaming, so I can learn and build these rules into my data mart and ensure that data is stored and structured in an analytics-friendly manner.

Presentation

Once the data is analyzed, the next and most important step in the life cycle of any application is the presentation/visualization of the results. Depending upon the target audience of the end business user, the data visualization can be achieved using a custom-built UI presentation layer, business insight reports, dashboards, charts, graphs, and so on.

The requirement could vary from autorefreshing UI widgets to canned reports and ADO queries.

Distributed batch processing

The first and foremost point to understand is what are the different kinds of processing that can be applied to data. Well, they fall in two broad categories:

- Batch processing
- Sequential or inline processing

The key difference between the two is that the sequential processing works on a per tuple basis, where the events are processed as they are generated or ingested into the system. In case of batch processing, they are executed in batches. This means tuples/events are not processed as they are generated or ingested. They're processed in fixed-size batches; for example, 100 credit card transactions are clubbed into a batch and then consolidated.

Some of the key aspects of batch processing systems are as follows:

- Size of a batch or the boundary of a batch
- Batching (starting a batch and terminating a batch)
- Sequencing of batches (if required by the use case)

The batch can be identified by size (which could be *x* number of records, for example, a 100-record batch). The batches can be more diverse and be divided into time ranges such as hourly batches, daily batches, and so on. They can be dynamic and data-driven, where a particular sequence/pattern in the input data demarcates the start of the batch and another particular one marks its end.

Once a batch boundary is demarcated, said bundle of records should be marked as a batch, which can be done by adding a header/trailer, or maybe one consolidated data structure, and so on, bundled with a batch identifier. The batching logic also performs bookkeeping and accounting for each batch being created and dispatched for processing.

In certain specific use cases, the order of records or the sequence needs to be maintained, leading to the need to sequence the batches. In these specialized scenarios, the batching logic has to do extra processing to sequence the batches, and extra caution needs to be applied to the bookkeeping for the same.

Now that we understand what batch processing is, the next step and an obvious one is to understand what distributed batch processing is. It's a computing paradigm where the tuples/records are batched and then distributed for processing across a cluster of nodes/processing units. Once each node completes the processing of its allocated batch, the results are collated and summarized for the final results. In today's application programming, when we are used to processing a huge amount of data and get results at lightning-fast speed, it is beyond the capability of a single node machine to meet these needs. We need a huge computational cluster. In computer theory, we can add computation or storage capability by two means:

- By adding more compute capability to a single node
- By adding more than one node to perform the task

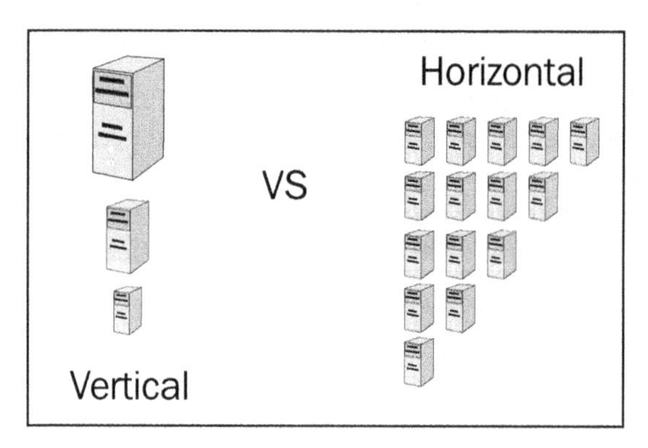

Source: `https://encrypted-tbn0.gstatic.com/images?q=tbn:ANd9GcSy_pG3f3Lq7spA6rp5aVZjxKxYzBI5y2xCn0XX_ClK49kH2IyG`

Vertical scaling is a paradigm where we add more compute capability; for example, add more CPUs or more RAM to an existing node or replace the existing node with a more powerful machine. This model works well only up to an extent. You may soon hit the ceiling and your needs would outgrow what the biggest possible machine can deliver. So, this model has a flaw in the scaling, and it's essentially an issue when it comes to a single point of failure because, as you see, the entire application is running on one machine.

So you can see that vertical scaling is limited and failure prone. The higher end machines are pretty expensive too. So, the solution is horizontal scaling. I rely on clustering, where the computational capability is basically not derived from a single node, but from a collection of nodes. In this paradigm, I am operating in a model that's scalable and there is no single point of failure.

Batch processing in distributed mode

For a very long time, Hadoop was synonymous with Big Data, but now Big Data has branched off to various specialized, non-Hadoop compute segments as well. At its core, Hadoop is a distributed, batch-processing compute framework that operates upon MapReduce principles.

It has the ability to process a huge amount of data by virtue of batching and parallel processing. The key aspect is that it moves the computation to the data, instead of how it works in the traditional world, where data is moved to the computation. A model that is operative on a cluster of nodes is horizontally scalable and fail-proof.

Hadoop is a solution for offline, batch data processing. Traditionally, the NameNode was a single point of failure, but the advent of newer versions and **YARN** (short for **Yet Another Resource Negotiator**) has actually changed that limitation. From a computational perspective, YARN has brought about a major shift that has decoupled MapReduce and Hadoop, and has provided the scope of integration with other real-time, parallel processing compute engines like Spark, **MPI** (short for **Message Processing Interface**), and so on.

Push code to data

So far, the general computational models have a data flow where the data is ingested and moved to the compute engine.

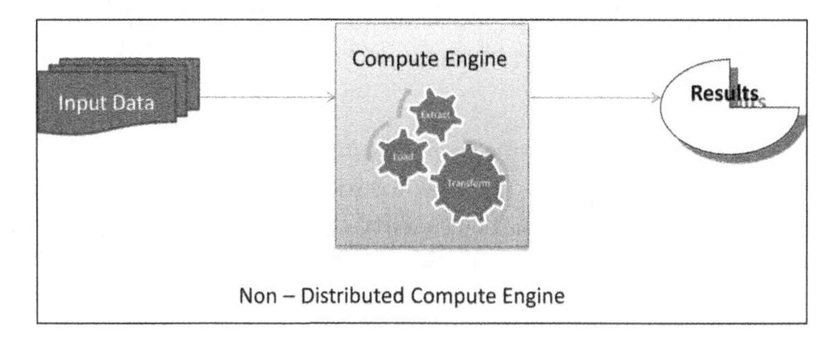

The advent of distributed batch processing made changes to this and this is depicted in the following figure. The batches of data were moved to various nodes in the compute-engine cluster. This shift was seen as a major advantage to the processing arena and has brought the power of parallel processing to the application.

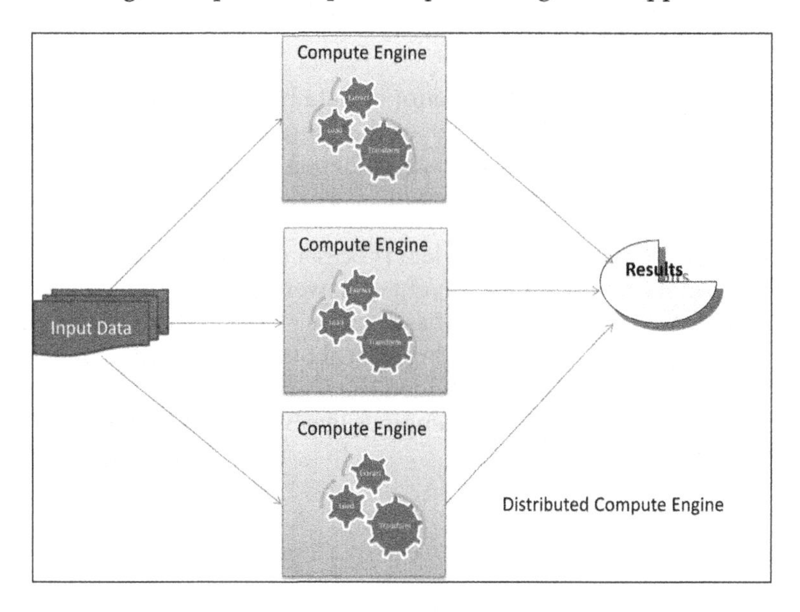

Moving data to compute makes sense for low volume data. But, for a Big Data use case that has humongous data computation, moving data to the compute engine may not be a sensible idea because network latency can cause a huge impact on the overall processing time. So Hadoop has shifted the world by creating batches of input data called blocks and distributing them to each node in the cluster. Take a look at this figure:

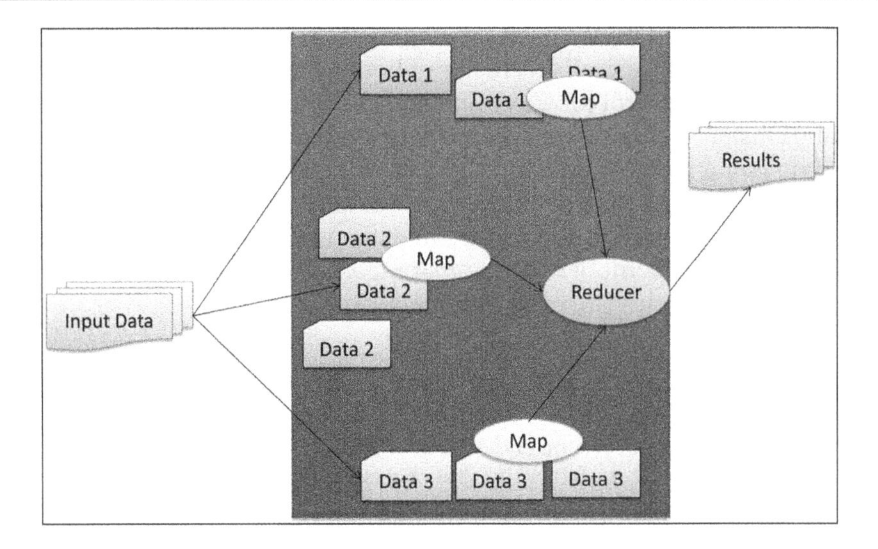

At the initialization stage, the Big Data file is pushed into HDFS. Then, the file is split into chunks (or file blocks) by the Hadoop NameNode (master node) and is placed onto individual DataNodes (slave nodes) in the cluster for concurrent processing.

The process in the cluster called Job Tracker moves execution code or processing to the data. The compute component includes a Mapper and a Reduce class. In very simple terms, a Mapper class does the job of data filtering, transformation, and splitting. By nature of a localized compute, a Mapper instance only processes the data blocks which are local to or co-located on the same data node. This concept is called data locality or proximity. Once the Mappers are executed, their outputs are shuffled through to the appropriate Reduce nodes. A Reduce class, by its functionality, is an aggregator for compiling all the results from the mappers.

Distributed databases (NoSQL)

We have discussed the paradigm shift from *data to computation* to the paradigm of *computation to data* in case of Hadoop. We understand on the conceptual level how to harness the power of distributed computation. The next step is to apply the same to database level in terms of having distributed databases.

In very simple terms, a database is actually a storage structure that lets us store the data in a very structured format. It can be in the form of various data structural representations internally, such as flat files, tables, blobs, and so on. Now when we talk about a database, we generally refer to single/clustered server class nodes with huge storage and specialized hardware to support the operations. So, this can be envisioned as a single unit of storage controlled by a centralized control unit.

Distributed database, on the contrary, is a database where there is no single control unit or storage unit. It's basically a cluster of homogenous/heterogeneous nodes, and the data and the control for execution and orchestration is distributed across all nodes in the cluster. So to understand it better, we can use an analogy that, instead of all the data going into a single huge box, now the data is spread across multiple boxes. The execution of this distribution, the bookkeeping and auditing of this data distribution, and the retrieval process are managed by multiple control units. In a way, there is no single point of control or storage. One important point is that these multiple distributed nodes can exist physically or virtually.

Do not relate this to the concept of parallel systems, where the processors are tightly coupled and it all constitutes a single database system. A distributed database system is a relatively loosely coupled entity that shares no physical components.

Now we understand the differentiating factors for distributed databases. However, it is necessary to understand that, due to their distributed nature, these systems have some added complexity to ensure correctness and the accuracy of the day. There are two processes that play a vital role:

- **Replication**: This is tracked by a special component of distributed databases. This piece of software does the tedious job of bookkeeping for all the updates/additions/deletions that are being made to the data. Once all changes are logged, this process updates so that all copies of the data look the same and represent the state of truth.
- **Duplication**: The popularity of distributed databases is due to the fact that they don't have a single point of failure and there is always more than one copy of data available to deal with a failure situation if it happens. The process that copies one instance of data to multiple locations on the cluster generally executes at some defined interval.

Both these processes ensure that at a given point in time, more than one copy of data exists in the cluster, and all the copies of the data have the same representation of the state of truth for the data.

A NoSQL database environment is a non-relational and predominately distributed database system. Its clear advantage is that it facilitates the rapid analysis of extremely high-volume, disparate data types. With the advent of Big Data, NoSQL databases have become the cheap and scalable alternative to traditional RDBMS. The USPs they have to offer are availability and fault tolerance, which are big differentiating factors.

NoSQL offers a flexible and extensible schema model with added advantages of endless scalability, distributed setup, and the liberty of interfacing with non-SQL interfaces.

We can distinguish NoSQL databases as follows:

- **Key-value store**: This type of database belongs to some of the least complex NoSQL options. Its USP is the design that allows the storage of data in a schemaless way. All the data in this store contains an index key and an associate value (as the name suggests). Popular examples of this type of database are Cassandra, DynamoDB, **Azure Table Storage** (**ATS**), Riak, Berkeley DB, and so on.
- **Column store or wide column store**: This is designed for storing the data in rows and its data in data tables, where there are columns of data rather than rows of data, like in a standard database. They are the exact opposite of row-based databases, and this design is highly scalable and offers very high performance. Examples are HBase and Hypertable.
- **Document database**: This is an extension to the basic idea of a key-value store where documents are more complex and elaborate. It's like each document has a unique ID associated with it. This ID is used for document retrieval. These are very widely used for storing and managing document-oriented information. Examples are MongoDB and CouchDB.
- **Graph database**: As the name suggests, it's based on the graph theory of discreet mathematics. It's well designed for data where relationships can be maintained as a graph and elements are interconnected based on relations. Examples are Neo4j, polyglot, and so on.

The following table lays out the key attributes and certain dimensions that can be used for selecting the appropriate NoSQL databases:

- **Column 1**: This captures the storage structure for the data model.
- **Column 2**: This captures the performance of the distributed database on the scale of low, medium, and high.
- **Column 3**: This captures the ease of scalability of the distributed database on the scale of low, medium, and high. It notes how easily the system can be scaled in terms of capacity and processing by adding more nodes to the cluster.
- **Column 4**: Here we talk about the scale of flexibility of use and the ability to cater to diverse structured or unstructured data and use cases.

- **Column 5**: Here we talk about how complex it is to work with the system in terms of the complexity of development and modeling, the complexity of operation and maintainability, and so on.

Data model	Performance	Scalability	Flexibility	Complexity
Key-value store	High	High	High	None
Column Store	High	High	Moderate	Low
Document Store	High	Variable (high)	High	Low
Graph Database	Variable	Variable	High	High

Advantages of NoSQL databases

Let's have a look at the key reasons for adopting an NoSQL database over a traditional RDBMS. Here are the key drivers that have been attributed to the shift:

- **Advent and growth of Big Data**: This is one of the prime attribute forces driving the growth and shift towards use of NoSQL.
- **High availability systems**: In today's highly competitive world, downtime can be deadly. The reality of business is that hardware failures will occur, but NoSQL database systems are built over a distributed architecture so there is no single point of failure. They also have replication to ensure redundancy of data that guarantees availability in the event of one or more nodes being down. With this mechanism, the availability across data centers is guaranteed, even in the case of localized failures. This all comes with guaranteed horizontal scaling and high performance.
- **Location independence**: This refers to the ability to perform read and write operations to the data store regardless of the physical location where that input-output operation actually occurs. Similarly, we have the ability to have any write percolated out from that location. This feature is a difficult wish to make in the RDBMS world. This is a very handy tool when it comes to designing an application that services customers in many different geographies and needs to keep data local for fast access.

- **Schemaless data models**: One of the major motivator for move to a NoSQL database system from an old-world relational database management system (RDBMS) is the ability to handle unstructured data and it's found in most NoSQL stores. The relational data model is based on strict relations defined between tables, which themselves are very strict in definition by a determined column structure. All of this then gets organized in a schema. The backbone of RDBMS is structure and it's the biggest limitation as this makes it fall short for handling and storing unstructured data that doesn't fit into strict table structure. A NoSQL data model on the contrary doesn't have any structure and it's flexible to fit in any form, so it's called **schemaless**. It's like one size fits all, and it's able to accept structured, semistructured, or unstructured data. All this flexibility comes along with a promise of low-cost scalability and high performance.

Choosing a NoSQL database

When it comes to making a choice, there are certain factors that can be taken into account, but the decision is still more use-case-driven and can vary from case to case. Migration of a data store or choosing a data store is an important, conscious decision, and should be made diligently and intelligently depending on the following factors:

- Input data diversity
- Scalability
- Performance
- Availability
- Cost
- Stability
- Community

Real-time processing

Now that we have talked so extensively about Big Data processing and Big Data persistence in the context of distributed, batch-oriented systems, the next obvious thing to talk about is real-time or near real-time processing. Big data processing processes huge datasets in offline batch mode. When real-time stream processing is executed on the most current set of data, we operate in the dimension of *now* or the immediate past; examples are credit card fraud detection, security, and so on. Latency is a key aspect in these analytics.

The two operatives here are velocity and latency, and that's where Hadoop and related distributed batch processing systems fall short. They are designed to deliver in batch mode and can't operate at a latency of nanoseconds/milliseconds. In use cases where we need accurate results in fractions of seconds, for example, credit card fraud, monitoring business activity, and so on, we need a **Complex Event Processing** (**CEP**) engine to process and derive results at lightning fast speed.

Storm, initially a project from the house of Twitter, has graduated to the league of Apache and was rechristened from Twitter Storm. It was a brainchild of Nathan Marz that's now been adopted by CDH, HDP, and so on.

Apache Storm is a highly scalable, distributed, fast, reliable real-time computing system designed to process high-velocity data. Cassandra complements the compute capability by providing lightning fast reads and writes, and this is the best combination available as of now for a data store with Storm. It helps the developer to create a data flow model in which tuples flow continuously through a topology (a collection of processing components). Data can be ingested to Storm using distributed messaging queues such as Kafka, RabbitMQ, and so on. Trident is another layer of abstraction API over Storm that brings microbatching capabilities into it.

Let's take a closer look at a couple of real-time, real-world use cases in various industrial segments.

The telecoms or cellular arena

We are living in an era where cell phones are no longer merely calling devices. In fact, they have evolved from being phones to *smartphones*, providing access to not just calling but also facilities such as data, photographs, tracking, GPS, and so on into the hands of the consumers. Now, the data generated by cell phones or telephones is not just call data; the typical **CDR** (short for **Call Data Record**) captures voice, data, and SMS transactions. Voice and SMS transactions have existed for more than a decade and are predominantly structured as they are because of telecoms protocols worldwide; for example, CIBER, SMPP, SMSC, and so on. However, the data or IP traffic flowing in/out of these smart devices is pretty unstructured and high volume. It could be a music track, a picture, a tweet, or just about anything in the data dimension. CDR processing and billing is generally a batch job, but a lot of other things are real-time:

- **Geo-tracking of the device**: Have you noticed how quickly we get an SMS whenever we cross a state border?

- **Usage and alerts**: Have you noticed how accurate and efficient the alert that informs you about the broadband consumption limit is and suggests that you top up the same?
- **Prepaid mobile cards**: If you have ever used a prepaid system, you must have been awed at the super-efficient charge-tracking system they have in place.

Transportation and logistics

Transportation and logistics is another useful segment that's using real-time analytics from vehicular data for transportation, logistics, and intelligent traffic management. Here's an example from McKinney's report that details how Big Data and real-time analytics are helping to handle traffic congestion on a major highway in Tel Aviv, the capital of Israel. Here's what they actually do: they monitor the receipts from the toll constantly and during the peak hours, to avert congestion, they hike the toll prices. This is a deterrent factor for the users. Once the congestion eases out during non-peak hours, the toll rates are reduced.

There may be many more use cases that can be built around the data from check-posts/tolls to develop intelligent management of traffic, thus preventing congestion, and make better utilization of public infrastructure.

The connected vehicle

An idea that was still in the realms of fiction until the last decade is now a reality that's being actively used by the consumer segment today. GPS and Google Maps are no news today, they are being imbibed and heavily used features.

My car's control unit has telemetry devices that capture various KPIs, such as engine temperature, fuel consumption pattern, RPM, and so on, and all this information is used by the manufacturers for analysis. In some of the cases, the user is also allowed to set and receive alerts on these KPI thresholds.

The financial sector

This is the sector that's emerging as the biggest consumer of real-time analytics for very obvious reasons. The volume of data is huge and quickly changing; the impact of analytics and its results boils down to the money aspect. This sector needs real-time instruments for rapid and precise data analysis for data from stock exchanges, various financial institutions, market prices and fluctuations, and so on.

Summary

In this chapter, we have discussed various aspects of the Big Data technology landscape. We have talked about the terminology, definitions, acronyms, components, and infrastructure used in context with Big Data. We have also described the architecture of a Big Data analytical platform. Further on in the chapter, we also discussed the various computational methodologies starting from sequential, to batch, to distributed, and then arrived at real time. At the end of this chapter, we are sure that our readers are now well acquainted with Big Data and its characteristics.

In the next chapter, we will embark on our journey towards the real-time technology—**Storm**—and will see how it fits well in the arena of real-time analytics platforms.

2
Getting Acquainted with Storm

The focus of this chapter is to acquaint readers with Storm, and explain the inception and the journey Storm has been through. It aims to make the user aware of the basic concepts and architecture of Apache Storm and explain with use cases how Storm can be used in real time Big Data analytics.

We will cover the following topics in this chapter:

- An overview of Storm
- The journey of Storm
- Storm abstractions
- Storm architecture and its components
- How and when to use Storm
- Storm internals

An overview of Storm

If someone would ask me to describe Storm in a line, I would use the well-known statement, "Storm is actually Hadoop of real time." Hadoop provides the solution to the volume dimension of Big Data, but it's essentially a batch processing platform. It doesn't come with speed and immediate results/analysis. Though Hadoop has been a turning point for the data storage and computation regime, it cannot be a solution to a problem requiring real-time analysis and results.

Storm addresses the velocity aspect of Big Data. This framework provides the capability to execute distributed computations at lightning fast speed in real-time streaming data. It's a widely used solution to provide real-time alerts and analytics over high velocity streaming data. Storm is a project that's now adopted by Apache. It is proven and known for its capabilities; being under the Apache canopy, it is free and open source. It is a distributed compute engine, which is highly scalable, reliable, and fault tolerant and comes with a guaranteed processing mechanism. It's capable of processing unbounded streaming data and provides extensive computation and micro batching facilities on the top of it.

Storm provides solutions to a very wide spectrum of use cases, ranging from alerts and real-time business analytics, machine learning, and ETL use cases to name a few.

Storm has a wide variety of input and output integration points. For input data, it conjuncts well with leading queuing mechanisms like RabbitMQ, JMS, Kafka, Krestel, Amazon Kinesis, and so on. For the output end points, it connects well with most of the traditional databases such as Oracle and MySQL. The adaptability is not limited to traditional RDBMS systems; Storm interfaces very well with Big Data stores such as Cassandra, HBase, and so on.

All these capabilities make Storm the most sought after framework when it comes to providing real-time solutions. Around high-velocity data, Storm is the perfect choice. The following diagram perfectly captures and describes Storm as a black box:

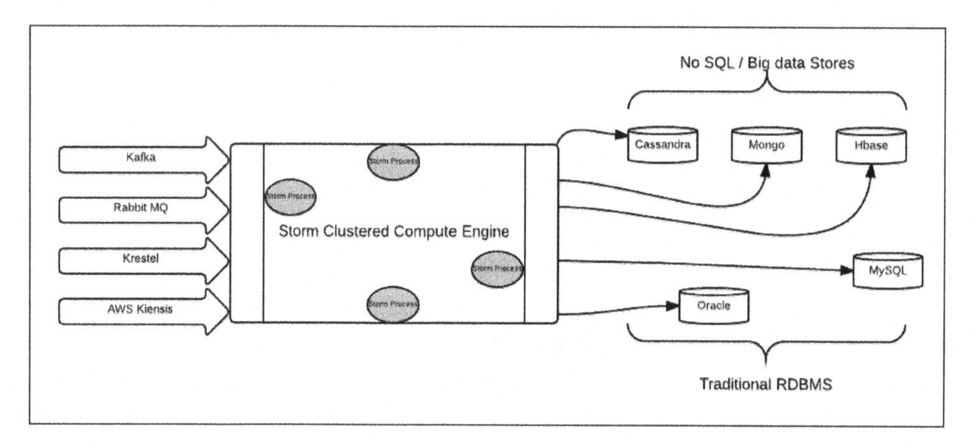

The journey of Storm

Now that we know about the capabilities of Storm, knowing a little history about this wonderful marvel of engineering will get us acquainted with how great frameworks are built and how small experiments become huge successes. Here is the excerpt of Storm's journey, which I learned from Nathan Marz's blog (`http://nathanmarz.com/blog/history-of-apache-storm-and-lessons-learned.html`).

Storm is Nathan's brainchild and in his words, there are two important aspects any successful initiative needs to abide by (Nathan has said that in the context of Storm, but I can see these are generic commandments that can be linked to the fundamental success of any invention):

- There should be a real problem that this solution/invention can solve effectively
- There must be a considerable number of people who believe in the solution/invention as a tool to handle the problem

The problem at hand that led to idea of Storm was the real-time analytics solution that was being used back in 2010-2011 for analyzing social media data and providing insight to business houses. Now the question here is what were the issues with their existing solution that led to inception of frameworks such as Storm? The long answer made short, as it's said, "*all good things come to an end*" and so "*all good solutions run into problems and eventually the end of life.*" Here, the existing solution at BackType was very complex. It was not scaling effectively and the business logic was hardwired into the application framework, thus making the life of developers a bigger challenge. They were actually using a solution wherein data from Twitter Firehose was pushed to a set of queues, and they had Python processes to subscribe to these queues, read and deserialize them, and then publish them to other queues and workers. Though the application had a distributed set of workers and brokers, orchestration and management was a very tedious and complicated code segment.

Step 1

That's when the idea struck Nathan Marz and he came up with a few abstracted concepts:

- **Stream**: This is a distributed abstraction of endless events, which has the ability to be produced and processed in parallel
- **Spout**: This is the abstract component that produces the streams
- **Bolt**: This is the abstract component that processes the streams

Step 2

Once the abstractions were in place, the next big leap in realization of the idea was actually figuring out the solution for the following:

- Intermediate brokers
- Solving the dilemma that comes with the promise of guaranteed processing in a real-time paradigm

The solution to these two aspects gave the vision to build the smartest component of this framework. Thereafter, the path to success was planned. Of course, it was not simple but the vision, thoughts, and ideas were in place.

It took around 5 months to get the first version in place. A few key aspects that were kept in mind right from the beginning are as follows:

- It was to be open source
- All APIs were in Java, thus making it easily accessible by the majority of the community and applications
- It was developed using Clojure which made the project development fast and efficient
- It should use the Thrift data structure and lend usability to non-JVM platforms and applications

In May 2011, BackType was acquired by Twitter and thus Storm became a prodigy of the Twitter powerhouse. It was officially released in September 2011. It was readily adopted by the industry and later adopted by industry majors such as Apache, HDP, Microsoft, and so on.

That was the short synopsis of the long journey of Apache Storm. Storm was a success because of the following six KPIs that no tool/technology/framework could offer in a package at that point of time:

- **Performance**: Storm is best suited for the velocity dimension of Big Data, where data arriving at tremendous rates has to be processed in strict SLA of order of seconds.
- **Scalability**: This is another dimension that's the key to the success of Storm. It provides massive parallel processing with linear scalability. That makes it very easy to build systems that can be easily scaled up/down depending on the need of the business.
- **Fail safe**: That's another differentiating factor of Storm. It's distributed and that comes with an advantage of being fault tolerant. This means that the application won't go down or stop processing if some component or node of the cluster snaps. The same process or the work unit would be handled by some other worker on some other node, thus making the processing seamless even in event of failure.
- **Reliability**: This framework provides the ability to process each event, once and exactly once by the application.
- **Ease**: This framework is built over very logical abstractions that are easy to understand and comprehend. Thus, the adoption or migration to Storm is simple, and that is one of the key attribute to its phenomenal success.

- **Open source**: This is the most lucrative feature that any software framework can offer—a reliable and scalable piece of excellent engineering without the tag of license fees.

After the synopsis of the long journey of Storm, let's understand some of its abstractions before delving deeper into its internals.

Storm abstractions

Now that we understand how Storm was born and how it completed the long journey from BackType Storm to Twitter Storm to Apache Storm, in this section, we'll introduce you to certain abstractions that are part of Storm.

Streams

A stream is one of the most basic abstraction and core concepts of Storm. It's basically unbounded (no start or end sequence) of data. Storm as a framework assumes that the streams can be created in parallel and processed in parallel by a set of distributed components. As an analogy, it can be co-related to a stream.

In the context of Storm, a stream is an endless sequence of tuples or data. A tuple is data comprising of key-value pairs. These streams conform to a schema. This schema is like a template to interpret and understand the data/tuple in the stream, and it has specifications such as fields. The fields can have primitive data types such as integer, long, bytes, string, Boolean, double, and so on. But Storm provides facility to developers to define support for custom data types by writing their own serializers.

- `Tuple`: These are data that form streams. It's the core data structure of Storm, and it's an interface under the `backtype.storm.tuple` package.
- `OutputFieldsDeclarer`: This is an interface under `backtype.storm.topology`. It is used for defining the schemas and declaring corresponding streams.

Topology

The entire Storm application is packaged and bundled together in Storm topology. The same analogy can be built for a MapReduce job. The only difference between a Storm topology and a MapReduce job is that while the latter terminates, the former runs forever. Yes you read that correctly, Storm topologies don't end unless terminated, because they are there to process data streams and streams don't end. Thus, the topologies stay alive forever, processing all incoming tuples.

A topology is actually a **DAG** (short for **Directed Acyclic Graph**), where spouts and bolts form the nodes and streams are the edges of the graph. Storm topologies are basically Thrift structures that have a wrapper layer of Java APIs to access and manipulate them. `TopologyBuilder` is the template class that exposes Java API for creating and submitting the topology.

Spouts

While describing the topology, we touched upon the spout abstraction of Storm. There are two types of node elements in a topology DAG, one of them is spout—the feeder of data streams into the topology. These are the components that connect to an external source in a queue and read the tuples from it and push them into the topology for processing. A topology essentially operates on tuples, thus the DAG always starts from one or more spouts that are basically source elements for getting tuples into the system.

Spouts come in two flavors with the Storm framework: reliable and unreliable. They function in exactly the same manner as their name suggests. The reliable spout remembers all the tuples that it pushes into the topology by the acknowledgement or acking method, and thus replays failed tuples. This is not possible in an unreliable spout, which doesn't remember or keeps track of the tuples it pushes into the topology:

- `IRichSpout`: This interface is used for implementation of spouts.
- `declareStream()`: This is a method under the `OutputFieldsDeclarer` interface and it's used to specify and bind the stream for emission to a spout.
- `emit()`: This is a method of the `SpoutOutputCollector` class, and was created with a purpose to expose Java APIs to emit tuples from `IRichSpout` instances.
- `nextTuple()`: This is the live wire method of the spout that's continuously called. When it has tuples that are read from external source, the same is emitted into the topology, else it simply returns.
- `ack()`: This method is called by the Storm framework when the emitted tuple is successfully processed by the topology.
- `fail()`: This method is called by the spout when the emitted tuple fails to be processed completely by the topology. Reliable spouts line up such failed tuples for replay.

Bolts

Bolts are the second types of nodes that exist in a Storm topology. These abstract components of the Storm framework are basically the key players in processing. They are the components that perform the processing in the topology. Thus, they are the hub of all logic, processing, merging, and transformation.

Bolts subscribe to streams for input tuples and once they are done with their execution logic, they emit the processed tuples to streams. These processing powerhouses have the capability to subscribe and emit to multiple streams:

- `declareStream()`: This method from `OutputFieldsDeclarer` is used to declare all the streams a particular bolt would emit to. Please note the functionality of bolts emitting to a stream is identical to a spout emitting on a stream.
- `emit()`: Similar to a spout, a bolt also uses an `emit` method to emit into the stream, but the difference here is that the bolt calls the `emit` method from `OutputCollector`.
- `InputDeclarer`: This interface has methods for defining various grouping (subscriptions on streams) that control the binding of bolts to input streams, thus ensuring bolts read tuples from the streams based on definitions in groupings.
- `execute()`: This method holds the crux of all processing, and it's executed for each input tuple for the bolt. Once the bolt completes the processing it calls the `ack()` method.
- `IRichBolt` and `IBasicBolt`: These are the two interfaces provided by the Storm framework for implementation of bolts.

Now that we have understood the basic paradigms and their functions with respect to Storm, the following diagram summarizes all of it:

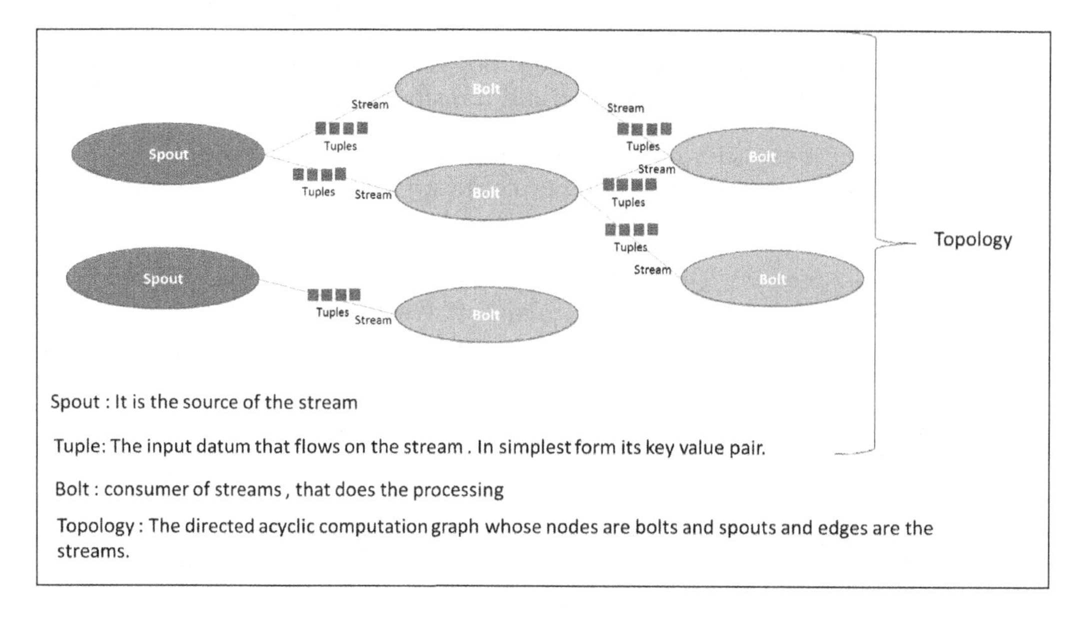

Tasks

Within the bolt and spout, the actual processing task is broken into smaller work items and is executed or computed in parallel. These threads of execution that actually perform the computation within the bolts or spouts are called **tasks**. One bolt and spout can spawn any number of tasks (of course, each node has a limit to resources in terms of RAM and CPU, but the framework itself does not levy any limit).

Workers

These are the processes which are spawned to cater to the execution of the topology. Each worker is executed in isolation from other workers in the topology and to achieve this, they are executed in different JVMs.

Storm architecture and its components

We have discussed enough about the history and theory of abstractions of Storm; it's now time to dive in and see the framework in execution and get hands on to the real code to actually see Storm in action. We are just one step away from the action part. Before we get there, let's understand what are the various components that get to play in Storm and what is their contribution in the building and orchestration of this framework.

Storm execution can be done in two flavors:

- **Local mode**: This is a single node and a nondistributed setup that is generally used for demo and testing. Here, the entire topology is executed in a single worker and thus a single JVM.
- **Distributed mode**: This is a multinode setup that is fully or partially distributed and this is the recommended mode for real-time application development and deployment.

The instructions can be referred to from the Apache Storm site at `https://storm.apache.org/documentation/Setting-up-a-Storm-cluster.html`. A typical Storm setup has the following components.

A Zookeeper cluster

Zookeeper is actually the orchestration engine and bookkeeper for Storm. Zookeeper actually does all the coordination such as submission of topology, creation of workers, keeping track and checking of dead nodes and processes, and restarting the execution on alternate choices in the cluster in the event of failures of supervisors or worker processes.

A Storm cluster

A Storm cluster is generally set up on multiple nodes and comprises the following processes:

- **Nimbus**: This is the master process of the Storm framework and can be considered analogous to the JobTracker of Hadoop. This is the process which owns the task of topology submission and distributes the entire code bundle to all other supervisor nodes of the cluster. It also distributes the workers across various supervisors in the cluster. A Storm cluster has one Nimbus daemon process.

- **Supervisors**: These are the processes that actually do the processing. A Storm cluster generally has multiple supervisors. Once the topology is submitted to the Nimbus and the worker assignment is done, worker processes within the supervisor nodes do all the processing; these worker processes are started by the Supervisor daemon.
- **UI**: The Storm framework provides the following browser based interface to monitor the cluster and various topologies. The UI process has to be started on any one node in the cluster and the web application is accessible at `http://ui-node-ip:8080`:

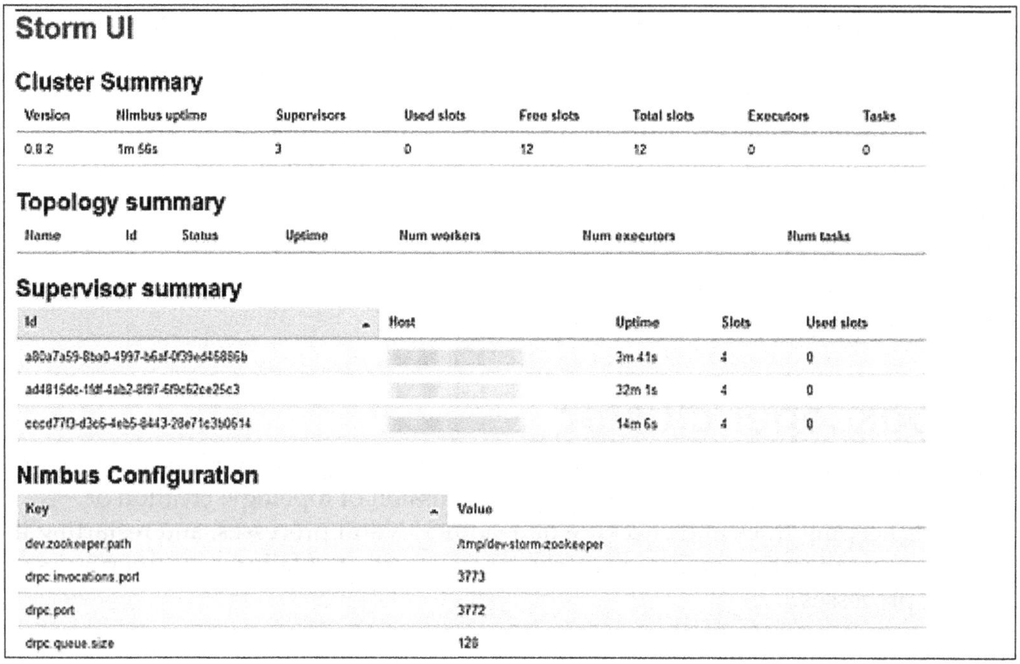

Storm UI

Cluster Summary

Version	Nimbus uptime	Supervisors	Used slots	Free slots	Total slots	Executors	Tasks
0.8.2	1m 56s	3	0	12	12	0	0

Topology summary

Name	Id	Status	Uptime	Num workers	Num executors	Num tasks

Supervisor summary

Id	Host	Uptime	Slots	Used slots
a80a7a59-8ba0-4997-b6af-0f39ed45886b		3m 41s	4	0
ad4815dc-1fdf-4ab2-8f97-6f9c62ce25c3		32m 1s	4	0
cecd77f3-d3e6-4eb5-8443-28e71e3b0614		14m 6s	4	0

Nimbus Configuration

Key	Value
dev.zookeeper.path	/tmp/dev-storm-zookeeper
drpc.invocations.port	3773
drpc.port	3772
drpc.queue.size	128

Now that we have an idea about the various processes and components of the Storm cluster, let's get further acquainted with how the various moving parts function together and what happens when a topology is submitted to the cluster.

Have a look at the following diagram:

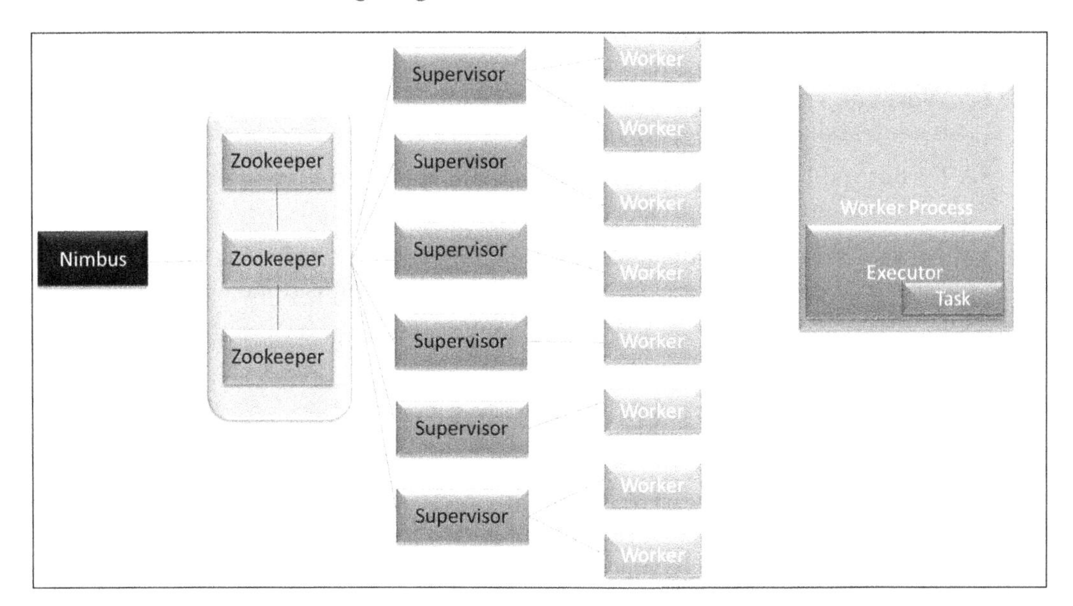

This diagram depicts the following:

- **Nimbus**: It is the master Storm process of the cluster, essentially a Thrift server.

  This is the Storm daemon where the topology is submitted by a Storm submitter. The code distribution (the JAR file and all its dependencies) is done from this node to all other nodes of the cluster. This node sets up all static information about the cluster and topology; it assigns all workers and starts the topology.

  This process also keeps a check and monitor on failure situations across the cluster. If a supervisor node goes down, the Nimbus reassigns the tasks executing on that node to other nodes in the cluster.

- **Zookeeper**: Once the topology is submitted (submission is done to the Nimbus Thrift server in JSON and Thrift), Zookeeper captures all worker assignments and thus keeps track of all processing components in the cluster.

  Cluster synchronization and heartbeat tracking is done by Zookeeper for all worker processes.

  This mechanism ensures that after the topology has been submitted, if the Nimbus goes down, the topology operations would still continue to function normally because the co-ordination and heartbeat is tracked by Zookeeper.

- **Supervisors**: These are the nodes that take up the processing job from the Nimbus and execute various workers according to the assignment to execute the same.
- **Workers**: These are the processes that execute within the supervisor nodes; the job assigned to them is to execute and complete a portion of the topology.
- **Executors**: These are Java threads that are spawned by worker processes within their JVM for processing of the topology.
- **Tasks**: These are the instances or the components within executor where actually a piece of work happens, or the processing is done.

How and when to use Storm

I am a believer of the fact that the quickest way to get acquainted to a tool or technology is to do it, and we have been doing a lot of theoretical talking so far rather than actually doing it, so let's actually begin the fun. We would start with the basic word count topology, I have lot of experience of using Storm on Linux, and there is a lot of online material available for the same. I have used a Windows VM for execution of the word count topology. Here are a couple of prerequisites:

- apache-storm-0.9.5-src.
- JDK 1.6+.
- Python 2.x. (I figured this out by a little trial and error. My Ubuntu always had Python and it never gave any trouble; for example, the word count uses a Python script for splitting sentences, so I set up Python 3 (the latest version), but later figured out that the compatible one is 2.x.)
- Maven.
- Eclipse.

Here we go.

Set up the following environment variables accurately:

- `JAVA_HOME`
- `MVN_HOME`
- `PATH`

The `PATH` variable should have the path to Python installation on your machine:

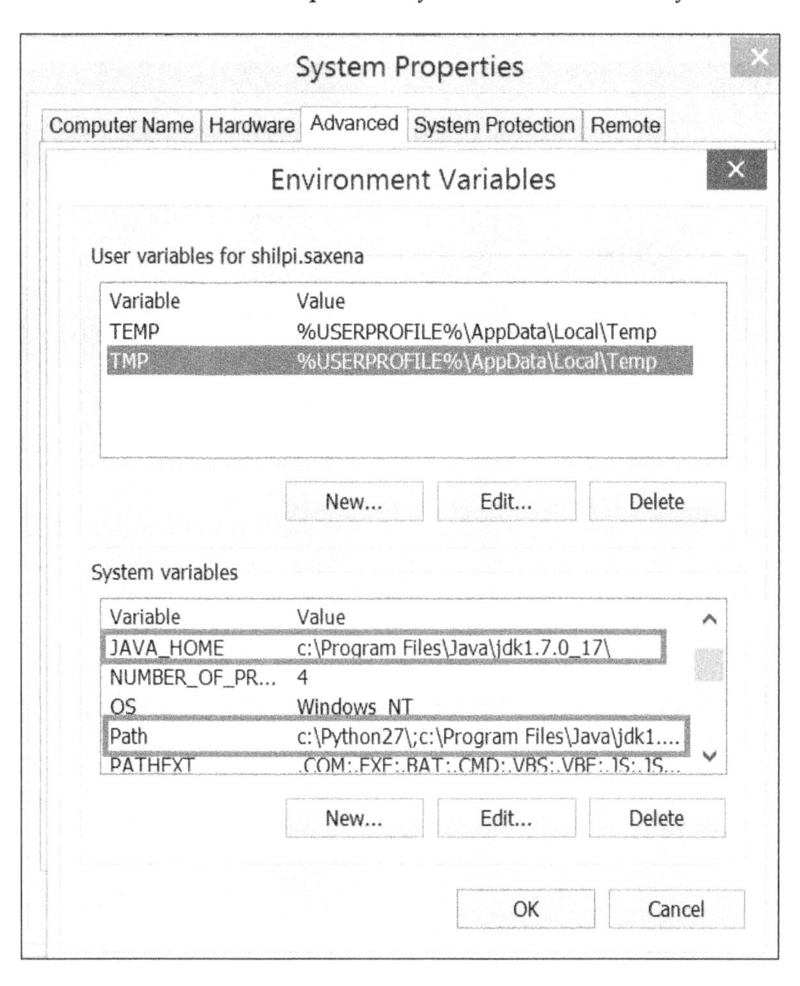

Just to crosscheck that everything is set up accurately, please issue the following commands on your command prompt and match the output:

```
C:\Users\shilpi.saxena>java -version
java version "1.7.0_17"
Java(TM) SE Runtime Environment (build 1.7.0_17-b02)
Java HotSpot(TM) 64-Bit Server VM (build 23.7-b01, mixed mode)

C:\Users\shilpi.saxena>mvn -version
Apache Maven 3.3.3 (7994120775791599e205a5524ec3e0dfe41d4a06; 2015-04-22T17:27:3
7+05:30)
Maven home: E:\softwares\maven\apache-maven-3.3.3-bin\apache-maven-3.3.3\bin\..
Java version: 1.7.0_17, vendor: Oracle Corporation
Java home: c:\Program Files\Java\jdk1.7.0_17\jre
Default locale: en_US, platform encoding: Cp1252
OS name: "windows 8", version: "6.2", arch: "amd64", family: "windows"

C:\Users\shilpi.saxena>python --version
Python 2.7.10
```

Now, we are all set to import the Storm starter project into Eclipse and actually see it executing. The following screenshot depicts the steps to be executed for importing and reaching the word count topology in the Storm source bundle:

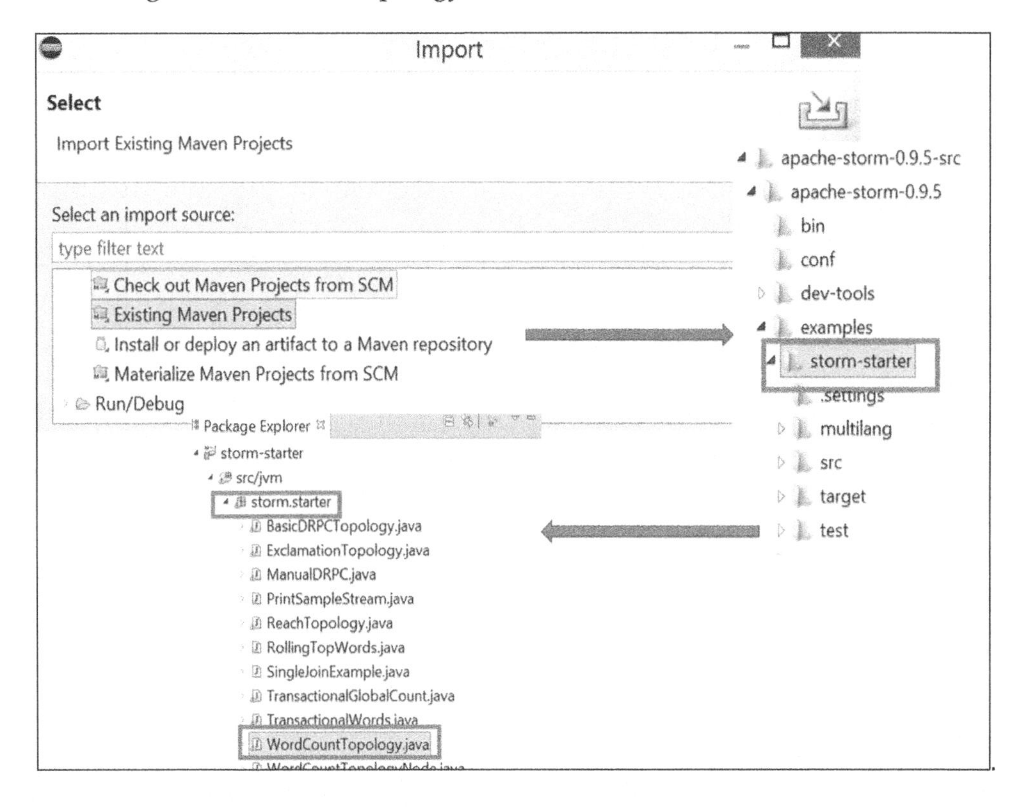

Now, we have the project ready to be built and executed. I will explain all the moving components of the topology in detail, but for now let's see what the output would be like.

```
[NIOServerCxn.Factory:0.0.0.0/0.0.0.0:2000] INFO  org.apache.storm.zookeeper.server.NIOServerCnxn - Closed socket connect
[main] INFO  backtype.storm.utils.StormBoundedExponentialBackoffRetry - The baseSleepTimeMs [1000] the maxSleepTimeMs [3
pache.storm.curator.framework.imps.CuratorFrameworkImpl - Starting
[main] INFO  org.apache.storm.zookeeper.ZooKeeper - Initiating client connection, connectString=localhost:2000/storm sess
[main-SendThread(127.0.0.1:2000)] INFO  org.apache.storm.zookeeper.ClientCnxn - Opening socket connection to server 127.
[main-SendThread(127.0.0.1:2000)] INFO  org.apache.storm.zookeeper.ClientCnxn - Socket connection established to 127.0.0.
ory:0.0.0.0/0.0.0.0:2000] INFO  org.apache.storm.zookeeper.server.NIOServerCnxnFactory - Accepted socke
ory:0.0.0.0/0.0.0.0:2000] INFO  org.apache.storm.zookeeper.server.ZooKeeperServer - Client attempting t
[SyncThread:0] INFO  org.apache.storm.zookeeper.server.ZooKeeperServer - Established session 0x15034fee1050005 with negot
[main-SendThread(127.0.0.1:2000)] INFO  org.apache.storm.zookeeper.ClientCnxn - Session establishment complete on server
) org.apache.storm.curator.framework.state.ConnectionStateManager - State change: CONNECTED
torm.daemon.supervisor - Starting Supervisor with conf {"dev.zookeeper.path" "/tmp/dev-storm-zooke

21594 [Thread-32] INFO  backtype.storm.daemon.task - Emitting: split default ["score"]
21594 [Thread-11-count] INFO  backtype.storm.daemon.task - Emitting: count default [four, 6]
21594 [Thread-11-count] INFO  bac executor - Processing received message sou
21595 [Thread-11-count] INFO  bac Emitting: count default [score, 6]
21595 [Thread-32] INFO  backtype.storm.daemon.task - Emitting: split default ["and"]
21595 [Thread-13-count] INFO  backtype.storm.daemon.executor - Processing received message sou
21595 [Thread-13-count] INFO  backtype.storm.daemon.task - Emitting: count default [and, 9]
```


We have seen the topology executing, so there are a couple of important observations I want you all to deduce from the previous screenshot of the Eclipse console.
Note that though it's a single-node Storm execution, you can still see the loggers pertaining to the creation of the following:

- Zookeeper connection
- Supervisor process startup
- Worker process creation
- Tuple emission after actual word count

Now let's take a closer look at understanding the wiring of the word count topology. The following diagram captures the essence of the flow and the relevant code snippets. The word count topology is basically a network of `RandomSentenceSpout`, `SplitSentenceBolt`, and `WordCountBolt`.

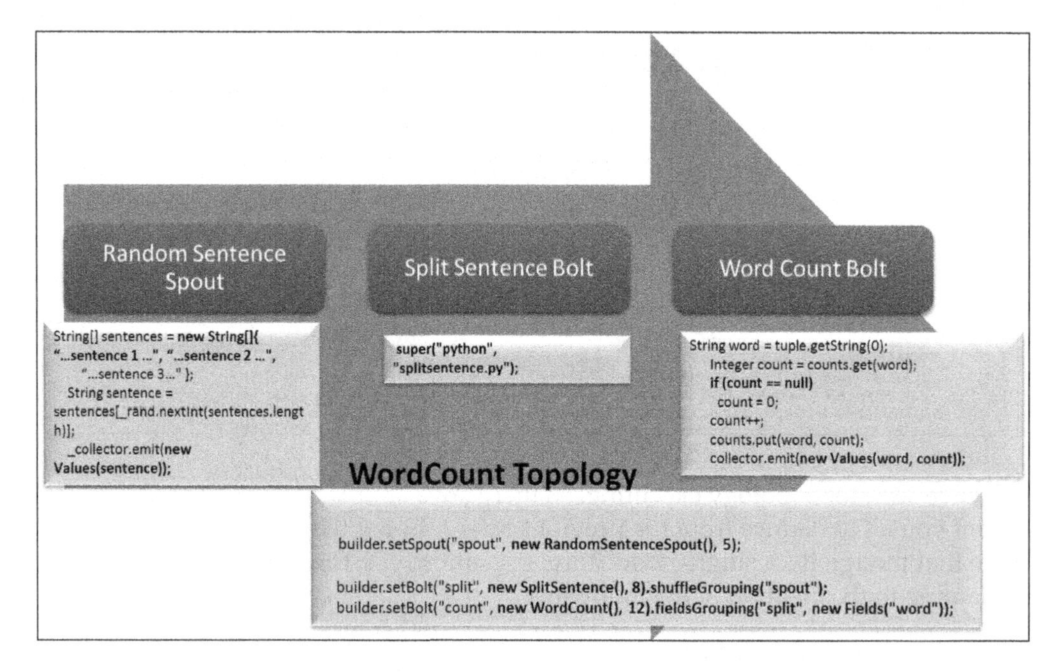

Though this diagram is self-explanatory in terms of the flow and action, I'll take up a few lines to elaborate on the code snippets:

- `WordCountTopology`: Here, we have actually done the networking or wiring of the various streams and processing components of the application:

```
// we are creating the topology builder template class
TopologyBuilder builder = new TopologyBuilder();
// we are setting the spout in here an instance of    //
RandomSentenceSpout
builder.setSpout("spout", new RandomSentenceSpout(), 5);
//Here the first bolt SplitSentence is being wired into //the
builder template
builder.setBolt("split", new SplitSentence(),
8).shuffleGrouping("spout");
//Here the second bolt WordCount is being wired into the //builder
template
builder.setBolt("count", new WordCount(), 12).
fieldsGrouping("split", new Fields("word"));
```

One item worth noting is how various groupings, `fieldsGrouping` and `shuffleGrouping`, in the preceding examples are being used for wiring and subscribing the streams. Another interesting point is the parallelism hint defined against each component while it's being wired into the topology.

```
builder.setBolt("count", new WordCount(), 12).
fieldsGrouping("split", new Fields("word"));
```

For example, in the preceding snippet, a new bolt `WordCount` is defined with a parallelism hint of `12`. That means 12 executor tasks would be spawned to handle the parallel processing for this bolt.

- `RandomSentenceSpout`: This is the spout or the feeder component of the topology. It picks up a random sentence from the group of sentences hardcoded in the code itself and emits that onto the topology for processing using the `collector.emit()` method. Here's an excerpt of the code for the same:

```
public void nextTuple() {
  Utils.sleep(100);
  String[] sentences = new String[]{ "the cow jumped over
    the moon", "an apple a day keeps the doctor away",
    "four score and seven years ago", "snow white and the
    seven dwarfs", "i am at two with nature" };
  String sentence = sentences[_rand.nextInt
    (sentences.length)];
  _collector.emit(new Values(sentence));
}
...
public void declareOutputFields(OutputFieldsDeclarer
  declarer) {
  declarer.declare(new Fields("word"));
}
```

The `nextTuple()` method is executed for every event or tuple that is read by the spout and pushed into the topology. I have also attached the snippet of the `declareOutputFields` method wherein a new stream emerging from this spout is being bound to.

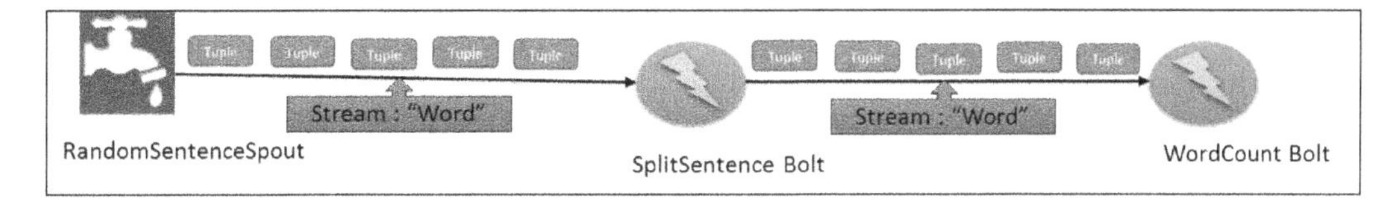

Now that we have seen the word count executing on our Storm setup, it's time to delve into storm internals and understand the nitty-gritties of Storm internals and its architecture, and dissect some of the key capabilities to discover the implementation for the same.

Storm internals

The moment people start talking about Storm, a few key aspects of this framework stand apart:

- Storm parallelism
- Storm internal message processing

Now, let's pick each of these attributes and figure out how Storm is able to deliver these capabilities.

Storm parallelism

If we want to enlist the processes that thrive within a Storm cluster, the following are key components to be tracked:

- **Worker process**: These are the processes executing on the supervisor node and process a subset of the topology. Each worker process executes in its own JVM. The number of workers allocated to a topology can be specified in the topology builder template and is applicable at the time of topology submission.
- **Executors**: These are the threads that are spawned within the worker processes for execution of a bolt or spout. Each executor can run multiple tasks, but being a single thread, these tasks on the executor are performed sequentially. The number of executors is specified while wiring in the bolts and spouts in the topology builder template. The default value is 1.
- **Tasks**: These are basic action hubs where actual processing is done. By default, Storm launches one task per executor. The number of tasks can also be specified at the time of setting up bolts and spouts in the topology builder template.

Consider the following line of code:

```
builder.setBolt("split", new SplitSentence(), 8).setNumTasks(16).
shuffleGrouping("spout"); //1
...
conf.setNumWorkers(3); //2
```

This code snippet captures the following:

- The `SplitSentence` bolt has been allocated eight executors.
- The `SplitSentence` bolt would launch 16 tasks during its execution, which means two tasks per executor. With each executor, these tasks would be executed sequentially.
- The topology is configured to be launched using three worker processes.

The following diagram also captures the relationship of these three components with respect to each other:

The worker processes are spawned within the supervisor node. The generic thumb rule is to have one worker per processor on the node. Within each of the worker processes, multiple executor processes are created—each executing in its own JVM and orchestrating their tasks.

Next, we should get into understanding the Storm parallelism concepts. Here we will try to infer the same using a sample example topology, and then figure out what happens when the same is submitted and how performance can be achieved:

```
Config topologyConf = new Config();
topologyConf.setNumWorkers(2);
topologyBuilder.setSpout("my-spout", new MySpout(), 2);
topologyBuilder.setBolt("first-bolt", new FirstBolt(),2)
.setNumTasks(4)
.shuffleGrouping("my-spout");
topologyBuilder.setBolt("second-bolt", new YellowSecondBolt(), 6)
                .shuffleGrouping("first-bolt");
```

Here, we have a plain vanilla topology that's allocated two workers and it has one spout with a parallelism hint of `2` and two bolts. The first bolt has a parallelism hint of `2` and number of tasks as `4`, while the second one has a parallelism hint of `6`.

Please note parallelism hint refers to number of executors, and by default, Storm spawns one task per executor. So here is some calculation that we will be looking at in the previous topology template configuration:

- Total combined parallelism (number of executors) for all components = 2 (spout parallelism) + 2 (first bolt parallelism) + 6 (second bolt parallelism) = 10
- Number of workers allocated = 2
- Number of executors to be spawned on each worker = 10/2 = 5
- Number of tasks for spout = 1 (default)
- Number of tasks for first bolt = 4
- Number of tasks for second bolt = 6

Have a look at the following diagram:

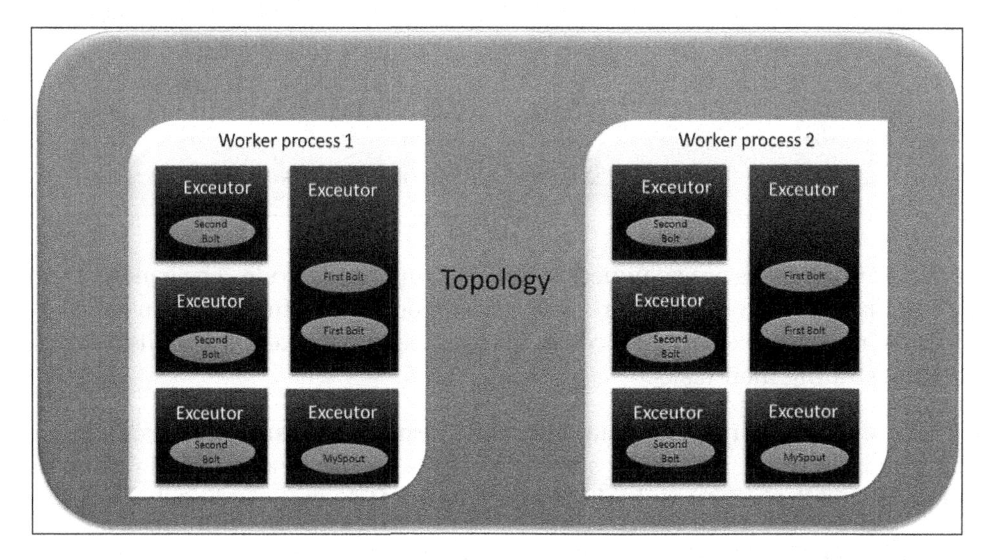

The preceding image captures the distribution of topology components across two workers.

Storm internal message processing

In the previous section, we discussed Storm parallelism and so you must have a sense of how distributed Storm topology components are across different nodes, workers, and threads.

Now, we need to understand that there is lot of inter-process communication that is in play for orchestrating such a distributed processing unit. While this communication is the essence of all processing, it has to be efficient and minimally loaded so that it doesn't become a load stone and bring down the throughput.

While we will discuss in detail each of these aspects in later chapters, it's fair to understand what are the various kinds of communication that are in play in a Storm cluster that holds a topology in execution:

- **Inter-worker communication**: We are referring to the information exchange that happens between two worker processes. There are two flavors attached to this kind of communication:
    - **Workers executing on same node**: This one doesn't involve network hop as here the exchange is happening between two worker nodes on the same supervisors. This is inter-JVM communication that is executed using ZeroMQ in earlier Storm versions and using Netty in Storm 0.9 and above.
    - **Workers executing across nodes**: Here, we are referring to exchange of information that happens between two worker nodes executing on different supervisors. This does involve network hop. It is executed using ZeroMQ in earlier Storm versions and using Netty in Storm 0.9 and above.
- **Intra-worker communication**: This refers to the information exchange that happens within the worker. This is the messaging communication between the executors that are spawned on the same worker. This kind of communication happens between different worker threads within a single JVM on single supervisor nodes. Storm uses **LMAX Disruptor** (a super-efficient, lightweight messaging framework for inter-thread communication).

A couple of aspects to be noted here are as follows:

- All internode communication is done using ZeroMQ, Netty, or Kyro. Serialization is used in here.
- All communication that's local to the node is done using LMAX Disruptor. No serialization is used in here.

- Effective use of a message exchange framework and serialization leads to the efficiency and performance that Storm is able to attain.

The next diagram shows the internal communication and message execution within a worker:

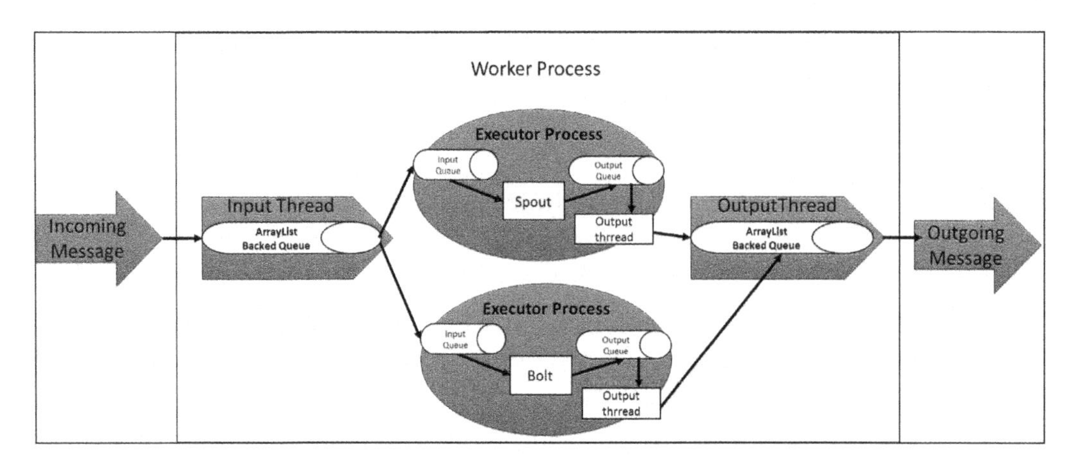

Each Storm supervisor has a TCP port allocated to it. This is defined under the `storm.yaml` configuration file. The worker input thread process as depicted in the preceding diagram continuously listens to the allocated port. This input thread, when it receives a message, reads it, and places it into the buffer (which is nothing but an `ArrayList` based queue). This input receiving thread is called the `receiver.buffer` thread and is responsible for reading incoming messages and batching them into `topology.receiver.buffer`.

More than one executor can be spawned within the same worker process. Again, referring to the preceding diagram, each executor process also has its own input queue, which is fed from `receiver.buffer`. Every executor has its own input queue. The processing logic is written in the `execute()` method of the bolt, or the `nextTuple()` method of the spout; this processing is performed on the messages waiting in the executor queue, and once the processing is done and the message needs to be transmitted, the output thread or the sender thread of the executor dispatches the message to the output thread of the worker.

This output thread of the worker receives the message and places it in an `ArrayList` output queue. Once the threshold is achieved, the message is transmitted out of the node on the outbound TCP port.

Summary

We covered quite a bit on Storm, its history, and its inception in this chapter. We introduced the components of Storm along with internal implementations of certain key aspects of Storm. We saw actual code and we now expect you to be able to set up Storm (local and cluster) and execute the basic examples as part of a Storm starter.

In the next chapter, we will initiate the users on various input data sources that are used in conjunction with Storm. We will discuss the reliability of Storm and how to persist data into some stable storage from Storm bolts.

3

Processing Data with Storm

This chapter will focus primarily on reading and processing the data using Storm. The key aspect being covered here will comprise of the ability of Storm to consume data from various sources, processing and transforming the same, and storing it to data stores. We will also help you to understand these concepts and give examples of filters, joins, and aggregators.

In this chapter, we will cover the following topics:

- Storm input sources
- Meet Kafka
- Reliability of data processing
- Storm simple patterns
- Storm persistence

Storm input sources

Storm works well with a variety of input data sources. Consider the following examples:

- Kafka
- RabbitMQ
- Kinesis

Storm is actually a consumer and process of the data. It has to be coupled with some data source. Most of the time, data sources are connected devices that generate streaming data, for example:

- Sensor data
- Traffic signal data

- Data from stock exchanges
- Data from production lines

The list can be virtually endless and so would be the use cases that can be served with the Storm-based solutions. But in the essence of designing cohesive but low coupling systems, it's very important that we keep the source and computation lightly coupled. It's highly advisable that we use a queue or broker service to integrate the streaming data source with Storm's computation unit. The following diagram quickly captures the basic flow for any Storm-based streaming application, where the data is collated from the source and ingested into Storm:

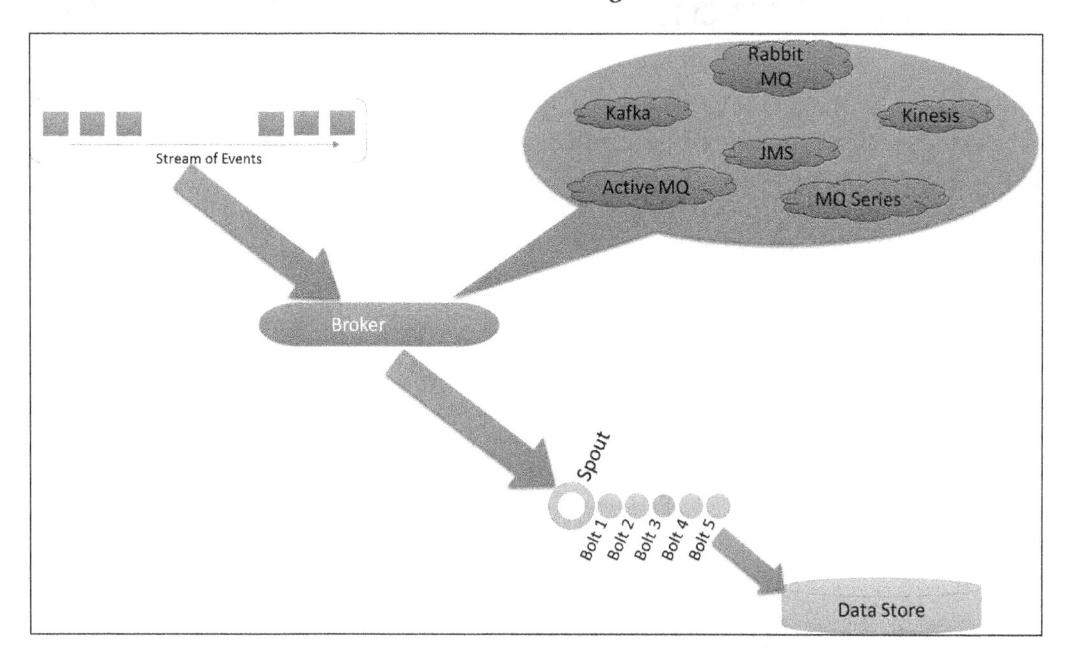

The data is consumed, parsed, processed, and dumped into the database. In the coming sections, we will delve a little deeper into the options that are available for a decoupled integration between a Storm compute unit and the data source.

Meet Kafka

Kafka is a distributed queuing system that operates on the principle of commit logs. Its execution is based on a traditional publisher-subscriber model and it's known for its built-in performance efficiency and durability. When we essentially mark a data structure as durable, it's due to the ability to retain or recover the messages or data even in the event of failure.

Before moving ahead, let's get acquainted with a few terms that will help us walk through Kafka better:

- Kafka being based on typical pub-sub model, there are Kafka producer processes that produce the messages and Kafka consumer processes that consume the messages.
- The feeds or streams of one or more messages are grouped into the Kafka topic to which the consumer process subscribes while the producer process publishes.
- We have said Kafka is distributed. Thus, it's sure that it executes in a clustered setup in production scenarios. It has one or more broker servers, which are stringed together to form a Kafka cluster.

The following diagram depicts a typical Kafka cluster and its components:

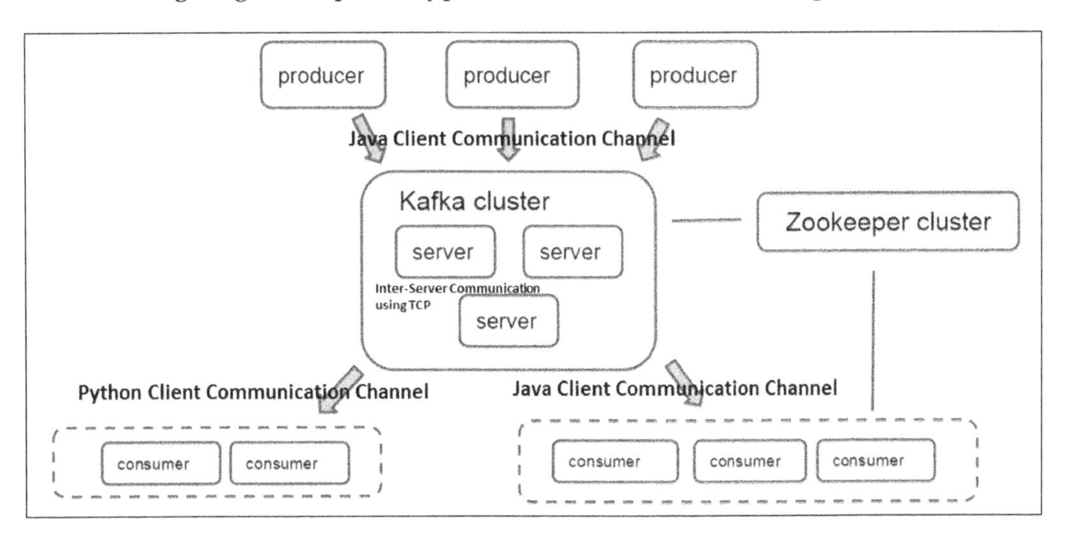

Though the diagram is self-explanatory, here is a brief explanation for the same. The Kafka cluster generally comprises of one or more Kafka servers that communicate with each other through the typical TCP protocol. The producer and consumer processes generally communicate to the servers through clients, which can be in Java, Python, or a variety of languages (Kafka clients can be found at `https://cwiki.apache.org/confluence/display/KAFKA/Clients`).

Getting to know more about Kafka

Kafka topics can be assumed to be like *named* letter boxes, where the messages are delivered by the Kafka producers. Talking about one Kafka cluster, one can have multiple topics, each of which is further portioned and chronologically ordered. Topics can be assumed as a logical collection of partitions that actually hold the physical files.

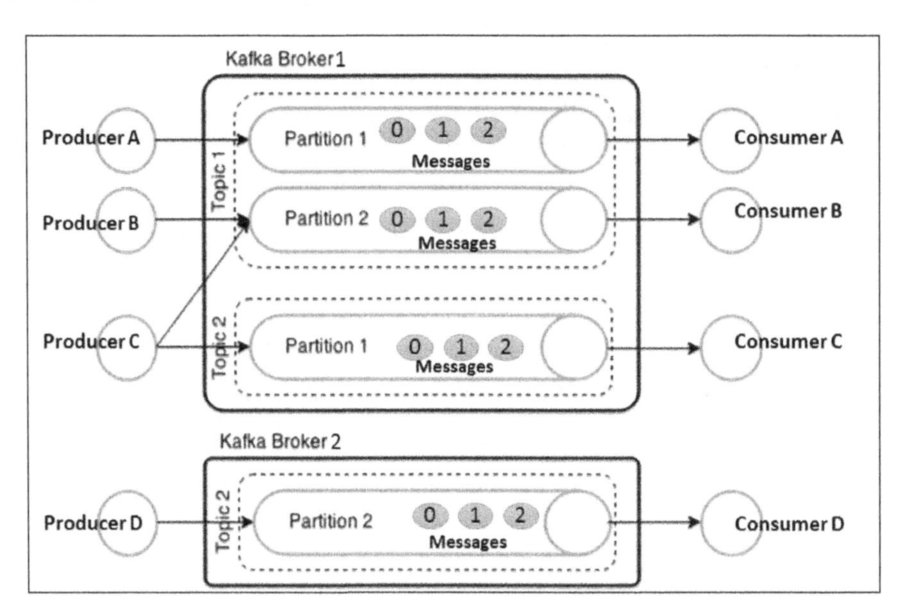

As depicted in the diagram, one Kafka broker can hold multiple partitions and each of the partitions hold multiple messages in a strict order. Ordering (where 0th message is oldest in order of time) is one of the greatest advantages that are provided by the Kafka message broking system. One or more producers can write to a partition and consumers subscribe to retrieve the messages of these partitions. All messages are distinguished by a unique offset ID (unique identifier associated to every message in the partition, and the uniqueness is maintained only within the partition).

Each message published is retained for a specific time denoted by **Time to live** (**TTL**) that has been configured. This behavior is irrespective of whether the message has been consumed by the consumer or retained by the partition. The next important attribute to be acquainted within Kafka is **topics**.

If I describe in simplest words, Kafka continuously writes the messages into a commit log. Each of the partition has its own immutable commit log. As said before, each message is marked with a sequence ID.

Talking about Kafka **consumers**, it's very important to understand that one of the reasons for Kafka's efficiency is that overloading for setting and maintaining the consumer context is minimal. It actually does what's necessary; per consumer, it just requires to maintain the **offset**. The consumer metadata is maintained on the server, and it's the job of the consumer to remember the offset. We need to understand a very important implication of the previous statement. Kafka stores all messages in the partition in the form of a commit log. Well, logs are essentially chronologically ordered, but as mentioned, Kafka consumers retain the right to maintain, manage, and advance the offset. Thus, they can read and handle the message the way they want to; for example, they can reset the offset to read from beginning of the queue, or they can move the offset to the end to consume at the end.

Another aspect that adds to the scalability of the Kafka solution is that while one partition is hosted on one machine, one topic can have any number of partitions, thus making it linearly scalable to store extended amounts of data in theory. This mechanism of distributed partitions, along with the replication of data across partitions of a topic, resonates two essential Big Data concepts: high availability and load balancing.

The handling of partitions is done in a very resilient and failsafe manner; each partition has its leader and followers—something very close and similar to the way the Zookeeper quorum operates. When the messages arrive to the topic, they are first written to the partition leader. In the background, there are writes that are replicated to the followers to maintain the replication factor. In the event of failure of the leader, the leader is re-elected and one of the followers becomes the leader. Each Kafka server node serves as a leader to one or more partitions spread across the cluster.

As said earlier, the entire responsibility of the consumption of messages is an equally important role that the Kafka producers execute. First and the foremost, they publish the message to the topic, but it's not as straight and simple as this. They have to make a choice to decide which message should be written to which partition of the topic. This decision is achieved by one of the configured algorithms; it could be round-robin, key-based, or even some custom algorithm.

Now that the messages have been published, we need to understand how essentially Kafka consumers operate and what are the finer dynamics. Traditionally, if we analyze the world of messaging services there are only two models that operate at gross level in theory. Others are more or less abstractions built around them with evolution in implementations. These are the two basic models:

- **Queue**: In this model, the messages are written to a single queue and the consumer can read the messages off the queue
- **Pub-sub**: In this model, where the messages are written to a topic, all subscribed consumers can read off from the same

I would like to reiterate that the preceding description is valid at the base level. Various implementations of a queue offer this behavior depending upon their implementations and aspects such as being push-based or pull-based services.

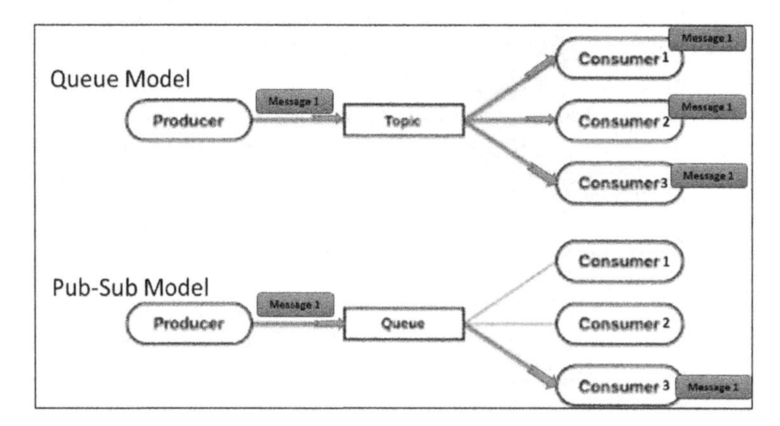

Kafka implementers have been smart enough to offer flexibility and capability of both by coming up with an amalgamation. In Kafka terminology, that's christened as a generalization called a **consumer group**.

This mechanism effectively implements both the queuing and pub-sub models described previously and provides the advantages of load balancing at the consumer end. This gets the control of rate of consumption and its scalability effectively on the client-consumer end. Each consumer is part of a consumer group, and any message that's published to a partition is consumed by one (note only one) consumer in each of the consumer group(s):

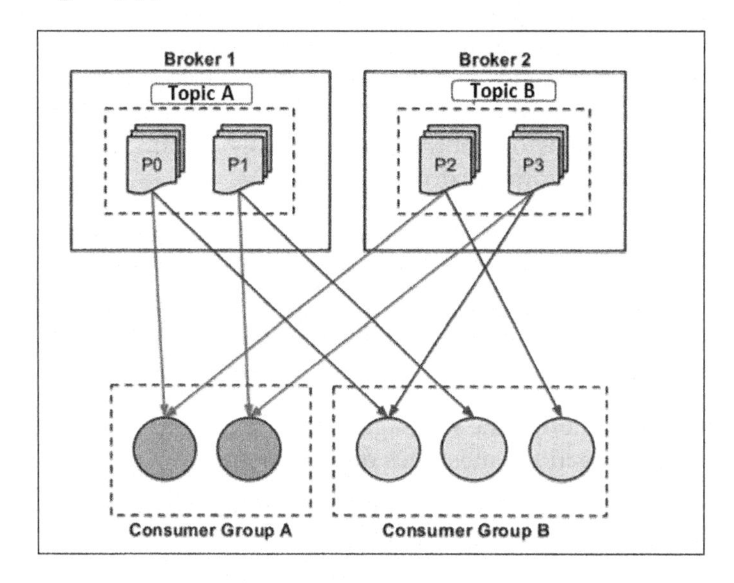

If we try to analyze the preceding diagram, we'd clearly see a graphical depiction of consumer groups and their behavior. Here, we have two Kafka brokers: broker A and broker B. Each of them has two topics: topic A and topic B. Each of the topics is partitioned into two partitions each: partition 0 and partition 1. If you look closely at the preceding diagram, you'll notice that the message from partition 0 in topic A is written to one consumer in consumer group A and one in consumer group B.

Similarly, for all other partitions, the queuing model can be achieved by having all the consumers in a single consumer group, thus achieving one message to be delivered to only one consumer process. Its direct implications are the achievement of load balancing.

If we happen to have a configuration where each consumer group has only a single consumer process in it, then the same behavior as publisher-subscriber model is exhibited and all the messages are published to all consumers.

Kafka comes with following commitments:

- The message ordering is maintained per producer per topic partition
- The messages are presented to consumers in the order they are written to the commit log
- With a replication factor of *N*, the cluster can overall withstand up to *N-1* failures

To set up Kafka on your system(s), download it from `http://kafka.apache.org/downloads.html`, and then run the following commands:

```
> tar -xzf kafka_2.11-0.9.0.0.tgz
> cd kafka_2.11-0.9.0.0
```

Kafka requires ZooKeeper to be set up. You can either use your existing ZooKeeper setup and integrate the same with Kafka, or you can use the quick quick-start ZooKeeper Kafka script for the same that comes bundled within the Kafka setup. Check out the following code:

```
> bin/zookeeper-server-start.sh config/zookeeper.properties
[2015-07-22 15:01:37,495] INFO Reading configuration from: config/
zookeeper.properties (org.apache.zookeeper.server.quorum.
QuorumPeerConfig)
```

Once we have the ZooKeeper up and running, we are all set to have the Kafka server started and running:

```
> bin/kafka-server-start.sh config/server.properties
[2015-07-22 15:01:47,028] INFO Verifying properties (kafka.utils.
VerifiableProperties)
[2015-07-22 15:01:47,051] INFO Property socket.send.buffer.bytes is
overridden to 1048576 (kafka.utils.VerifiableProperties)
```

Once we have Kafka up and running, the next step is to create a Kafka topic:

```
> bin/kafka-topics.sh --create --zookeeper localhost:2181 --replication-
factor 1 --partitions 1 --topic test
```

Once the topic is created the same can be verified using the following commands:

```
> bin/kafka-topics.sh --list --zookeeper localhost:2181
Test
```

Here, we have created a topic called `test`, where the replication factor for the same is kept as `1` and the topic has a single partition.

Now, we are all set to publish the messages and we will run the Kafka command line producer:

```
> bin/kafka-console-producer.sh --broker-list localhost:9092 --topic test
This is message 1
This is message 2
```

Now, we can have the command-line consumer consume these messages. Kafka also has a command-line consumer that will dump out messages to a standard output:

```
> bin/kafka-console-consumer.sh --zookeeper localhost:2181 --topic test
--from-beginning
This is message 1
This is message 2
```

With Kafka set up, let's move back to Storm and work through Storm-Kafka integration in the next sections.

Other sources for input to Storm

In our earlier example, we have seen integrated with Storm, one of them being Kafka (just discussed in the previous section). In Storm samples, the word count topology (which we covered in detail in an earlier chapter) doesn't use any data source for input. Instead, some sentences are hardcoded in the spout itself and this seed data is emitted to the topology. This may be fine for test cases and samples, but for real-world implementations this is neither ideal nor expected. Storm has to feed a stream of live events into the topology in almost all of the real-world implementations. We can have a variety of input sources that can be integrated with Storm. Let's have a closer look at code snippets on what all we can plug in with Storm to feed the data.

A file as an input source

We can use a Storm spout to be effectively reading from a file; though that's not a real use case for a streaming app, but we can have Storm very well read in from the file. All we need to do is to write a custom spout for the same.

The following code segment captures the snippet for the same, followed by an explanation:

```
/**
 * This spout reads data from a CSV file.
 */
public class myLineSpout extends BaseRichSpout {
  private static final Logger LOG = LoggerFactory.
getLogger(myLineSpout.class);
  private String fileName;
  private SpoutOutputCollector _collector;
  private BufferedReader reader;
  private AtomicLong linesRead;

  /**
   * Prepare the spout. This method is called once when the topology
is submitted
   * @param conf
   * @param context
   * @param collector
   */
  @Override
  public void open(Map conf, TopologyContext context,
SpoutOutputCollector collector) {
    linesRead = new AtomicLong(0);
```

```
        _collector = collector;
        try {
          fileName= (String) conf.get("myLineSpout.file");
          reader = new BufferedReader(new FileReader(fileName));
          // read and ignore the header if one exists
        } catch (Exception e) {
          throw new RuntimeException(e);
        }
      }

      ...
      /**
       * Storm will call this method repeatedly to pull tuples from the
    spout
       */
      @Override
      public void nextTuple() {
        try {
          String line = reader.readLine();
          if (line != null) {
            long id = linesRead.incrementAndGet();
            _collector.emit(new Values(line), id);
          } else {
            System.out.println("Finished reading file, " + linesRead.get()
    + " lines read");
            Thread.sleep(10000);
          }
        } catch (Exception e) {
          e.printStackTrace();
        }
      }

     ...
```

The preceding snippet captures the two very important code sections of the `myLineSpout` class that reads line by line from my CSV file—the first one being the `open()` method that is executed the moment the spout is initialized. In the `open()` method, we are reading the file name and setting up the file reader for the same. The second method is the `nextTuple()` method that is executed for each new data that's read from the file. Here, we are actually reading the lines from the file and emitting them to the topology. Well, it's straightforward and simple; why don't you try it with the word count Storm sample example and instead of seeded data, read the data from a file and execute the topology.

A socket as an input source

Similarly, we can use a Storm spout to be effectively reading from a socket. Here's a snippet from my custom socket spout. Again, we have captured only two of the significant methods via `open()` and `nextTuple()`. The code is as follows:

```
public class mySocketSpout extends BaseRichSpout{
        ...
        public void open(Map conf,TopologyContext context,
SpoutOutputCollector collector){
          _collector=collector;
          _serverSocket=new ServerSocket(_port);
        }

        public void nextTuple(){
           _clientSocket=_serverSocket.accept();
           InputStream incomingIS=_clientSocket.getInputStream();
           byte[] b=new byte[8196];
           int len=b.incomingIS.read(b);
           _collector.emit(new Values(b));
     }
}
```

In the `open()` method, we instantiate and create the server socket. In the `nextTuple()` method, we get the incoming bytes and then emit them to the topology.

Kafka as an input source

Well, this one is a straightforward and almost out-of-the-box, and that is because Storm comes with a Kafka spout. Let's go through the following snippet to understand the same in the word count context:

```
public StormTopology buildTopology(...) {
  SpoutConfig kafkaConfig = new SpoutConfig(abc,TOPIC_NAME,
    "192.168.213.85", "storm");
  kafkaConfig.scheme = new SchemeAsMultiScheme(new
    StringScheme());
  TopologyBuilder builder = new TopologyBuilder();
  builder.setSpout(WORD_COUNTER_SPOUT_ID, new
    KafkaSpout(kafkaConfig), 1);
...
  return builder.createTopology();
}
```

In the preceding snippet, we are creating a topology where we are:

- Setting up a Kafka config where we specify the topic name, host ID of Kafka broker(s), and the spout identifier
- Specifying the scheme details
- Setting the spout in the topology builder along with other bolts
- Taking a look at the actual segment that wires in all the topology aspects together

Check out the following code:

```
public static void main(String[] args) throws Exception {
  ...
KafkaStormTopoLogy kafkaStormTopoLogy = new
KafkaStormTopoLogy(kafkaZk);
...
StormTopology stormTopology = kafkaStormTopoLogy.buildTopology(wn, wc,
pb);
String dockerIp = args[1];
List<String> zList = new ArrayList<String>();
zList.add(ZKNODE1);
// configure how often a tick tuple will be sent to our bolt
config.put(Config.TOPOLOGY_TICK_TUPLE_FREQ_SECS, 30);
config.put(Config.NIMBUS_HOST, dockerIp);
config.put(Config.NIMBUS_THRIFT_PORT, 6627);
config.put(Config.STORM_ZOOKEEPER_PORT, 2181);
config.put(Config.STORM_ZOOKEEPER_SERVERS, zList);
config.setNumWorkers(1);
try {
System.out.println("Submitting Topology... ");
StormSubmitter.submitTopology(TOPOLOGY_NAME, config,
         stormTopology);
System.out.println("Topology submitted successfully  !! ");
    ...
  }
```

Well, the preceding snippet doesn't need any explanation as that's the regular topology submission. The only item noteworthy is `tick tuple`. It is a very handy tool when we want the topology to do something at a said interval. Let's take an example; let's say I have a bolt that has data loaded from a cache and I want the bolt to refresh from the cache every 30 seconds. In that case, I can mention that my topology generates a `tick tuple` event. This is done at the time of topology configuration:

```
config.put(Config.TOPOLOGY_TICK_TUPLE_FREQ_SECS, 30);
```

In the bolt, you can identify this special event, this truth combination, and perform the necessary action:

```
return tuple.getSourceComponent().equals(Constants.SYSTEM_COMPONENT_
ID)
  && tuple.getSourceStreamId().equals(Constants.SYSTEM_TICK_STREAM_
ID);
```

Reliability of data processing

One of the USPs of Storm is guaranteed message processing that makes it a very lucrative solution. Having said that, we as programmers have to make certain modeling to use or not use to the reliability provided for by Storm.

First of all, it's very important to understand what happens when a tuple is emitted into the topology and how its corresponding DAG is constructed. The following diagram captures a typical case in this context:

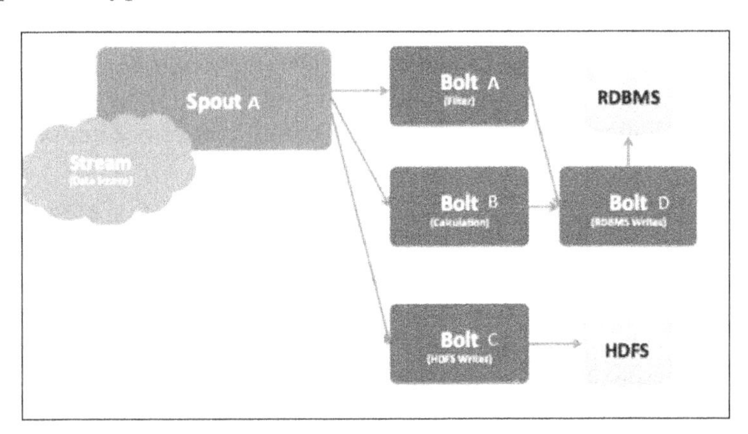

Here, the function of the topology is very clear: every emitted tuple has to be filtered, calculated, and written to the HDFS and database. Now, let's take an implication of DAG with respect to a single tuple being emitted into the topology.

Every single tuple that is emitted into the topology moves as follows:

- Spout A -> Bolt A -> Bolt D -> Database
- Spout A -> Bolt B -> Bolt D -> Database
- Spout A -> Bolt C -> HDFS

So, one tuple from spout A is replicated at step 1 into three tuples that move to Bolt A, Bolt B, and Bolt 3 (three tuples). In the next step, there's no change in number, and a single tuple is resonated to the next step as single tuple only (three tuples, total 3+3 = six tuples). In the next step at Bolt D, two streams are joined so it's like it consumes to tuples but emits one so it would be like 6 +1 = 7 tuples.

So, for one event to be successfully processed, Storm has to internally generate, propagate, and manage multiple tuples based on the topology structure, parallelism, and grouping. In the previous example, we have assumed all parallelism to be *1* and shuffle grouping binding of bolts and spouts. Thus, we kept it very simple for the sake of illustration.

Another noteworthy aspect is that to acknowledge an event to be successfully processed, Storm accepts `ack()` from all nodes in the DAG the tuple is being executed. All the `ack()` should arrive within the `Config.TOPOLOGY_MESSAGE_TIMEOUT_SECS` configured in Storm; the default value of the same attribute is 30 seconds. If `ack()` doesn't happen in 30 seconds, Storm assumes it as a failure and re-emits the tuple into the topology.

Replay the failed messages based on how we design our topologies. If we create reliable topologies with anchoring, then Storm replays all failed messages. In case of unreliable topologies (as the name suggests), replay does not happen.

The concept of anchoring and reliability

So far, we have understood very well the function of the `nextTuple()` method in the spout. It fetches the next event that becomes available at the source and emits it into the topology. The `open()` method of the spout holds the definition of the **spout collector** that's used to actually emit the tuple from the spout into the topology. Every tuple/event that is emitted by the spout into the topology is tagged with a message ID, which is the identifier for the tuple. Whenever the spouts emit the messages into the topology, it tags them with `messageId`, as shown here:

```
_collector.emit(new Values(...),msgId);
```

This `messageId` tag is actually an identifier for the tuple. Storm tracks and tags the tuples using this `messageID` as it plays the tuple through the bolt tree.

In case the event is successfully played through the DAG, it's acknowledged. Please note that this acknowledging of the tuple is done at the spout level by the spout that emitted the tuple. If the tuple is timed out, then the originating spout executes a `fail()` method on the tuple.

Now, we need to understand a very important aspect of replay. The question is, "how does Storm replay the tuples that are already emitted?" The answer is that the spout reads a tuple from the queue, but the tuple remains in the queue until it's successfully played and then once `ack()` is received only then does Storm acknowledge the tuple to the queue and thus removes the same. In case of `fail()`, the message is queued back to the queue for consumption and replay:

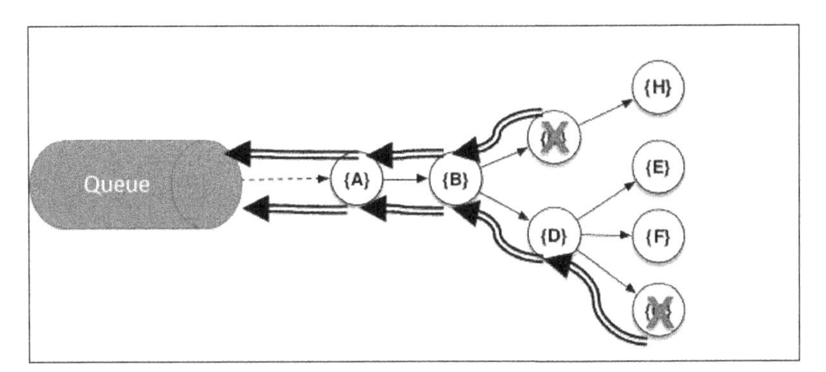

As depicted in the diagram, the failed tuples are propagated back to the spout and are lined back into the queue. When the messages are read from the queue by the spout, they are marked as *un-acked*. During this duration, they are still in the queue but not available to be read by any other spout/topology/client. If such a un-acked message is played successfully through the topology it's *acked* and removed from the queue. In case the event fails to complete its execution through the topology, it's failed and re-queued and made available for consumption to the spout again.

One of the most important points to note is **anchoring**. It's tagging of all edges of the DAG through which the tuple is played. Anchoring is a choice of the developer who wires in the topology, but Storm can replay the messages only in anchored topologies. Now the two logical questions to be asked are:

- How to do the anchoring of tuples along the DAG of topology during execution?
- Why would a developer create an un-anchored topology?

Let's answer these one by one. Anchoring is pretty simple and we as developers have to be cognizant of the same during emitting the tuples from the bolts and spouts. Here are two code snippets that would make it very clear:

```
_collector.emit(new Values(word));
```

The above snippet is the un-anchored version from unreliable topologies, where the tuples could not be replayed in the event of failure.

```
//simple anchoring
_collector.emit(new Values(1, 2, 3),msgID);
List<Tuple> anchors = new ArrayList<Tuple>();
anchors.add(tuple1);
anchors.add(tuple2);
//multiple anchoring output tuple is anchored to two //input tuples
viz tuple1 and tuple2
_collector.emit(anchors, new Values(1, 2, 3));
```

This second snippet captures the anchored version, where the tuples are tied together using the anchor list, and in case of any failure, this reliable topology would be able to replay all the events.

Now coming to our second question, having anchoring and reliable topology is a little expensive in terms of book keeping and message size that's being propagated through the topology. There could be numerous scenarios where reliability is not required and hence there are unreliable topologies where no anchoring is done.

Storm bolts can be broadly classified into two segments: the basic bolts and the ones that do the aggregation and joins. The basic bolts are plain and clearly depicted in the following diagram; `prepare()` sets up the output collector to which tuples are emitted immediately after they are processed. All the bolts following this general pattern are actually implemented using the `IBasicBolt` interface. The diagram also captures the second variety of not-so-simple Storm bolts that perform the tasks such as *aggregation* and *joins*. The tuples are anchored to multiple input tuples and sometimes they are emitted after a preprogrammed delay such as in the case of aggregates:

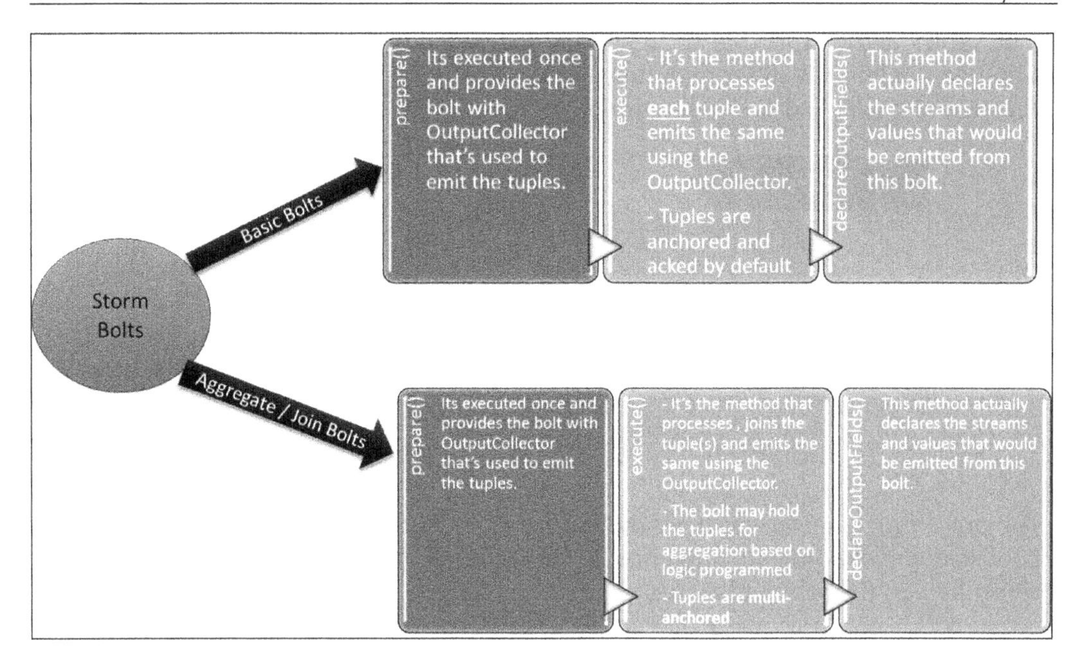

Now that we have understood Storm reliability, let's touch upon the most important component that makes sure that all updates about ack or fail reach the spout successfully. They are acker processes.

The Storm acking framework

Now that we have understood Storm reliability, let's discuss the most important component that makes sure that all updates about ack or fail reach the spout successfully. They are acker processes. These are lightweight tasks that coexist with spouts and bolts, and are responsible for acking all successfully executed messages to the spout. There, the number is controlled by a property in Storm config called `TOPLOGY_ACKER_EXECUTORS`; by default, it's equal to the number of workers defined in the topology. If the topology operates at a less TPS, the num ackers should be reduced. However, for high-TPS topologies, this number should be increased so that tuples are acknowledged at the rate of arrival and processing.

Ackers follow the following algorithm to track the completion of the tuple tree for each tuple being played through the topology:

- Maintain a checksum hash
- For each executed tuple XOR it to the value of checksum hash

If all tuples in the tuple tree are acked the checksum would be 0; or else, it would be a non-zero value, the latter denoting a failure in the topology. Its working is largely driven and controlled using tick tuple:

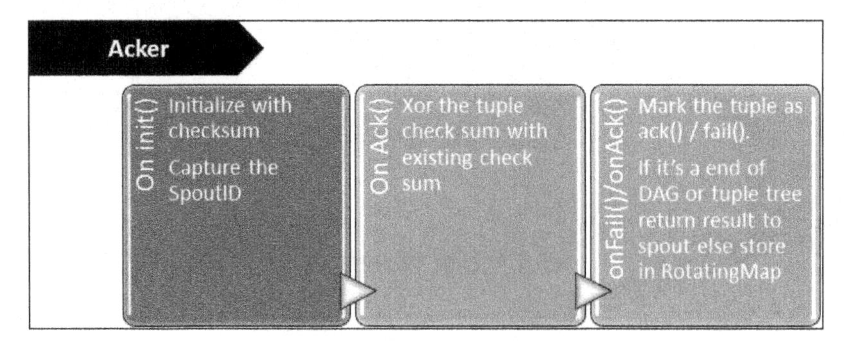

The preceding diagram captures the flow of the acker process. Note that it has a book keeping component, ledger or `rotatingMap`, and the entire flow of things is controlled on the basis of tick tuples.

Storm simple patterns

While we work with Storm, there are a variety of patterns you can recognize. In the segment here, without using Trident, we are attempting to capture some common patterns with Storm topologies.

Joins

As the name suggests, this is the most common pattern. The output from two or more different streams is joined on some common field and is emitted as a single tuple. In Storm, that's effectively achieved using fields grouping, which ensures that all the tuples with same field value are emitted to the same task. The following figure and code snippet captures its essence:

```
 TopologyBuilder builder = new TopologyBuilder();
    builder.setSpout("gender", genderSpout);
    builder.setSpout("age", ageSpout);
    builder.setBolt("join", new SingleJoinBolt(new Fields("gender",
"age"))).fieldsGrouping("gender", new Fields("id"))
        .fieldsGrouping("age", new Fields("id"));
```

That's effectively achieved using the fields grouping, which ensures that all tuples with the same value in a common field are emitted by the join bolt.

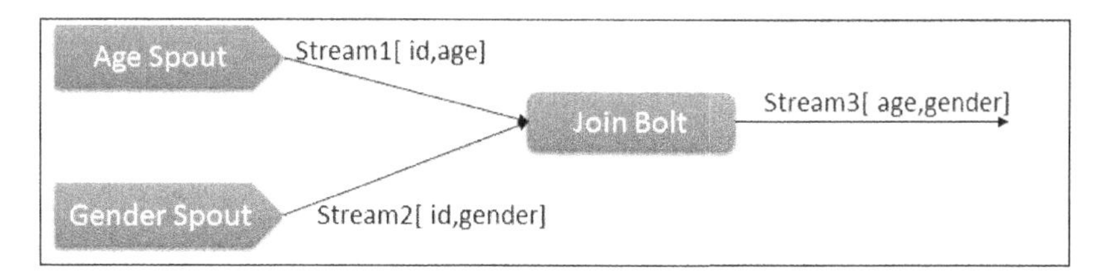

Here, we have two streams arriving from two spouts: the gender spout and age spout. The common field is *d*, over which the streams are joined by the joiner bolt and emitted as a new stream that has fields as *age* and *gender*.

Batching

This is another very common pattern that comes into play when we have to hold and perform processing in batches. Let's take an example to understand it better; I have a Storm application that dumps the tuples into database. For efficient utilization of network bandwidth, I would want the database to write in batches of 100. Unless we are using transactional Trident topologies, the simplest mechanism is to hold the records into a local instance data structure and track the count and write to databases in batches. In general, there are two different variants of batching that can be executed:

- **Count-based batching**: Create a batch based on the number of records. A plain count initialized in the prepare method that's incremented in the execute method on arrival of the tuple could be used for tracking of the same.
- **Time-based batching**: Create a batch based on time. Let's say a batch of five minutes, and if we want to keep the implementation as simple we would create a mechanism to emit a tick tuple to the topology every five minutes.

Storm persistence

Now that we know Storm and its internals very well, let's wire in persistence to Storm. Well we have done all the computation and code, so now it's very important to store the computed results or intermediate references into a database or some persistence store. You have the choice of writing your own JDBC bolts or you can actually use the implementation provided for using Storm persistence.

Let's start with writing our own JDBC persistence first. Once we have touched upon the nitty gritty, then we can look at and appreciate what Storm provides for. Let's say we are setting up software system at toll gates that could monitor the emission rates of vehicles and track the details of the vehicles that are running at emissions beyond the prescribed limit.

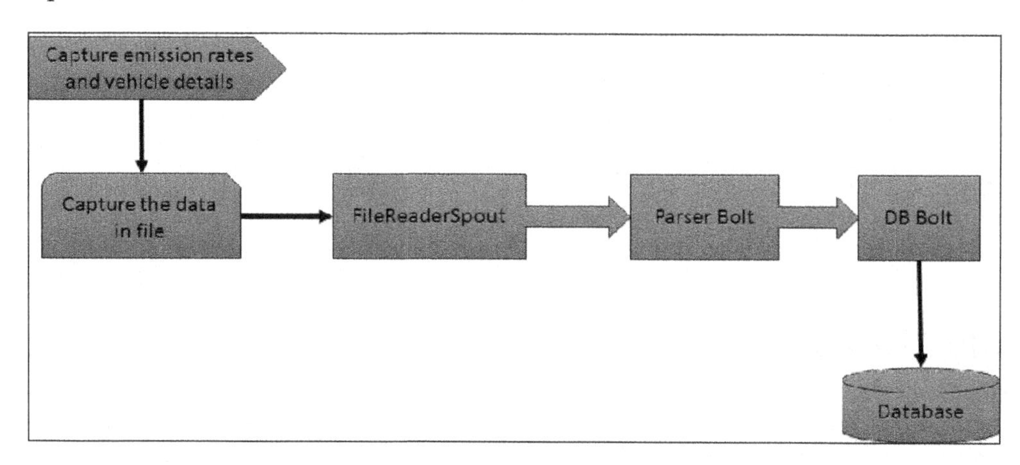

Here, all the vehicle details and their emissions are captured in the file that is being read by the file reader spout. The spout then reads the record and feeds it into the topology where it is consumed by the parser bolt, which converts the record into POJO and hands it off to the database bolt. This bolt checks the emission thresholds and if it's beyond the prescribed limit, the record is persisted into the database.

The following snippets show what the input to the topology in the file would look like:

`#Vehicle Registration number, emission rate, state`

`UP14 123, 60, UP`

`DL12 2653, 70, DELHI`

`DL2C 2354, 40, DELHI`

Here's the snippet that handles the database part and persistence by setting up the connection to the database. Here, we used MySQL database for simplicity, and Storm works well with SQL stores like Oracle or SQL server as well as NoSQL options such as Cassandra. The code is as follows:

```
try
{
connection driverManager.getConnection(
"jdbc:mysql://"+databaseIP+":"+databasePort+"/"+databaseName,
userName, pwd);
```

```
connection.prepareStatement("DROP TABLE IF EXISTS "+tableName).
execute();

StringBuilder createQuery = new StringBuilder(
"CREATE TABLE IF NOT EXISTS "+tableName+"(");
for(Field fields : tupleInfo.getFieldList())
{
if(fields.getColumnType().equalsIgnoreCase("String"))
createQuery.append(fields.getColumnName()+" VARCHAR(500),");



connection.prepareStatement(createQuery.toString()).execute();

// Insert Query
StringBuilder insertQuery = new StringBuilder("INSERT INTO
"+tableName+"(");
String tempCreateQuery = new String();
for(Field fields : tupleInfo.getFieldList())
{
insertQuery.append(fields.getColumnName()+",");
}
...

prepStatement = connection.prepareStatement(insertQuery.toString());
}
```

In the preceding snippet, we are actually creating a prepared statement using a query builder and adding fields to the template.

The next step actually captures the snippet where we format and execute the insert query by filling the template with actual values from the tuple, forming a batch of events, and writing them to the database once the batch size is attained. The code is as follows:

```
if(tuple!=null)
{
List<Object> inputTupleList = (List<Object>) tuple.getValues();
int dbIndex=0;
for(int i=0;i<tupleInfo.getFieldList().size();i++)
{
Field field = tupleInfo.getFieldList().get(i);
...
if(field.getColumnType().equalsIgnoreCase("String"))
prepStatement.setString(dbIndex, inputTupleList.get(i).toString());
```

```
else if(field.getColumnType().equalsIgnoreCase("int"))
prepStatement.setInt(dbIndex,
Integer.parseInt(inputTupleList.get(i).toString()));
...
...
else if(field.getColumnType().equalsIgnoreCase("boolean"))
prepStatement.setBoolean(dbIndex,
Boolean.parseBoolean(inputTupleList.get(i).toString()));
...
...

Date now = new Date();
try
{
prepStatement.setTimestamp(dbIndex+1, new java.sql.Timestamp(now.
getTime()));
prepStatement.addBatch();
counter.incrementAndGet();
if (counter.get()== batchSize)
executeBatch();
}
...


}

public void executeBatch() throws SQLException
{
batchExecuted=true;
prepStatement.executeBatch();
counter = new AtomicInteger(0);
}
```

The next step is to wire in all the spouts and bolts together so that we can actually see the topology in action:

```
MyFileSpout myFileSpout = new MyFileSpout ();

ParserBolt parserBolt = new ParserBolt ();
DBWriterBolt dbWriterBolt = new DBWriterBolt();
TopologyBuilder builder = new TopologyBuilder();
builder.setSpout("spout", myFileSpout, 1);
builder.setBolt("parserBolt ", parserBolt,1).shuffleGrouping("spout");
builder.setBolt("dbWriterBolt",dbWriterBolt,1).shuffleGrouping("thres
holdBolt");
```

The preceding snippets are actually included with the intention to serve as a do-it-yourself template so that readers can try executing this topology themselves.

Storm's JDBC persistence framework

In the previous section, we have wired in the Storm persistence ourselves. We will now discuss Storm's persistence provider framework so that we, as developers, are saved a lot of work. Using this template-based framework, we can quickly wire persistence into our Storm topology.

Some of the key components of this framework are as follows:

- **The ConnectionProvider interface**: This facilitates the usage of a user-driven connection pooling. By default, the Storm persistence framework supports an implementation of HikariCP.
- **The JdbcMapper interface**: This is the main component that basically maps the tuple to columns of the table. `SimpleJDBCMapper` is an out-of-the-box, simple implementation of the same. The following snippet from the Storm sample emphasis more on the same:

```
Map hikariConfigMap = Maps.newHashMap();
hikariConfigMap.put("dataSourceClassName","com.mysql.jdbc.jdbc2.
optional.MysqlDataSource");
hikariConfigMap.put("dataSource.url", "jdbc:mysql://localhost/
test");
hikariConfigMap.put("dataSource.user","root");
hikariConfigMap.put("dataSource.password","password");
ConnectionProvider connectionProvider = new HikariCPConnectionProv
ider(hikariConfigMap);
String tableName = "user_details";
JdbcMapper simpleJdbcMapper = new SimpleJdbcMapper(tableName,
connectionProvider);
```

Then, we have `JDBCLookupbolt` to read from the database and `JDBCInsertBolt` for inserting data into the database. Here's how all is wired in together with the help of some code snippet:

```
JdbcLookupBolt departmentLookupBolt = new JdbcLookupBolt(
connectionProvider, SELECT_QUERY, this.jdbcLookupMapper);
// must specify column schema when providing custom query.
List<Column> schemaColumns = Lists.newArrayList(new Column(
"create_date", Types.DATE), new Column("dept_name",
Types.VARCHAR), new Column("user_id", Types.INTEGER),
new Column("user_name", Types.VARCHAR));
JdbcMapper mapper = new SimpleJdbcMapper(schemaColumns);
JdbcInsertBolt userPersistanceBolt = new JdbcInsertBolt(
connectionProvider, mapper)
```

```
.withInsertQuery("insert into user (create_date, dept_name, user_
id, user_name) values (?,?,?,?)");
// userSpout ==> jdbcBolt
TopologyBuilder builder = new TopologyBuilder();
builder.setSpout(USER_SPOUT, this.userSpout, 1);
builder.setBolt(LOOKUP_BOLT, departmentLookupBolt,
1).shuffleGrouping(
USER_SPOUT);
builder.setBolt(PERSISTANCE_BOLT, userPersistanceBolt, 1)
.shuffleGrouping(LOOKUP_BOLT);
```

Here, we have provided for a code snippet that simply uses the bolts provided by the Storm persistence framework and writes them into the database. The spout emits the tuple to insert the bolt where the tuple values are mapped into fields of the insert query, then the lookup bolt fetches the department values and the persistence bolt finally inserts the data into the table.

Downloading the example code

You can download the example code files for this book from your account at `http://www.packtpub.com`. If you purchased this book elsewhere, you can visit `http://www.packtpub.com/support` and register to have the files e-mailed directly to you.

You can download the code files by following these steps:

- Log in or register to our website using your e-mail address and password.
- Hover the mouse pointer on the **SUPPORT** tab at the top.
- Click on **Code Downloads & Errata**.
- Enter the name of the book in the **Search** box.
- Select the book for which you're looking to download the code files.
- Choose from the drop-down menu where you purchased this book from.
- Click on **Code Download**.

Once the file is downloaded, please make sure that you unzip or extract the folder using the latest version of:

- WinRAR / 7-Zip for Windows
- Zipeg / iZip / UnRarX for Mac
- 7-Zip / PeaZip for Linux

Summary

This chapter emphasizes on getting the readers acquainted to Kafka and its basics. We also integrated Kafka and Storm. We explored the other data sources for Storm such as file and socket. Then, we walked our readers through the concept of reliability acking and anchoring. We also understood Storm joins and batching. Then, at the end, we moved to understand and implement persistence in Storm by integrating it with a database. This chapter touched upon couple of do-it-yourself exercises that the readers are recommended to try and implement.

In the next chapter, we will introduce the Trident abstraction that is built as an extension to Storm, for providing transactional and microbatching capabilities. We will also look into internals of Lmax, 0MQ, and Netty, and learn about Storm optimizations.

4
Introduction to Trident and Optimizing Storm Performance

In this chapter, we will get acquainted with the Trident framework of Storm before we embark on the journey of Storm optimization. We will get acquainted with the various parameters that impact the performance of a Storm job and make recommendations to identify and tune the relevant parameters. We will also look into the tools that are used industry-wide for Storm monitoring and benchmarking.

- Trident framework
- State management
- Understanding LMAX
- Storm internode communication (ZeroMQ versus Netty)
- Understanding Storm UI
- Optimizing Storm performance

Working with Trident

Throughout the book, we have portrayed Storm as a solution to be used as a high-performant, real-time stream computational tool. But, in reality, all real-time use cases are not actually real-time; they are an extension to real-time and use an amalgamation of micro batching. Let's give you some examples.

Let's say we want to know the names of the top five performing stocks. This data should reflect the stock performance over the last 10 minutes. We also want to know which is the most liked picture on Facebook for each 5-minute period.

There are numerous scenarios that require small unit batching over real-time streaming data and computations around the same; thus, the need for the extension of Storm.

Trident, like its predecessor, Storm, was also incepted at the Twitter technology house. At a high level, it's an extension and abstraction over the top of the Storm framework, with some additional capability for batching, stateful processing, and querying of the streaming data. It lets the users execute queries against streaming data batched over count/time, and it is high on performance due to the distributed nature of its execution.

It has an extensive variety of functions, filters, joins, and aggregations that provide all the tools necessary for creating great solutions for microbatching time window problems. Like Storm, Trident uses spouts and bolts, but the Trident abstraction generates them automatically before the topology execution.

Transactions

Trident executes transactions that are actually streaming data chunked into batches, so the key difference from Storm is that Storm processes tuple by tuple, while Trident processes the items after batching the tuples into transactions. Conceptually, these transactions are very similar to database transactions:

- Each transaction has a transaction ID
- It begins by executing `beginCommit`
- Each transaction is marked as successful once all the events in that batch are executed successfully
- If any event/tuple of the transaction fails, the entire batch is rolled back and re-queued for re-execution
- It ends with a commit on completion of successful execution

Trident topology

Trident abstraction is exposed as an API that provides the developers with the class to create a topology. In our snippet, we will use the `TridentTopology` class provided by the framework. Before moving further, let's draw an analogy between Storm and Trident to get a better understanding of the Trident concepts:

- Storm topology bolts execute every tuple emitted by spout
- Trident topology performs operations such as filter, aggregate, grouping and so on in orderly manner on the input stream

- So a Storm tuple is a single event, while a Trident tuple is a batch of events/transactions
- In Storm, the computation/processing happens in the execute method of bolts, and in Trident it happens in the form of an operation

Simple Trident topology can be spawned using the following snippet:

```
TridentTopology myTridentTopology = new TridentTopology();
```

Trident tuples

Extending the preceding analogy, the Trident tuple can be described as the single unit of data that the Trident topology can process. Talking about the API, it's exposed as an interface `TridentTuple`, which forms the data model for the topology.

Trident spout

In basic terms, we can say that the Trident spout has some extra features than `IRichSpout` that we used in Storm. One such capability is the exhibition of transactional features. We will be using an extension of the interface called `ITridentSpout` provided by the API. Trident provides a variety of generic spouts and some sample spouts. For example, `FeederBatchSpout` names a list of tuples to a batch and emits them into the topology:

```
TridentTopology myTridentTopology = new TridentTopology();
FeederBatchSpout myTestSpout = new FeederBatchSpout(
   ImmutableList.of("fromMobile", "toMobile", "duration"));
myTridentTopology.newStream("fixed-batch-spout", myTestSpout)
myTestSpout.feed(ImmutableList.of(new Values("981100000",
"9800110011", 200))); // from Mobile No, To Mobile No, duration in ms
```

Here, we have created a simple Trident topology and added an instance of `feederbatch` spout to the same using the name of `myTestSpout`, then we have fed a single tuple into the same.

Trident operations

As said earlier, the unit of processing/execution in Trident is an operation, which actually processes an input stream of Trident tuples. It has a vast and robust set of operations for performing a range and variety of simple and complex computations on streaming data. In the following section, we will get you acquainted with some of the frequently used Trident operations.

Merging and joining

The merging and joining operation is used for combining one or more streams into one single stream. It's performed using the merge function call. Joining is similar to database joins. It uses the Trident tuple field from both sides to check and then it joins the two streams:

```
TridentTopology myTridentTopology = new TridentTopology();
myTridentTopology.merge(stream1, stream2, stream3);
myTridentTopology.join(stream1, new Fields("key"), stream2, new
Fields("x"),
   new Fields("key", "a", "b", "c"));
```

Filter

This operation does what its name suggests and is generally used in situations of input validation. As an input, the Trident filter gets a subset of Trident tuple fields and, as a result, it returns the Boolean value true or false depending on whether certain conditions are satisfied or not. The tuple is retained in output stream in true scenarios and in false scenarios, it's dropped off. Here's a snippet that walks us through the example implementation of the same:

```
public class MyTestFilter extends BaseFilter {
   public boolean isKeep(TridentTuple tuple) {
      return tuple.getInteger(1) % 2 == 0;
   }
}

//input

[1, 4]
[1, 5]
[1, 8]

//output

[1, 4]
[1, 8]
```

Here's the snippet capturing the call to the same topology for each Trident tuple:

```
 TridentTopology myTidentTopology = new TridentTopology();
myTidentTopology.newStream("spout", spout)
.each(new Fields("a", "b"), new MyTestFilter())
```

Function

It's inherited from the `BaseFunction` class and executes on a single Trident tuple. It exhibits the following key characteristics in that it takes a single input value and emits zero or more tuples as output. The output from the function operation is appended to the last of the input tuple and the same is emitted to the output stream:

```
public class MyTestFunction extends BaseFunction {
   public void execute(TridentTuple tuple, TridentCollector collector)
{
      int a = tuple.getInteger(0);
      int b = tuple.getInteger(1);
      collector.emit(new Values(a + b));
   }
}

//input
[1, 2]
[1, 3]
[1, 4]

//output
[1, 2, 3]
[1, 3, 4]
[1, 4, 5]
```

This snippet captures the call to the same topology for each Trident tuple:

```
TridentTopology myTidentTopology = new TridentTopology();
myTidentTopology.newStream("spout", spout)
   .each(new Fields("a, b"), new MyTestFunction(), new Fields("d")));
```

Aggregation

Aggregations are basically Trident operations that perform an aggregate or summation operation on an input Trident batch (transaction), stream, or partition. The following figure captures the three kinds of Trident aggregations:

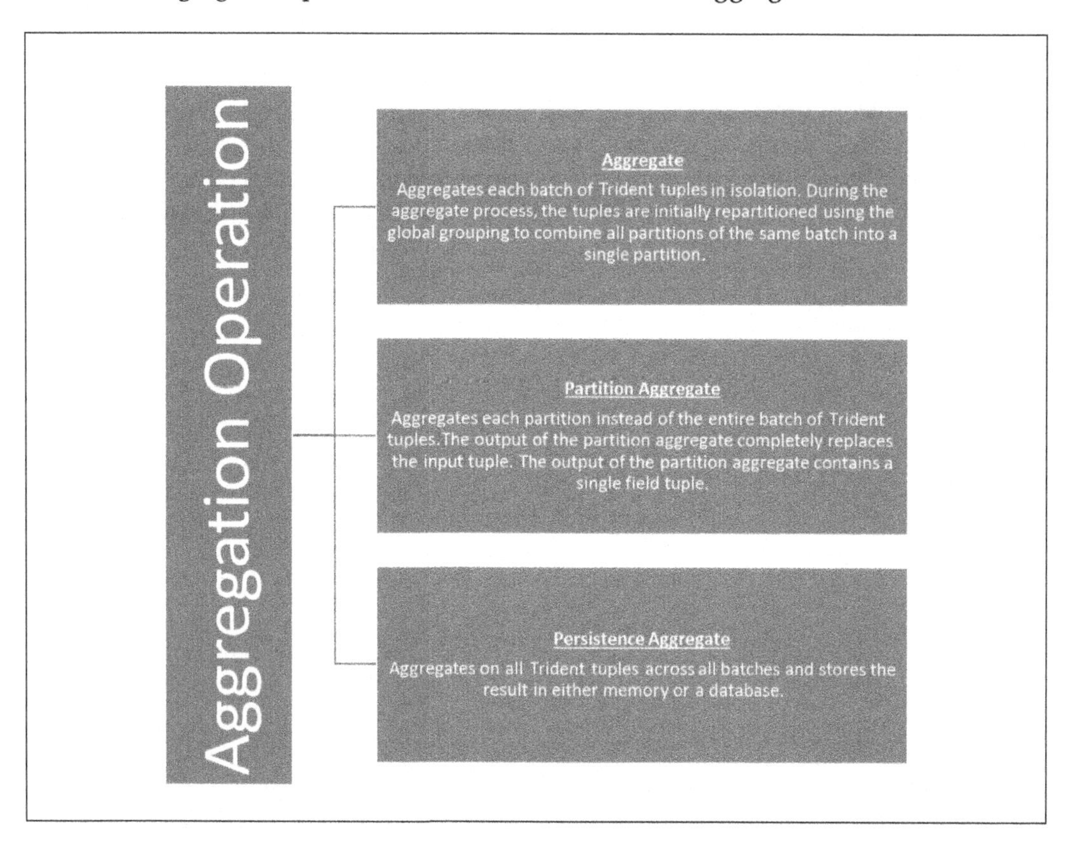

The following snippet is an easy-to-comprehend code capture of the aggregate operation provided by the Trident framework:

```
TridentTopology myTidentTopology = new TridentTopology();

// aggregate operation
myTidentTopology.newStream("MySpout", spout)
    .each(new Fields("a, b"), new MyFunction(), new Fields("d"))
    .aggregate(new Count(), new Fields("count"))
```

```
// partitionAggregate operation
myTidentTopology.newStream("MySpout", spout)
   .each(new Fields("a, b"), new MyFunction(), new Fields("d"))
   .partitionAggregate(new Count(), new Fields("count"))

// persistentAggregate - saving the count to memory
myTidentTopology.newStream("MySpout", spout)
   .each(new Fields("a, b"), new MyFunction(), new Fields("d"))
   .persistentAggregate(new MemoryMapState.Factory(), new Count(), new
Fields("count"));
```

In the preceding example, the count aggregator is used. It is one of the in-built aggregators provided by the Trident framework. It's implemented using the `CombinerAggregator`. Alternatively, you can create an aggregation operation using `CombinerAggregator`, `ReducerAggregator`, or the generic aggregator interface. The following snippet captures the quick implementation of the same:

```
public class Count implements CombinerAggregator<Long> {
   @Override
   public Long init(TridentTuple tuple) {
      return 1L;
   }

   @Override
   public Long combine(Long val1, Long val2) {
      return val1 + val2;
   }

   @Override
   public Long zero() {
      return 0L;
   }
}
```

Grouping

These operations from the Trident framework are like `groupBy` operations in a relational model with the only difference being that the ones in here execute over a stream of tuples from the input source, while in relational databases they execute on records in a table.

This is a built-in operation and is executed by calling the `groupBy` method. This method repartitions the input stream by executing a `partitionBy` operation on the specified fields. Once this is done, within each partition it groups tuples together whose group fields are same. The sample code is as follows:

```
TridentTopology myTridentTopology = new TridentTopology();

// persistentAggregate - saving the count to memory
myTridentTopology.newStream("spout", spout)
    .each(new Fields("a, b"), new MyFunction(), new Fields("d"))
    .groupBy(new Fields("d")
    .persistentAggregate(new MemoryMapState.Factory(), new Count(), new
Fields("count"));
```

State maintenance

One of the key features of Trident is that it provides a mechanism to store the state information in the topology, in a cache, or in a separate database. This is a necessary implication of the functionality provided by the framework because if a tuple fails, it has to be replayed. Because the execution is happening in batches, the entire transaction has to be rolled back and replayed. Developers are generally recommended to create a small size batch of tuples where each batch is marked by a unique ID. The system maintains and executes the updates to the batches in an ordered manner.

The sample example covers all aspects of Trident as is practical. In the next sections, we will discuss a couple of internals of Storm that are actually key to the performance.

Understanding LMAX

One of the key aspects that attributes to the speed of Storm is the use of LMAX disruptor versus queues. We did touch upon this topic in one of the earlier chapters, but now we are going to dive deep into the same. To be able to appreciate the use of LMAX in Storm, we first need to get acquainted with LMAX as an exchange platform.

Just to reiterate what's been stated in one of the earlier chapters, this is how internal Storm communication happens:

- Communication within different processes executing on the same worker (in a way, its inter-thread communication on a single Storm node); the Storm framework is designed to used LMAX disruptor
- Communication between different workers across the node might be on the same node (here, ZeroMQ or Netty is used)
- Communication between two topologies is attained by external and non-Storm mechanisms such as queues (for example, RabbitMQ, Kafka, and so on) or distributed caching mechanisms (for example, Hazelcast, Memcache, and so on)

LMAX is basically the world's most performance-optimized and thus the fastest trading platform so far. It's recognized for its low latency, simplified design, and high throughput. Well, the answer as to what makes LMAX disruptors so fast is in the key to what made traditional data exchange systems slow: it's the queues. Traditionally, all data exchange systems had data passed between components during the various stages of processing. Queues were used and they actually introduced the latency. Disruptor has attempted to optimize this area by focusing on contention issues with queues and on optimizing/eliminating the same with the new ring buffer disruptor data structure. This disruptor data structure is actually the heart of LMAX framework.

At the core, it's nothing but an open source Java library created by LMAX. It's all about reusing memory, and it's purely sequential in nature. The more we learn about it, the more fascinating it gets in terms of its simplicity and non-concurrent implementation. The philosophy is straightforward: you need to understand the hardware well to write the piece of software that can exploit and make the most efficient solutions on it. I would like to quote Henry Petroski from Martin Fowler's blog:

> *"The most amazing achievement of the computer software industry is its continuing cancellation of the steady and staggering gains made by the computer hardware industry."*

Memory and cache

Let's revisit the memory organization of our operating system. This is the quick picture that comes to mind:

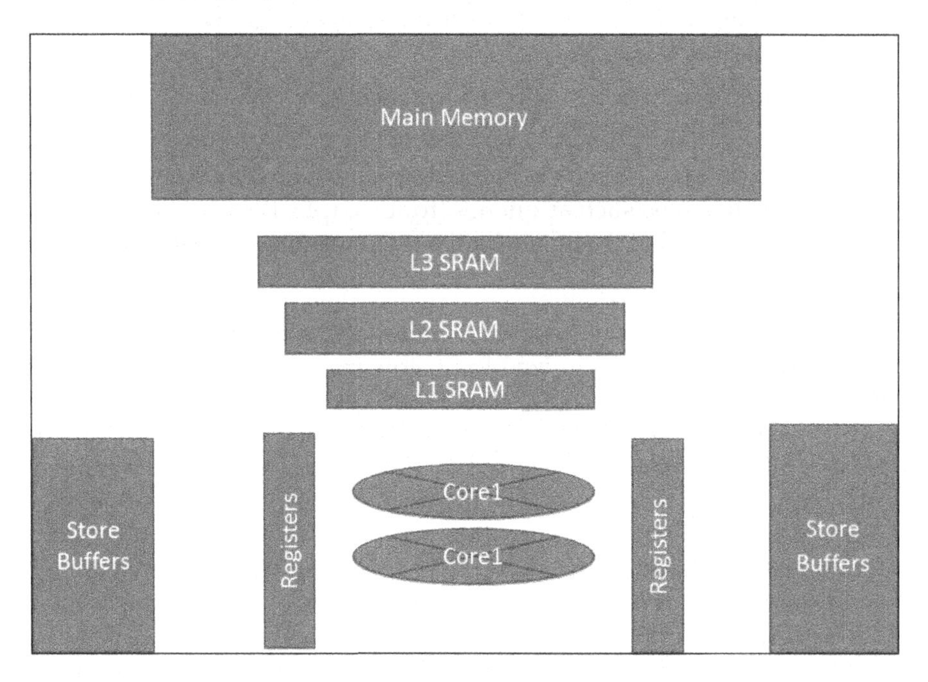

The preceding diagram depicts the main memory along with the SRAM/cache and its three levels, along with store buffers.

Now, let's go a step further to detail how memory and caching is used by the core and the data locality around cores. Registers are the closest to the cores for access, and then come the store buffers. These store buffers disambiguate the memory access in order of execution. Often, the operands and intermediate results from the previous operations are moved from the registers to accommodate the operands. A trip down memory lane to touch upon assembly language would help you remember and recall how we used to load and save the data from the register. We have a limited number of registers and all data that needs to be executed has to be in registers; thus, we have this frequent loading and embarking of intermediate results/data into store buffers during the execution of instructions. One thing that is sure and universally accepted is that these registers are closest to the core and the fastest. All the caches let us stage data away from the core at various levels, so the caches are faster than the main memory, but still not as fast as registers.

Let's learn about this efficiency using a simple example. I will write an instruction set for an iteration of six items (now what happens is that we have four store buffers, and the data for four items are held in store buffers, while for the other two, the data is stored out of the store buffers). Each application has access to four store buffers in general, so iterating six items in one loop is slower than having three each in two loops (it's been benchmarked and is available on Martin Thompson's blog, `http://mechanical-sympathy.blogspot.in/`). I found it shocking to my modular programming mind as well, but yes, context switching and load/unload play havoc with performance. At the hardware level, the preceding example does make sense and has been proved. I suggest that all programmers read more extensively about mechanical sympathy so that we can make use of the efficiency hardware provides. This has been very fundamental to the LMAX disruptor.

Moving away from registers to memory increases the latency from the order of nanoseconds to microseconds, and thus the code/instructions should be written with a conscious effort to keep the data needed for execution more local to the core, which gives lighting fast execution.

Now, let's move to cache and try to understand a couple of key aspects about it as captured in the following diagram:

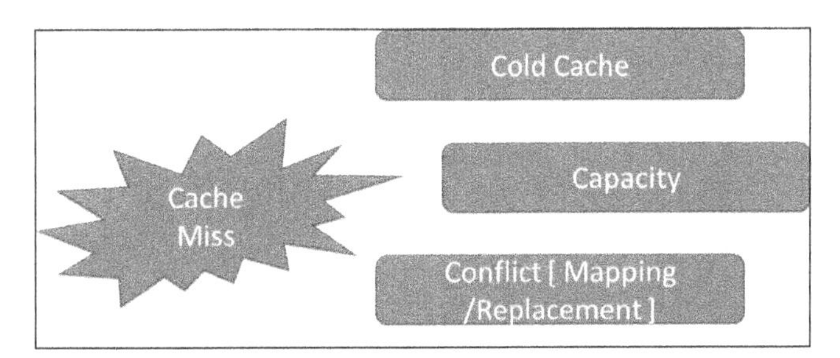

We all know and acknowledge that cache misses are expensive operations and should be avoided, but we also know why they are bound to happen. We always have more data than the cache can hold and, based on our caching strategy (however good and efficient its is), there are bound to be cache misses. As to why, in more technical terms, we have to touch upon the terms depicted in the preceding diagram:

- **Cold cache**: This refers to the part of the cache which is occupied, but has never been accessed or read.
- **Capacity**: Cache is limited so there has to be an eviction to accommodate new data. Loads of algorithms are available around the same.
- **Conflict for mapping/replacement**: This is related to associativity with data. Specific data has to be in specific places else we get a miss. The other contender for replacement is eviction.

Another significant point to be noted is that when we read from cache, what is returned is always a 64-bit/32-bit cache line depending on the architecture. In the case of a multiprocessor setup, there is contention between processors for updates to cache lines even when they are actually accessing different data on the same cache line.

For high performance, the following points need to be taken care of:

- Do not to share the cache line to avoid contention.
- Be sequential in the data organization and let the hardware perfect the data. For example, when iterating in a list, the data structure is sequential by definition and thus it's perfected in the cache.
- GC and compaction—especially old gen should be attempted to be avoided; for example, write code that refers data only from Eden/young generation.
- Restart every day so that we don't need compaction

The people at LMAX have taken care of this and designed an interesting data structure, called disruptor, for us. The following diagram captures some key contributors to the performance of disruptor:

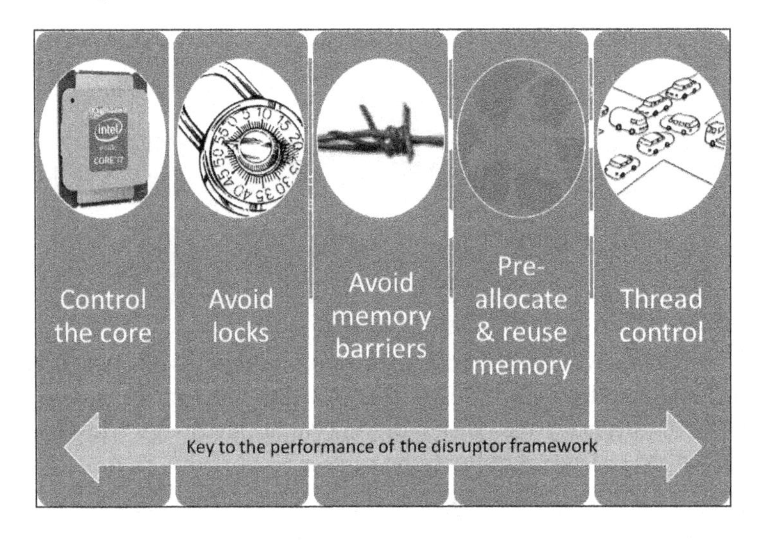

A brief description of the key contributors is as follows:

- Control the core and never release the core to the kernel (thus maintaining your L3 cache).
- Write the code in a non-contending manner; locks are extremely non-performing due to context switching in the kernel, which suspends threads waiting on a lock until it is released.

Note that during a kernel context switch, the OS may decide to perform other tasks not related to your process, and thus lose valuable cycles.

- Avoid memory barriers. Before we delve deeper into why, let's recollect what memory barriers are from the classic definition at `https://en.wikipedia.org/wiki/Memory_barrier`. It is very self-explanatory:

  > *A* **memory barrier**, *also known as a* **membar**, **memory fence** *or* **fence instruction**, *is a type of barrier instruction that causes a central processing unit (CPU) or compiler to enforce an ordering constraint on memory operations issued before and after the barrier instruction.*

  Processors used membars to demarcate the sections in the code where the ordering of updates to the memory mattered and should be adhered to. One item to note is that compilers also add membars cited example is volatile keyword in Java.

- Preallocate and use the sequential memory. The main reason for asking this is prefetching of the data in the cache, avoiding cache line contention, and reuse reduces the cost impact caused by GC and compaction.
- Thread control is an extremely important task to be taken care of while developing low-latency, high-throughput systems.

An obvious and enlightening question to ask here is: why not queues? What makes them non-efficient as compared to a disruptor framework? Here are a few prominent reasons:

- When we get to the realm of unbounded queues, we end up using linked lists that are not contiguous and thus, as a consequence, do not support striding (prefetching cache lines).
- Now, the obvious choice could be bounded queues that rely on arrays. We have a head (which reads the messages of the queue) and a tail (where messages are fed into the queue), which are the classic enqueue and dequeue operations. But we need to understand that both these basic queue operations are not only the primary points of write contention but also have a tendency to share cache lines. In Java, queues are known as GC-heavy data structures. For a bounded queue, the memory for data must be allocated, and, if unbounded, the linked list node must also be allocated. When dereferenced or marked for GC, all of these objects must be reclaimed.

- Smart use of mechanical sympathy in the way disruptors are modeled, as in a data structure and a framework:
    - It's a system that's designed to utilize the caches as effectively as possible by the nature of the hardware.
    - It starts by creating a large ring buffer of arrays at the start-up and data is copied into it as it's received.
    - Sequencing is vital. What you need next is loaded into the cache sequentially by effectively using padding where needed.
    - Avoid false sharing of cache lines.

They start allocating memory to create ring buffers, which have million entries, where they reuse the memory spaces as they work their way around the memory buffers. So, they don't have to worry about GC and compaction.

The sequencing of data around these buffers to make use of the cache lines is a very important aspect and LMAX uses padding to ensure non-sharing of cache lines to avoid contention.

Ring buffer – the heart of the disruptor

It's an array-based circular data structure that is used as a buffer to pass the data between contexts (one thread to another). In very simple terms, it's an array that has a pointer to the next available slot. Producers and consumers have the ability to write and read data from this data structure without locking/contention. The sequence/pointer keeps wrapping around the ring. What makes it different from the other circular buffers is the lack of an end pointer. These data structures are highly reliable as messages, once written, are not removed. They stay in there until they are marked to be overwritten. In the case of failures, replays are very easy: a simple example consumer. A request to replay from the message at slot 4 when the producer is writing message 10 replays all messages from slots 4 to 10 and retains them as non-overwritable till it gets an ack from the consumer.

The following diagram captures the significant aspects, as well as giving a common depiction of a ring buffer:

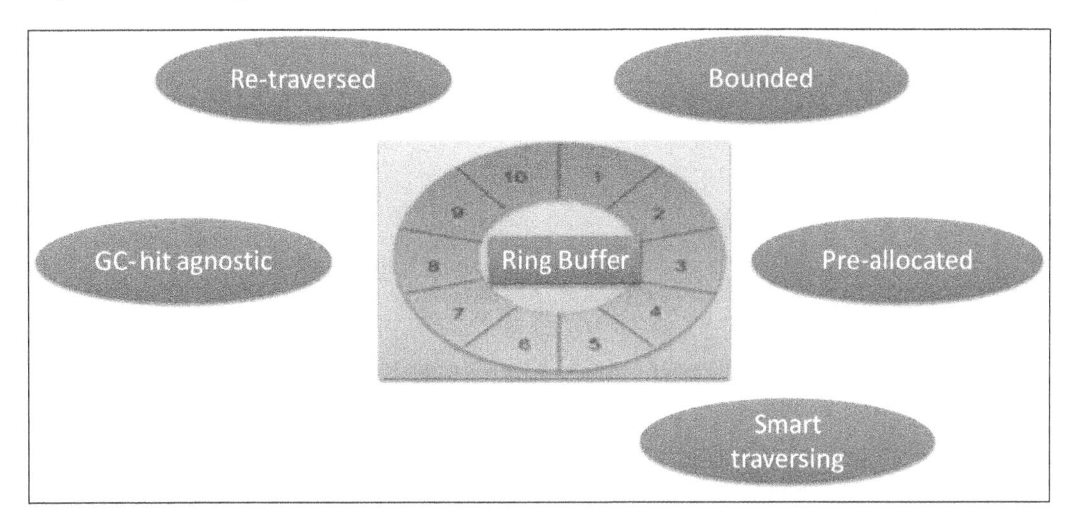

Talking about the implementation and salient features, it's a bounded array that is retraversed and modeled to behave as if it's virtually unbounded. How does this happen? It goes from 1 to 10 and then starts again at 1. It uses an interesting concept of bit mask modulus—it starts reusing the memory from 1 after reaching 10, but the sequence of numbers aren't restarted from 1. They proceed as 11, 12, 20, 21, and so on, to maintain the notion of virtual unboundedness. It can use modulus to figure out the next available number, but it's an expensive operation as compared to a bit mask operation. So it uses bitmap modulus (with a size of ring buffer of `-1` being applied to the sequence number) to compute next available element. This approach is yet another operation that demonstrates the mindset to exhibit efficiency driven programming. This is called **smart traversing**.

Note that ring buffers aren't doing anything new, but they are built with a mindset for taking advantage of hardware concepts. The network card we have been using has had two of them ever since it was created. LMAX has brought that same hardware concept, packaged in a software bundle for software programmers, to do efficient programming.

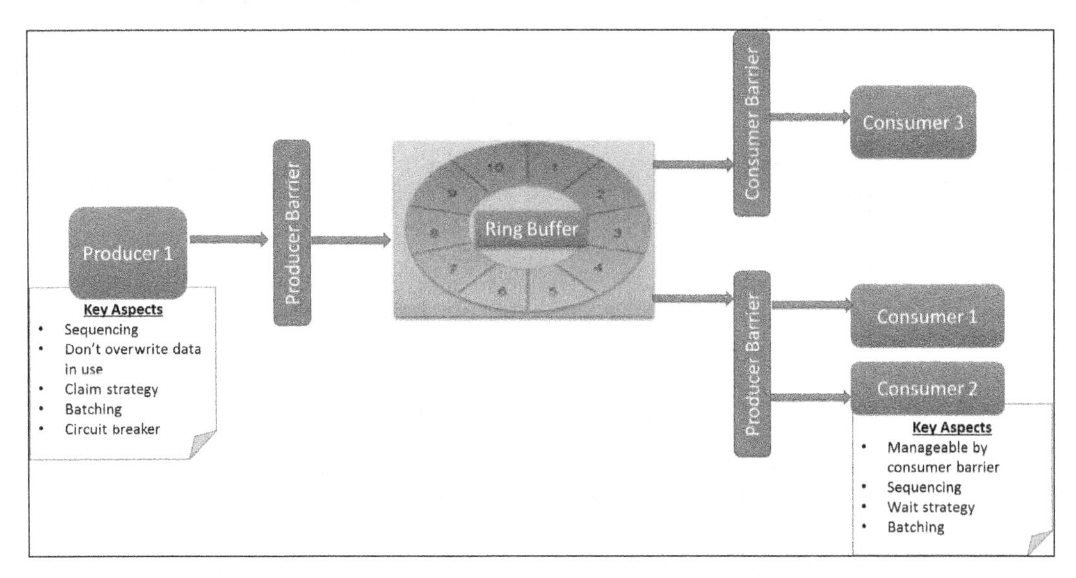

The preceding diagram depicts the typical moving components in a disruptor: producers and consumers.

Producers

The producers basically do what the name suggests. They dump the data into the ring buffer in sequence, say 1, 2, 3, and so on. Obviously, the producer has to be cognizant of the next available slot to be sure that they don't overwrite the data that's still not been consumed or read by the consumer. The consumers can provide notification that up to what sequence slot the producer is to fill the buffer. For example, if we go ahead and put data all the way up to slot 5, then the producers have to be intelligent enough to ensure they don't end up overwriting the data. Here, the claim strategy comes into play. It could be single-threaded or multithreaded. Single-threaded is absolutely great in a single producer model. However, if we have multiple producers in the mix, we need a multithreaded claim strategy to be deployed, which will help the producers to figure out the next available slot on the buffer. This uses a compare followed by a swap and is an expensive operation.

Before moving to batching, let's talk about claim strategy and write operations in the case of producer contention:

- In a multiple producer environment, we have a **CAS** (short for **content-addressed storage**) instead of a basic pointer to protect the counter
- In race condition, they can race and use the CAS for the next available slot
- When a producer reclaims a slot in the ring buffer, it copies the data into one of the preallocated elements using a two-step process, as follows:
    - Get the sequence number and copy the data
    - Explicitly commit it to the producer barrier thus making the data visible
- Producers can check with consumers to see where they are so they don't overwrite ring buffer slots still in use

The batching effect is another feature used by the producers to be efficient on latency. Here, the producer knows which slot the consumer is working on. Let's say that the consumer is consuming data from slot 9, while they have put data up to 4. It can definitely go and write the data in bursts till 9 or up to the point when the slots are empty in the ring buffer.

We definitely need timeouts or circuit breakers built inside the producers so that they can override and break the circle in a case where latency starts to build in the system.

Consumers

Consumers are basically the components to read the data from the ring. Let's say data has been put in slots 1, 2, 3, 4, and 5 by the producers, and there are two consumers in the system (C1 and C2) sitting behind the single consumer barrier (CB1). They can operate in complete independence of each other until they hit the last slot that's been filled in by the producer. The third consumer, here consumer 3, is sitting behind consumer barrier 2 with a dependency on anyone CB1 here. This consumer can't actually access any slot until C1 and C2 are finished with it, so we can establish dependencies judicially using consumer barriers.

Batching plays a very important role here as well; if C1 is working on 1 and its taking a long time, the producer starts putting elements at 6. When C2 is done with 2, 3, and 4, it can run and simply start reading the elements from point 6 upward. It's intelligent enough to sense and act in batches.

We have a single data structure for all components; the smart-batching to catch up has an effect on both the producer and consumers help beat the latency in the most unconventional manner. It performs better with increased loads and we don't get the J shaped graph that we do with queues that have surging loads. The Storm framework internally uses this clever framework for data transfer and communication between workers.

Storm internode communication

To begin with, Storm has been using ZeroMQ as the communication channel for internode communications. In version 0.9, it was experimentally replaced by Netty and in version 0.9.2, Netty has been completely adopted as a replacement for ZeroMQ. In this section we will touch upon both ZeroMQ and Netty because it's very important to understand what makes them different and why these were chosen by the implementers of Storm over their peers.

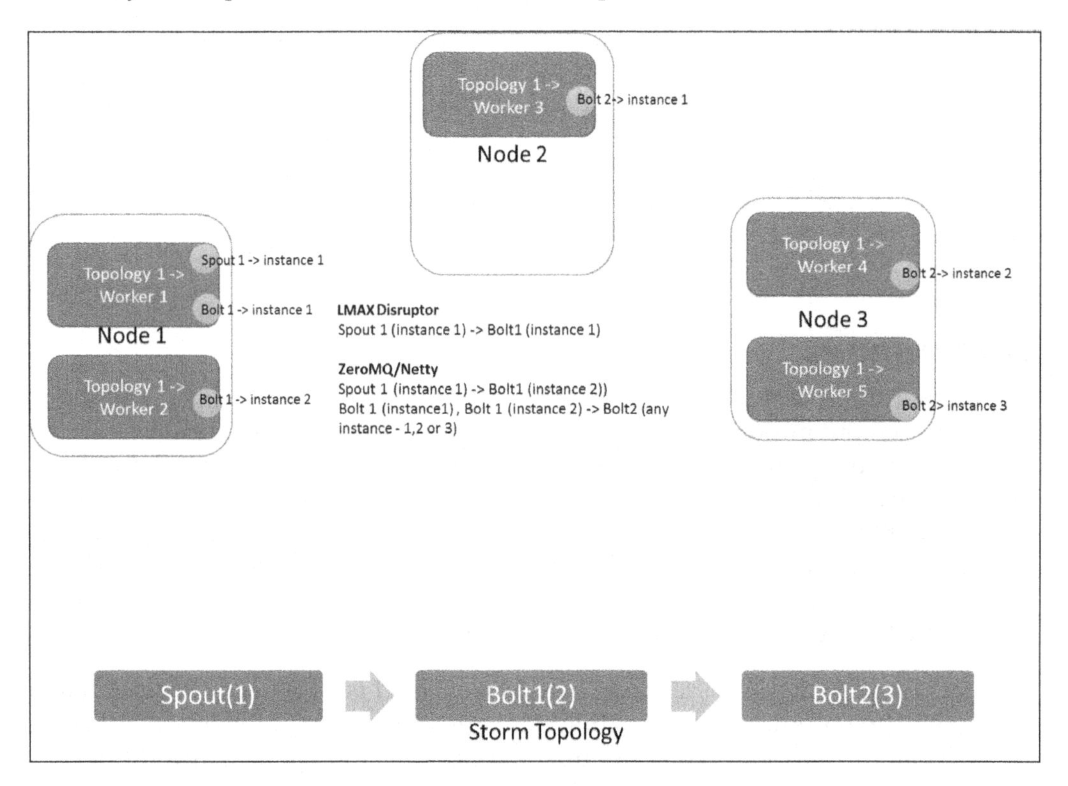

The preceding figure clearly describes how the different components communicate with each other using LMAX, ZeroMQ, or Netty based on whether they are executing within same worker on same node or not.

ZeroMQ

ZeroMQ is not a fully fledged messaging system such as AMQP, Rabbit MQ, and so on. It's a library that can be extended and used in building truly performance-oriented messaging systems for lean, mean situations. It's not a full-fledged framework, and it's an extensible toolkit—an asynchronous messaging library that serves the purpose fairly well. It is highly performant without any overkilling of extra baggage of the various layers that are transient to the frameworks. This library has all the necessary components that can be used to arrive at a quick messaging solution that is efficient and can be integrated with a large number of programming components through variety of adapters. It is a lightweight, asynchronous, and ultrafast messaging toolkit that can be used by developers for crafting high-performing solutions.

The implementation of ZeroMQ is in C++, so it doesn't run into the performance and GC issues that, generally, JVM-based applications do.

Here are some of the key aspects that make this library a choice above the rest for communication between different workers on same node or different nodes:

- It's a lightweight, asynchronous socket library that can be crafted to behave as a high performing concurrency framework
- It's faster than TCP, and ideal for internode communication in clustered setups
- It's not a networking protocol, but adapts to a wide variety such as IPC, TCP, multicast, and so on
- An asynchronous flavor helps to build a scalable I/O model for multicore message transferring apps
- It has a variety of inbuilt messaging patterns such as fan-out, pub-sub, request-reply, pipeline, and so on

Storm ZeroMQ configurations

Well, there are very simple configurations that are marked in under `storm.yaml`:

```
//Local mode is to use ZeroMQ as a message system, if set to false,
using the Java message system. The default is false
storm.local.mode.zmq : false
// Each worker process used in zeromq communication number of threads
zmq.threads : 1
```

The first one `storm.local.mode.zmq` controls whether ZeroMQ or Netty has to be used. In the latest version, by default, the inter-worker and inter-node communication is handled using Netty; thus, this value is false.

The `zmq.threads` parameter controls the number of threads that will be spawned for every worker. The more the merrier doesn't always work. We should never end up spawning more than our cores can handle, else there will be loads of cycles lost due to contention. The default value is one per worker.

Netty

The preceding section that describes ZeroMQ clearly states that ZeroMQ was a perfect choice for Storm. But, over the course of time, Storm adopters have realized that the issues that using ZeroMQ as a transport layer was posing and, being a native library, it ran into platform specific issues. In the early days, the installation of Storm with ZeroMQ was not simple, and it was downloaded and built for every installation. One more significant issue was that Storm was tightly coupled to ZeroMQ and worked with the relatively old 2.1.7 version.

After understanding the need, let's get introduced to Netty. Netty is a client-server messaging solution that's based on an NIO framework. It enables quick development and boasts ease of use with a relatively simplified design. It's high performing and scalable, along with having features like extensibility and flexibility.

The aspects that make Netty better than its peers are as follows:

- Low latency operations with non-blocking async operations
- Higher throughput
- Resource consumption is low
- Memory copy is minimized
- Secure SSL and TLS support

It provides a pluggability to Storm where the developers can choose between the two transport layer options that are ZeroMQ and Netty, just by means of a few settings in `storm.yaml`:

```
storm.messaging.transport: "backtype.storm.messaging.netty.Context"
storm.messaging.netty.server_worker_threads: 1
storm.messaging.netty.client_worker_threads: 1
storm.messaging.netty.buffer_size: 5242880
storm.messaging.netty.max_retries: 100
storm.messaging.netty.max_wait_ms: 1000
storm.messaging.netty.min_wait_ms: 100
```

The configuration starts by telling Storm that the transport layer is Netty. We will have to keep `storm.local.mode.zmq` as `false` and `storm.messaging.transport` as `backtype.storm.messaging.netty.context`.

Understanding the Storm UI

The Storm UI depicts some very vital and important aspects of the Storm cluster and topology. Some of the aspects that Storm depicts form the cardinal rules for optimizing the performance. But, before we talk about the performance, let's befriend the Storm UI and its parameters through series of captures from the Storm UI and descriptions of the same.

Storm UI landing page

The landing page on Storm UI first talks about **Cluster Summary**, as shown in the following screenshot:

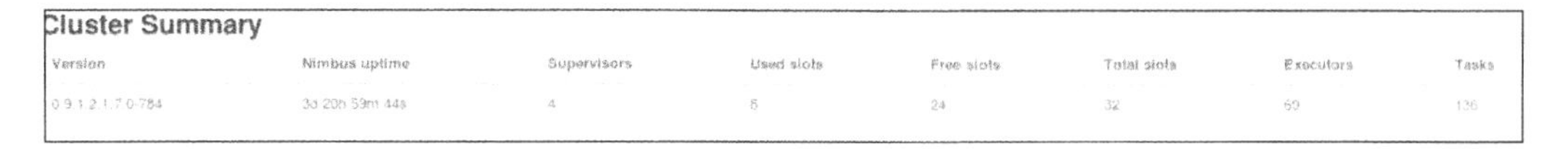

Cluster Summary

Version	Nimbus uptime	Supervisors	Used slots	Free slots	Total slots	Executors	Tasks
0.9.1.2.1.7.0-784	3d 20h 59m 44s	4	8	24	32	60	136

A brief description of the columns available in **Cluster Summary**, is as follows:

- **Version**: As the name suggests, this captures the version of Storm on the UI node. One of the prerequisites for a cluster is that the version of Storm should be same on all the nodes. Thus, this clearly denotes the version of Storm in the cluster.
- **Nimbus uptime**: This denotes the duration (in days, hours, minutes, and seconds) for which the Nimbus instance has been running. Nimbus being the coordinator daemon that essentially submits the topology to the cluster; it's uptime denotes the cluster uptime. However, there are situations where this value may not denote the cluster uptime. For instance, if Nimbus restarted at some later point in time after the topology submission.
- **Supervisors**: This is the number of nodes in the Storm cluster where the supervisor processes are up and running.
- **Total slots**: This is the number of workers in the cluster. This comes from the number of slots defined in `storm.yaml` for each of the supervisor nodes. The number of slots are generally kept equal to number of cores in the supervisor machines:

```
supervisor.slots.ports:
    - 6700
    - 6701
    - 6702
    - 6703
```

- **Used slots**: This is the number of workers that are in use by the bolts and spouts of the running topologies on the cluster.
- **Free slots**: This is the number of workers that are free and available in the cluster. This one is simple math. This number actually helps us predict how much is capacity and how much is HA capability. Let's take an example: I have a four-node Storm cluster, with each node having four slots, and two topologies that are executing on this cluster, which consume four slots each. So my total number of consumed slots is eight and the number of available unused slots is eight. Now, I have following capabilities in my cluster:
    - I can launch one or more topologies that consume cumulatively all the eight slots and the cluster will operate at 100 percent occupancy.
    - I can leave these eight slots as a HA capability for the cluster where my two topologies can run unimpacted; even if two of the nodes crash, they can always halt and rebalance over the remaining eight slots across the survivor nodes.
- **Tasks**: This parameter denotes the sum of running tasks in the cluster across all live topologies. It's basically the sum of the parallelism of all bolts and spouts.
- **Executors**: This represents the total number of threads that reside in the worker processes.

The **Topology summary** section is as shown in the following screenshot:

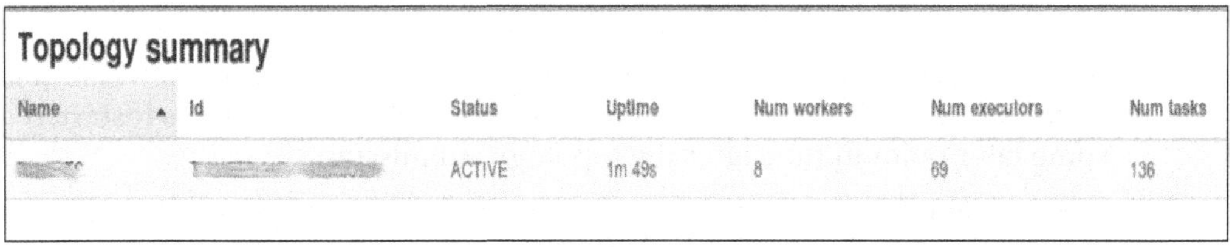

Topology summary

Name	Id	Status	Uptime	Num workers	Num executors	Num tasks
[illegible]	[illegible]	ACTIVE	1m 49s	8	69	136

A brief description of the columns available in **Topology summary** is as follows:

- **Name**: This is the name of the topology that was assigned at the submission of the topology to Nimbus. This is the user-defined identifier for the topology.
- **Id**: This is an identifier that was assigned by Storm to the topology at the time it was launched or submitted to the cluster for execution.
- **Status**: This depicts the various states of the topology and what it could be:
    - **ACTIVE**: A live and running topology.
    - **INACTIVE**: A live topology which is in a suspended state and is actually not processing any live traffic.

    - **KILLED**: A topology that was killed, and it was processing the tuples that were in the flow of execution when the kill command was issued. It's shutting down, and will exit and be removed from the UI.
    - **REBALANCING**: This state denotes that the topology is on hold and is not consuming any data; instead, it's being rebalanced across the cluster. This happens in situations where we modify the number of workers and executors for a running topology, or when one of the supervisor processes on which the topology workers were running is killed. Thus, the topology rebalances its processes across the other workers on live supervisors.

- **Uptime**: This depicts the time elapsed since the topology submission.
- **Num workers**: This denotes the number of workers assigned to the topology. This value is defined under the topology configuration.
- **Num executors**: This denotes the number of executors used by the topology.
- **Num tasks**: This is the number of tasks executing within the topology.

The **Supervisor summary** section is as shown in the following screenshot:

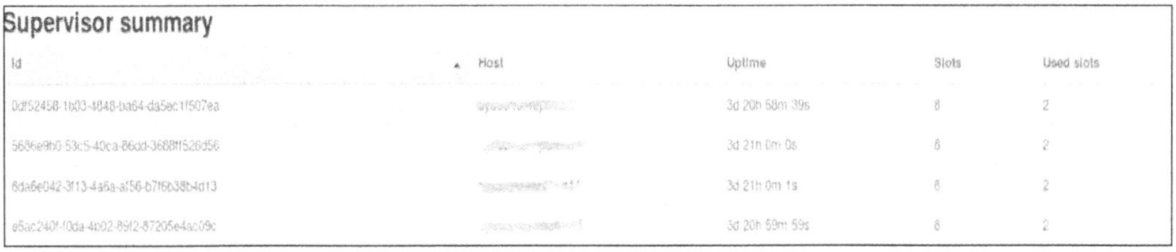

Supervisor summary

Id	Host	Uptime	Slots	Used slots
0df52458-1b03-4848-ba64-da5ec1f507ea	[illegible]	3d 20h 58m 39s	8	2
5686e9b0-53c5-40ca-86dd-3688ff526d56	[illegible]	3d 21h 0m 0s	8	2
6da6e042-3f13-4a6a-af56-b7f6b38b4d13	[illegible]	3d 21h 0m 1s	8	2
e5ac240f-f0da-4b02-89f2-87205e4ac09c	[illegible]	3d 20h 59m 59s	8	2

A brief description of the columns available in **Supervisor summary** is as follows:

- **Id**: This is a unique identifier that Storm assigns to every supervisor node that joins the cluster.
- **Host**: This is the hostname of the machine on which the supervisor process is executing.
- **Uptime**: This is the duration for which the Storm supervisor has been up and running as part of this cluster.
- **Slots**: The slots actually denote how many workers are launched on the supervisor at the time the supervisor process is started. In general, the number is kept as one worker per core.
- **Used slots**: This is the number of workers that are executing some topology components.

Topology home page

We have reached here after clicking on the topology name in the landing page. The first segment of the page talks about the **Topology actions**:

This segment explains the various actions that can be performed using the Storm UI on the topology:

- **Activate**: This is used to reactivate a deactivated topology.
- **Deactivate**: This action sends the topology into suspension. It's alive, but not processing or executing any tuples.
- **Rebalance**: This action is used to increase or decrease the number of workers and executors assigned to an active or running topology.
- **Kill**: This action is used to stop and terminate the topology. Storm guarantees processing, so **Kill** doesn't kill and remove the topology from Storm instantaneously, rather it happens in a phased manner and can take a while to execute. First, the topology stops reading data into the spout. It continues processing and draining out what was in execution at the time the command was issued. Once all tuples have been successfully executed and drained from the topology DAG, it then terminates and is removed from Storm.

The second segment of the topology home page on the Storm UI describes the **Topology stats**:

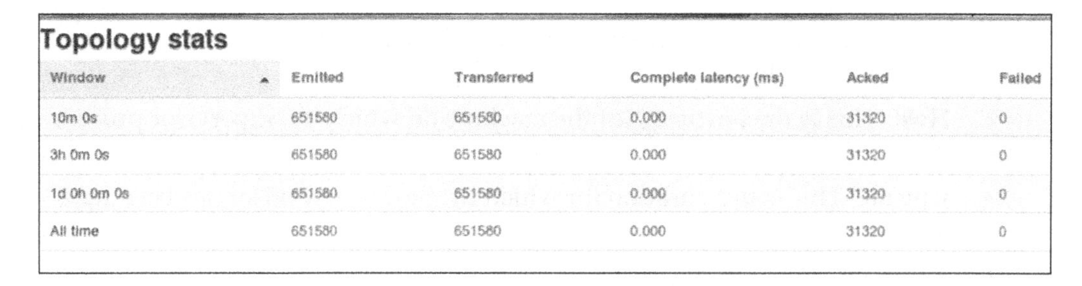

Topology stats

Window	Emitted	Transferred	Complete latency (ms)	Acked	Failed
10m 0s	651580	651580	0.000	31320	0
3h 0m 0s	651580	651580	0.000	31320	0
1d 0h 0m 0s	651580	651580	0.000	31320	0
All time	651580	651580	0.000	31320	0

A brief description of the columns available in **Topology stats** is as follows:

- **Window**: This interesting parameter denotes the time range over which the stats in rest of the column are. You can click and choose on what range suits them.

- **Emitted**: This statistic captures the sum total number of tuples emitted in the topology, rounded to an order of 10.
- **Transferred**: This denotes the number of tuples that were emitted and sent to one or more bolts, again rounded to an order of 10.
- **Complete latency (ms)**: It will be `0` if acking is off. But if tuples are to be explicitly acked, this is a very interesting parameter, as it captures the average time an event or tuple takes to complete its execution through the topology directed acyclic graph.
- **Acked**: This depicts the total number of tuples that executed successfully and were acked back to the spout. It's `0` in the case of no acking scenarios.
- **Failed**: This captures the number of tuples that were failed or timed out during the executions before acking was completed. This value is `0` in the case of no acking scenarios. Storm requeues all these failed tuples back to the queue so that they can be reprocessed in the topology.

The following screenshot captures the next section of the page, which has the **Spout (All time)** stats captured:

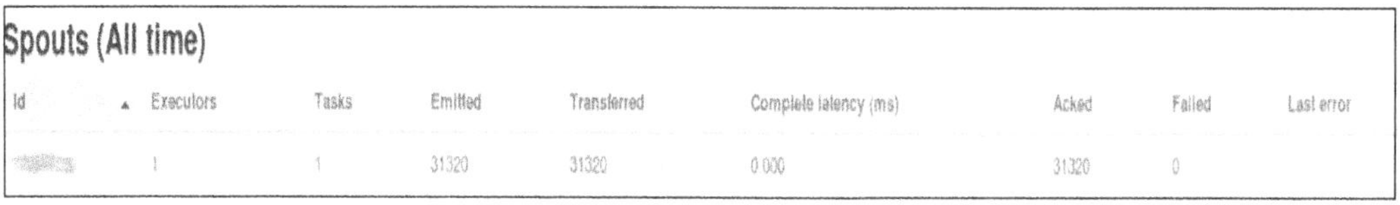

Spouts (All time)

Id	Executors	Tasks	Emitted	Transferred	Complete latency (ms)	Acked	Failed	Last error
[illegible]	1	1	31320	31320	0.000	31320	0	

The following section will walk you through the various parameters depicted here in and their inference:

- **Id**: This is the Storm-provided identifier for the topology component (spout/bolt)
- **Executors**: This captures how many executors are assigned by Storm for the execution of this component (bolt/spout)
- **Tasks**: This denotes the number of tasks that are spawned by the framework for the execution of this component (bolt/spout)

The remaining parameters keep the same meaning as discussed previously, except for **Last error**. This one captures the last error that occurred on this component (bolt/spout).

The following screenshot captures the section of the page that has the **Bolt (All time)** stats captured. The following section will walk you through the various parameters depicted here in and their inference:

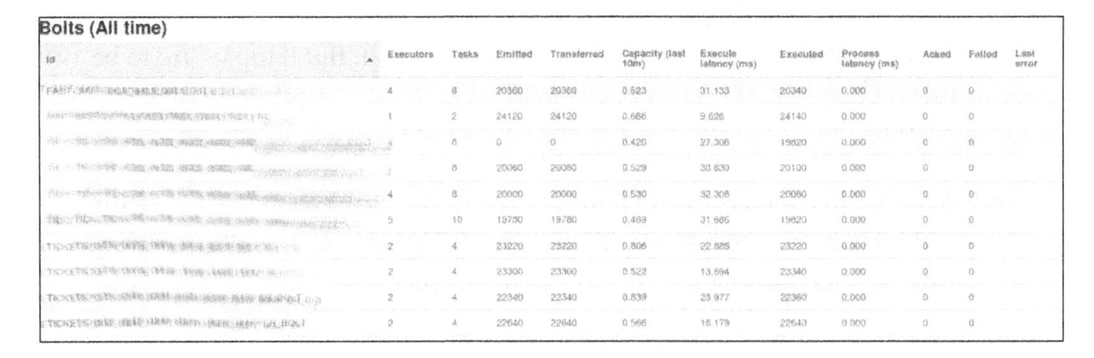

Bolts (All time)

Id	Executors	Tasks	Emitted	Transferred	Capacity (last 10m)	Execute latency (ms)	Executed	Process latency (ms)	Acked	Failed	Last error
[illegible]	4	8	20360	20360	0.523	31.133	20340	0.000	0	0	
[illegible]	1	2	24120	24120	0.666	9.626	24140	0.000	0	0	
[illegible]	[illegible]	8	0	0	0.420	27.306	19620	0.000	0	0	
[illegible]	[illegible]	8	20060	20080	0.529	30.630	20100	0.000	0	0	
[illegible]	4	8	20000	20000	0.530	32.308	20060	0.000	0	0	
[illegible]	5	10	19780	19780	0.468	31.665	19620	0.000	0	0	
[illegible]	2	4	23220	23220	0.806	22.825	23220	0.000	0	0	
[illegible]	2	4	23300	23300	0.522	13.694	23340	0.000	0	0	
[illegible]	2	4	22340	22340	0.839	23.977	22360	0.000	0	0	
[illegible]	2	4	22640	22640	0.566	16.179	22640	0.000	0	0	

I will omit the parameters that keep the same meaning as above and focus only on the relevant ones:

- **Emitted**: This captures the total number of tuples emitted from the bolt, rounded to an order of 10.
- **Capacity (last 10m)**: This basically denotes the efficiency factor of the component (bolt/spout) and, in ideal scenarios, should be less than `1`. At `1`, it's taken as an alert scenario and increasing the parallelism of the bolt should be attempted. Mathematically, it's the number of tuples executed by the bolt multiplied by age, latency, or time.
- **Execute latency (ms)**: This is the average time the tuple takes to complete the processing through the execute method of the bolt.
- **Executed**: This is the number of input tuples processed by the bolt.
- **Process latency (ms)**: This is a very important parameter, and it's the time taken by the tuple from its arrival at the bolt to the time it's acked. If this value is high, it will cause the complete latency to shoot up, even if your execute latency is low, which means that the tuple is spending more time in the queue waiting for execution through the bolt's execute method, and we should consider adding more ackers to make the acking faster.

Now that we have understood the basic and key aspects depicted in the Storm UI, the next obvious thing to talk about is optimizing Storm performance.

Optimizing Storm performance

To be able to optimize the performance of Storm, it's very important to understand what are or could be the performance bottlenecks. If we know the pitfalls, only then can we avoid them. Another noteworthy aspect of Storm, like all other Big Data frameworks, is that there is no rule of thumb for performance; every scenario is unique and so the performance optimization plan for every scenario is also unique.

So this section is more about pointers and classic dos and don'ts. What will actually work in your use case to serve as performance booster will have to be uncovered after several rounds of tweaks to the system and after observations.

Fundamentally, Storm is a high-performing, distributed processing system. The moment the work distribution comes into play, it brings with it its own Pandora's box that can be performance glitches such as the interaction between different processes on the same node, or different processes on different nodes that require channels, sources and sinks. In our topology, we can look at each node as a source for the next one in the graph. In this distributed setup, the following can go wrong:

- The sink bolt may be slow or clogged. For example, my bolt is operating at capacity 1, which is 100 percent efficiency, and thus it's not picking up any messages from the ZeroMQ or Netty channel.
- The source bolt is unaware of this fact, and it is super-efficiently pumping more and more tuples into the queue.
- The consequence is that the queue capacity is reached and there is spillage or a burst. Messages are failed and thus requeued for replay as per the nature of Storm. So, it's a vicious circle of infinite churn.
- The takeaway is that you should observe your latencies: both the execute and process latency. Attempt to keep your capacity under 1.

You can do so by increasing parallelism, but, of course, being cognizant of the number of workers and core, lest you increase the parallelism incredibly, and all processes and threads die of contention.

Latency should be seen in red by all programmers, so it's very important to get acquainted with the well-known latencies of the system. Here is a capture of this from `https://gist.github.com/jboner/2841832`:

```
Latency Comparison Numbers
--------------------------
L1 cache reference                          0.5 ns
Branch mispredict                           5   ns
L2 cache reference                          7   ns
14x L1 cache
```

```
Mutex lock/unlock                            25    ns
Main memory reference                       100    ns
20x L2 cache, 200x L1 cache
Compress 1K bytes with Zippy              3,000    ns        3 us
Send 1K bytes over 1 Gbps network        10,000    ns       10 us
Read 4K randomly from SSD*              150,000    ns      150 us
~1GB/sec SSD
Read 1 MB sequentially from memory      250,000    ns      250 us
Round trip within same datacenter       500,000    ns      500 us
Read 1 MB sequentially from SSD*      1,000,000    ns    1,000 us     1
ms  ~1GB/sec SSD, 4X memory
Disk seek                            10,000,000    ns   10,000 us    10
ms  20x datacenter roundtrip
Read 1 MB sequentially from disk     20,000,000    ns   20,000 us    20
ms  80x memory, 20X SSD
Send packet CA->Netherlands->CA     150,000,000    ns  150,000 us   150
ms
```

The Storm cluster should be built, scaled, and sized as per the requirements of the use case, and here are the important caveats that should be taken notice of:

- Number and variety of input sources
- Rate of arrival of data, TPS or transactions per second
- Size of each event
- Which is the component (bolt/spout) that is the most efficient and which one is the least

The cardinal rules for performance optimization are as follows:

- Be cognizant of network transfer and only do it when it's actually required. Network latencies are huge and generally not in a programmer's control. So, in taking one topology where all the bolts and spouts are only spread on a single node versus one where they are scattered across an `x` node cluster, the former will have better performance because it saves on network hop. While the latter has a higher chance of survival in the event of failure because it's spread across the cluster not just on a single node.
- The number of ackers should be kept equal to the number of supervisors.
- The number of executors should generally be kept to `1` per core—for CPU intensive topologies.

  Let's say I have 10 supervisors, each of which has 16 cores. So how many parallel units do I have? The answer is 10 * 16 = 160.

  Rule of 1 acker per node = 10 acker processes

Remaining parallel units = 160 - 10 = 150

Assign more parallel units to slower tasks and less to faster ones:

Emit -> Compute -> Persist [three components in topology]

So, with the persist being the slowest task (I/O bound), we can have parallelism as follows:

Emit [Parallelism 10] -> Compute [Parallelism 50] -> Persist [Parallelism 90]

- Increase parallelism whenever the capacity rises to reach `1`.
- Keep a tab on the number of unacked tuples by tweaking the following parameter in the configuration:

  ```
  topology.max.spout.pending
  ```

  The default value of this parameter is unset, so there is no limit, but based on the use case we need throttling so that, when we reach the point where the number of unacked messages is equal to the max spout pending, we halt reading more and let the processing catch up and ack all messages, and then proceed further. This value should:

  - Not be so small that the topology is waiting idle
  - Not be so big that the topology is swamped with messages before it can process and ack them

  Optimally, start from 1,000, and then tweak this and find out what works best for your use case. In the case of Trident, start low with something like 15-20.

- How much should be my timeout? Not too high and not too low. Observe the complete latency in the topology and then tweak the parameter.

  ```
  Topology.message.timeout.secs
  ```

- Machine sizing:
  - **Nimbus**: Lightweight and a medium quadcore node will suffice.
  - **Supervisors**: High-end nodes, more memory, and more core (depending the nature of the use case, whether it is CPU intensive, memory intensive, or may be both).

The silent orchestrator of the Storm cluster is **ZooKeeper**. This is the heart of all control and coordination, and all operations here are generally I/O-bound disk operations. Thus, the following generally helps to keep ZooKeeper efficient and the Storm cluster happy:

- Use ZooKeeper quorum (at least a three-node setup)
- Use dedicated hardware
- Use dedicated SSD for improved performance

Summary

This chapter's main emphasis was on getting the readers acquainted with the Trident framework as an extension of Storm as a microbatching abstraction. We have seen various key concepts and operations of Trident. Then, we took you into the inside of Storm with LMAX, ZeroMQ, and Netty. Lastly, we have concluded the chapter on the performance optimization aspects of Storm.

The next chapter will focus on the users to get you initiated on the AWS-based streaming framework: the Kinesis processing stream data on the Amazon cloud using Kinesis services.

5
Getting Acquainted with Kinesis

Optimum utilization of resources has always been one of the key business objectives. It becomes more important for corporations where the cost of infrastructure is almost 50% of the overall IT budget. Cloud computing is a key concept that is changing the face of corporate IT, where it not only helps in achieving coherence and economies at scale but also provides enterprise-class functionalities such as upgrades, maintenance, failover, load balancers, and so on. Of course, all these features come at a cost, but you only pay for what you use.

It did not take much time for enterprises to realize the benefits of cloud computing and they started adapting/implementing/hosting their services and products by leveraging either **IaaS** (`https://en.wikipedia.org/wiki/Cloud_computing#Infrastructure_as_a_service_.28IaaS.29`) or **PaaS** (`https://en.wikipedia.org/wiki/Platform_as_a_service`). The benefits of IaaS/PaaS were so noticeable that soon it was extended to cloud-based streaming analytics. Cloud-based streaming analytics is a service in the cloud that helps in developing/deploying low-cost analytics solutions to uncover real-time insights from the various data feeds received from varied data sources, such as devices, sensors, infrastructure, applications, and more. The objective is to scale to any volume of data with high or customizable throughput, low latency, and guaranteed resiliency, with hassle-free installation and setup within few minutes.

In late 2013, Amazon launched Kinesis as a fully managed, cloud-based service (PaaS) for performing cloud-based streaming analytics on the real-time data received from distributed data streams. It also allowed developers to write custom applications for performing near real-time analytics on the data feeds received in real time.

Let's move forward and find out more about Kinesis.

This chapter will cover the following points that will help us to understand the overall architecture and various components of Kinesis:

- Architectural overview of Kinesis
- Creating a Kinesis streaming service

Architectural overview of Kinesis

In this section, we will talk about the overall architecture and various components of Kinesis. This section will help us to understand the terminology and various components of Amazon Kinesis.

Benefits and use cases of Amazon Kinesis

Amazon Kinesis is a service provided by Amazon in the cloud that allows developers to consume data from multiple data sources, such as streaming news feeds, financial data, social media applications, logs, or sensor data, and subsequently write applications that respond to these real-time data feeds. The data received from Kinesis can be further consumed, transformed, and finally persisted in various data stores such as Amazon S3, Amazon DynamoDB, Amazon Redshift, or any other NoSQL database either in its raw form or filtered according to predefined business rules.

Kinesis can be integrated with real-time dashboards and business intelligence software, which thereby enables the scripting of alerts and decision making protocols that respond to the trajectories of incoming real-time data.

Amazon Kinesis is a highly available service where it replicates its data across different AWS availability zones within an AWS region. Amazon Kinesis is offered as a "managed service" (`https://en.wikipedia.org/wiki/Managed_services`) for dealing with incoming streams of real-time data that includes load balancing, failover, autoscaling, and orchestration.

Amazon Kinesis is undoubtedly categorized as a disruptive innovation/technology (`https://en.wikipedia.org/wiki/Disruptive_innovation`) in the area of real-time or near real-time data processing, where it provides the following benefits:

- **Ease of use**: Hosted as a managed service, Kinesis streams can be created just by a few clicks. Further applications can be developed for consuming and processing data in no time with the help of the AWS SDK.

- **Parallel processing**: It is common to process the data feeds for different purposes; for example, in a network monitoring use case, the processed network logs are shown on the real-time dashboards for identification of any security breaches/anomalies and at the same time it also stores the data in the database for deep analytics. Kinesis streams can be consumed by multiple applications concurrently, which may have different purposes or problems to solve.
- **Scalable**: Kinesis streams are elastic in nature and can scale from MBs to GBs per second, and from thousands to millions of messages per second. Based on the volume of data, throughput can be adjusted dynamically at any point in time without disturbing the existing applications/streams. Moreover, these streams can be created.
- **Cost effective**: There is no setup or upfront cost involved in setting up Kinesis streams. We pay only for what we use and that can be as little as $0.015 per hour with a 1 MB/second ingestion rate and a 2 MB/second consumption rate.
- **Fault tolerant and highly available**: Amazon Kinesis preserves data for 24 hours and synchronously replicates the streaming data across three facilities in an AWS region, preventing data loss in the case of application or infrastructure failure.

Apart from the benefits listed here, Kinesis can be leveraged for a variety of business and infrastructure use cases where we need to consume and process the incoming data feeds within seconds or milliseconds. Here are few of the prominent verticals and the associated use cases for Kinesis:

- **Telecommunication**: Analyzing **call data records** (**CDRs**) is one of the prominent and most discussed business use cases. Telecom companies analyze CDRs for actionable insights, which not only optimize the overall costs but, at the same time, introduce new business lines/trends, resulting in better customer satisfaction.

  The key challenge with CDRs is the volume and velocity, which varies from day to day or even hour to hour, and at the same time the CDRs are used to solve multiple business problems. Kinesis can undoubtedly be a best-fit solution as it provides an elegant solution to the key challenges very well.
- **Healthcare**: One of the prominent and best-suited use cases in healthcare for Kinesis is to analyze the privacy-protected streams of medical device data for detecting early signs of diseases and, at the same time, identify correlations among multiple patients and measure efficacy of the treatments.

- **Automotive**: Automotive is a growing industry in which we have seen a lot of innovation over the past few years. Lot of sensors are embedded in our vehicles that are constantly collecting various kinds of information such as distance, speed, geo-spatial/GPS locations, driving patterns, parking style, and so on. All this information can be pushed in to Kinesis streams in real-time, and consumer applications can process this information and can provide some real and actionable insights, such as assessing the driver risk for potential accidents or alerts for insurance companies, which can further generate personalized insurance pricing.

The preceding use cases are only a few examples of where Kinesis can be leveraged for storing/processing real-time or streaming data feeds. There could be many more use cases based on the industry and its needs.

Let's move forward and discuss the architecture and various components of Kinesis.

High-level architecture

A fully fledged deployment of Kinesis-based, real-time/streaming data processing applications will involve many components that closely interact with each other. The following diagram illustrates the high-level architecture of such deployments. It also defines the role played by each and every component:

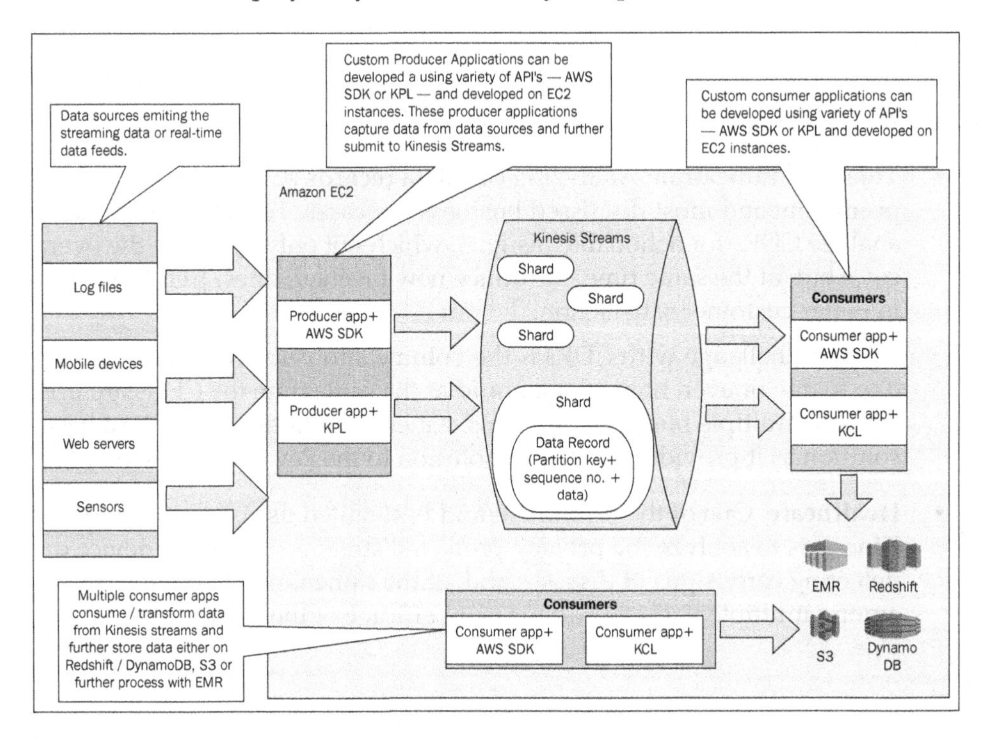

This diagram shows the architecture of the Kinesis-based, real-time/streaming data processing applications. At a high level, the producers fetch/consume the data from the data sources and continually push data to the Amazon Kinesis streams. Consumers at the other end continually consume the data from the Kinesis streams and further process it, and they can store their results using an AWS service such as Amazon DynamoDB, Amazon Redshift, Amazon S3, or any other NoSQL database, or maybe push it in to another Kinesis stream.

Let's move on to the next section where we will discuss the role and purpose of each and every component of the Kinesis architecture.

Components of Kinesis

In this section, we will discuss the various components of Kinesis-based applications. Amazon Kinesis provides the capability to store the streaming data, but there are various other components that play a pivotal role in developing full-blown, Kinesis-based, real-time data processing applications. Let's understand the various components of Kinesis.

Data sources

Data sources are those applications that are producing the data in real time and providing the means to access or consume the data in real or near real-time; for example, data emitted by various sensors or web servers emitting logs.

Producers

Producers are custom applications that consume the data from the data sources and then submit the data to Kinesis streams for further storage. The role of producers in the overall architecture is to consume the data and implement various strategies to efficiently submit the data to Kinesis streams. One of the recommended strategies is to create batches of data and then submit the records to the Kinesis streams. Producers optionally may perform minimal transformation, but we should ensure that any processing should not degrade the performance of the producers. The primary role of producers is to fetch data and optimally submit it to Kinesis streams. The producers are recommended to be deployed on the EC2 instances themselves, so that there is optimal performance and no latency while submitting the records to Kinesis. Producers can optionally be implemented using the APIs directly exposed by the AWS SDK or Kinesis Producer Library.

Consumers

Consumer applications are custom applications that connect and consume the data from Kinesis streams. Consumer applications further transform or enrich the data and can store it in some persistent storage services/devices such as DynamoDB (`https://aws.amazon.com/dynamodb/`), Redshift (`https://aws.amazon.com/redshift/`), S3 (`https://aws.amazon.com/s3/`), or may submit it to EMR, which is short for Elastic MapReduce, (`https://aws.amazon.com/elasticmapreduce/`) for further processing.

AWS SDK

Amazon provides a **software development kit** (**SDK**) that contains easy-to-use and high-level APIs so that users can seamlessly integrate the AWS services within their existing applications. The SDK contains APIs for many AWS services, including Amazon S3, Amazon EC2, DynamoDB, Kinesis, and others. Apart from the APIs, it also includes code samples and documentation. Producers and consumers of Kinesis streams can be developed using the Amazon Kinesis APIs exposed by AWS SDK, but these APIs provide basic functionality to connect, and submit or consume data to/from Kinesis streams. Other advanced functionalities, such as batching or aggregation, either need to be developed by the developer or he/she may also optionally use high-level libraries such as **Kinesis Producer Library** (**KPL**) or **Kinesis Client Library** (**KCL**).

Refer to `https://aws.amazon.com/tools/?nc1=f_dr` for more information about the available SDKs and `http://docs.aws.amazon.com/kinesis/latest/APIReference/Welcome.html` for more information about Amazon Kinesis API.

KPL

KPL is a high-level API developed over AWS SDK that can be used by developers to write the code for ingesting data into Kinesis streams. The Amazon KPL simplifies producer application development through which developers can achieve a high write throughput to an Amazon Kinesis stream that can be further monitored using Amazon CloudWatch (`https://aws.amazon.com/cloudwatch/`). Apart from providing a simplified mechanism for connecting and submitting data to Kinesis streams, KPL also provides the following features:

- **Retry mechanism**: Provides an automatic and configurable retry mechanism in scenarios where data packets are dropped or rejected by the Kinesis streams due to lack of availability of sufficient bandwidth.

- **Batching of records**: It provides the APIs for writing multiple records to multiple shards in one single request.
- **Aggregation**: Aggregates the records and increases the payload size to achieve the optimum utilization of available throughput.
- **Deaggregation**: Integrates seamlessly with the Amazon KCL and deaggregates the batched records.
- **Monitoring**: Submit the various metrics to Amazon CloudWatch to monitor the performance and overall throughput of the producer application.

It is also important to understand that KPL should not be confused with the Amazon Kinesis API that is available with the AWS SDK. The Amazon Kinesis API provides various functionalities, such as creating streams, resharding, and putting/getting records, but KPL just provides a layer of abstraction specifically for optimized data ingestion.

Refer to `http://docs.aws.amazon.com/kinesis/latest/dev/developing-producers-with-kpl.html` for more information on KPL.

KCL

KCL is the high-level API that was developed by extending the Amazon Kinesis API (included in AWS SDK) for consuming data from the Kinesis streams. KCL provides various design patterns for accessing and processing data in an efficient manner. It also incorporates various features such as load balancing across multiple instances, handling instance failures, checkpointing processed records, and resharding, which eventually helps developers to focus on the real business logic for processing the records received from the Kinesis streams. KCL is entirely written in Java, but it also provides support for other languages via its **MultiLangDaemon** interface.

Refer to `http://docs.aws.amazon.com/kinesis/latest/dev/developing-consumers-with-kcl.html` for more information on KCL, its role, and its support for multiple languages.

Kinesis streams

One of the most important components of the complete architecture is the Kinesis streams. Understanding the design of Kinesis streams is important for architecting and designing a scalable and performance-efficient real-time message processing system. Kinesis streams define four main components, which are used in the structuring and storing of the data received from producer: shards, data records, partition keys, and sequence numbers. Let's move forward and look at all these components of Kinesis streams.

Shards

A shard stores a uniquely identified group of data records in an Amazon Kinesis stream. A Kinesis stream is composed of multiple shards and each shard provides a fixed unit of capacity. Every record, when submitted to a Kinesis stream, is stored in one of the shards of the same stream. Each shard has its own capacity to handle read and write requests, and the eventual number of shards defined for a stream is the total capacity of the Amazon Kinesis stream. We need to be careful in defining the total number of shards for a stream because we are charged on a per-shard basis. Here's the capacity for reads and writes for one shard:

- **For reads**: Every shard has a maximum capacity to support up to 5 transactions per second with a maximum limit of 2 MB per second.
- **For writes**: Every shard has a maximum capacity to accept 1,000 writes per second, with a limit of 1 MB per second (including partition keys).

Let's take an example where you define 20 shards for your Amazon Kinesis stream. So the maximum capacity of your reads will be 1000 (20 shards * 5) transactions per second, where the total size of all reads should not be more than 40 MB (20*2) per second, which means that the size of each transaction, if equally divided, should not be more than 40 KB. For writes, there will be a maximum of 20,000 (1000*20) writes per second, where each write request should not be more than 1 MB per second.

Shards need to be defined at the time of initializing the Kinesis stream itself. To decide the total number of required shards, we need the following inputs, either from the user or developers who will be reading or writing records to the stream:

- **Total size of each record**: Let's assume that each record is 2 KB
- **Total required reads and writes per second**: Assume 1000 writes and reads per second

Considering the preceding numbers, we will require at least two shards. Here's the formula for calculating the total number of shards:

```
number_of_shards = max(incoming_write_bandwidth_in_KB/1000, outgoing_
read_bandwidth_in_KB/2000)
```

This will eventually result in the following calculation:

```
2 = max((1000*2KB)/1000,(1000*2KB)/2000)
```

Once we define the shards and streams are created, we can spin off multiple clients for reading and writing to the same streams.

Let's move forward and discuss the format of data stored within the streams/shards. The data within the shards is stored in form of data records, which are comprised of partition keys, sequence numbers and the actual data. Let's move forward and study each of the components of the data records.

Partition keys

Partition keys are the user-defined Unicode strings, each with a maximum length of 256 characters, which map the data records to a particular shard. Each shard stores the data for a specific set of partition keys only. The mapping of shard and data records is derived by providing partition keys as an input to a hash function (internal to Kinesis) that maps the partition key and associates the data with a specific shard. Amazon Kinesis leverages the MD5 hash function for converting partition keys (strings) to 128-bit integer values and then to further associate data records with shards. Every time producers submit records to Kinesis streams, a hashing mechanism is applied over the partition keys and then the data records are stored on the specific shards that are responsible for handling those keys.

Sequence Numbers

Sequence numbers are unique numbers assigned by Kinesis to each data record once it is submitted by the producers. The sequence numbers for the same partition key generally increase over a period of time, which means the longer the time period between write requests, the larger will be the sequence numbers.

In this section, we have discussed the various components and their role in the overall architecture of Kinesis streams. Let's move forward to the next section where we will see the usage of these components with the help of appropriate examples.

Creating a Kinesis streaming service

In this section, we will see some real-world examples which will produce the streaming data and then will store it in a Kinesis stream. At the same time, we will also see Kinesis consumers that will consume and process the streaming data from Kinesis streams.

Access to AWS Kinesis

The very first step in working with Kinesis streams is getting access to **Amazon Web Services** (**AWS**). Please perform the following steps for getting access to AWS:

1. Open `https://aws.amazon.com` and click on **Create an AWS Account**:

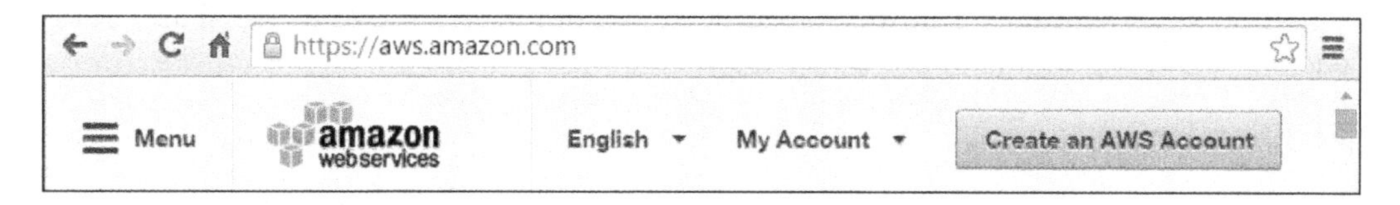

2. Follow the rest of the instructions as they appear on your screen.

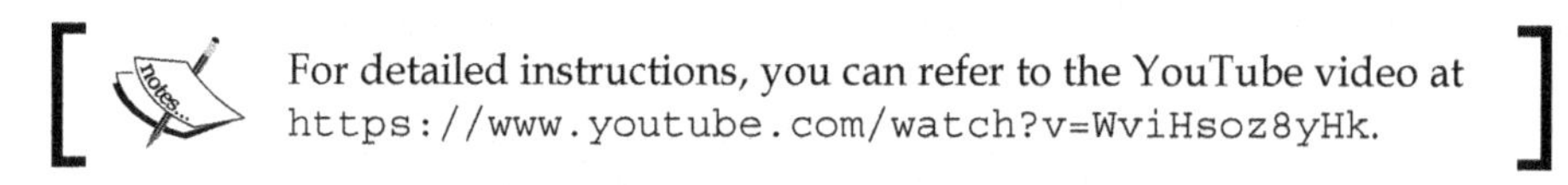

For detailed instructions, you can refer to the YouTube video at `https://www.youtube.com/watch?v=WviHsoz8yHk`.

The sign-up process may involve receiving a phone call and entering the temporary verification pin number.

At the end, you will be provided with the username and password for accessing and managing your AWS account and all its associated services.

Once we complete the sign up process successfully, we will have access to AWS and all its services, including Kinesis.

AWS provides a free tier for some of the services where we are not charged till we reach a certain limit; for example, launching and using micro instances for 750 hours a month is not charged.

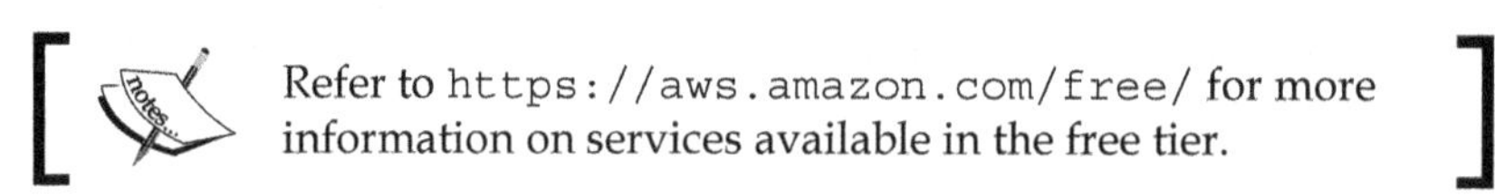

Refer to `https://aws.amazon.com/free/` for more information on services available in the free tier.

Kinesis is not part of the free tier, so it's chargeable, but the good part is that only we have to pay for what we use. We can start using Kinesis streams for as low as $0.015 per hour.

Refer to `https://aws.amazon.com/kinesis/pricing/` for more information on Kinesis pricing.

Assuming that we now have access to AWS, let's move forward and set up our development environment for working with Kinesis streams.

Configuring the development environment

In this section, we will talk about all the essential libraries required for working with Amazon Kinesis, and we will also configure our development environment. This will help us in the development of consumers and producers for our Kinesis streams.

Perform the following steps for configuring your development environment:

1. Download and install Oracle Java 7 from `http://www.oracle.com/technetwork/java/javase/install-linux-self-extracting-138783.html`.
2. Open your Linux console and execute the following command to configure `JAVA_HOME` as the environment variable:

   ```
   export JAVA_HOME=<Path of Java install Dir>
   ```

3. Download Eclipse Luna from `http://www.eclipse.org/downloads/packages/eclipse-ide-java-ee-developers/lunasr2` and extract it. Let's refer to the directory where we extracted it as `ECLIPSE_HOME`.
4. Open Eclipse and follow the instructions provided at `http://docs.aws.amazon.com/AWSToolkitEclipse/latest/GettingStartedGuide/tke_setup_install.html` for installing the AWS Toolkit for Eclipse.

   You might need to restart your Eclipse instance once the AWS toolkit is installed.

5. Next, download KCL from AWS's GitHub page (`https://github.com/awslabs/amazon-kinesis-client/archive/v1.6.0.zip`).
6. GitHub provides the source files that we need to compile with MVN (`https://maven.apache.org/`). If you do not want to do that, you can also download the compiled binaries with all dependencies from `https://drive.google.com/file/d/0B5oLQERok6YHdnlGb0dWLWZmMmc/view?usp=sharing`.

7. Open your Eclipse instance, create a Java project, and set its name to `RealTimeAnalytics-Kinesis`.
8. In your Eclipse project, create a package called `chapter.five`. Open the Eclipse project properties window and provide the dependencies of KCL, as shown in the following screenshot:

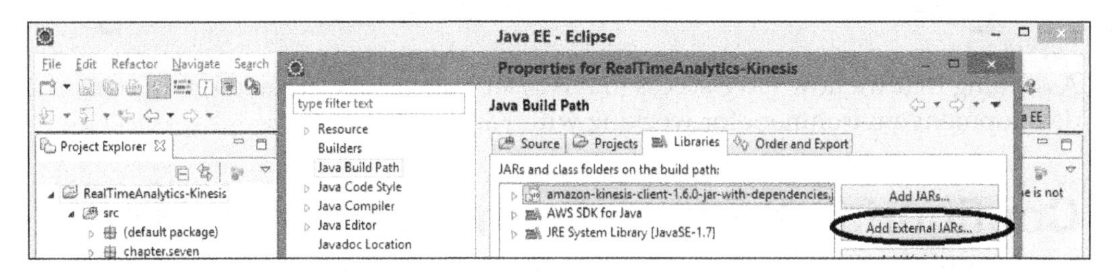

The preceding screenshot shows the Eclipse project and its dependencies that need to be added for compiling and running the code for Kinesis streams.

9. Next, follow the instructions provided at `http://docs.aws.amazon.com/AWSToolkitEclipse/latest/GettingStartedGuide/tke_setup_creds.html` and configure your Eclipse environment with the AWS access credentials. This is required so that you can directly connect to AWS from Eclipse itself.

That's it! We are done with the configurations. Our development is ready for working with Kinesis streams.

Let's move forward to the next sections where we will create streams, and write producers and consumers for developing a streaming service.

Creating Kinesis streams

In this section, you will learn various ways of creating or hosting Kinesis streams.

Kinesis streams can be created by two different methods: one is using the AWS SDK/toolkit, and the second is directly logging into the AWS and then using the user interface for creating Kinesis streams.

Perform the following steps for creating Kinesis streams using the AWS user interface:

1. Log into your AWS console and go to `https://console.aws.amazon.com/kinesis/home`. It will take you the home page for Kinesis streams.

2. Click on the **Create Stream** button, as shown on the home page of Kinesis, and you will see the following screen where you have to define the stream configurations:

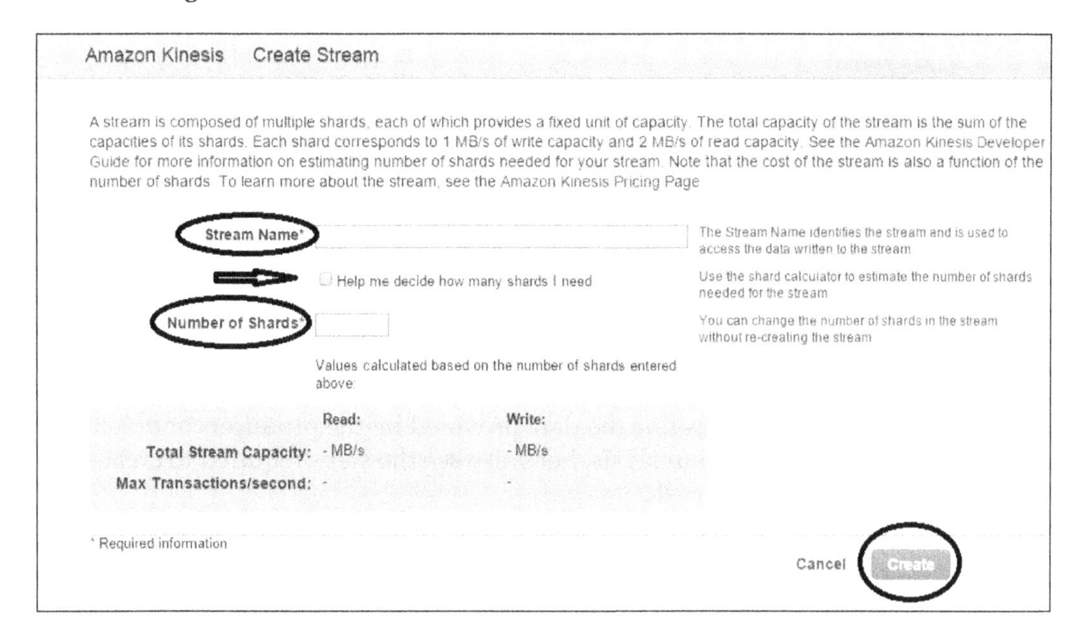

The preceding screenshot shows the Kinesis stream configuration page where we need to specify two configurations:

- **Stream Name**: This is the user-defined name of the stream. We will refer to this in our producers and consumers, which we will create in the subsequent sections. Let's set its name as `StreamingService`.
- **Number of Shards**: This is the most important configuration where we specify the number of shards. We need to be extra cautious in defining the number of shards as Amazon will charge based on the number of shards we have configured for a stream. We can also click on the **Help me decide how many shards I need** link and AWS will provide a GUI where we can provide the size of each record and the maximum reads/writes. AWS will calculate and suggest the appropriate number of shards.

3. Once all configurations are provided, the final step is to click on the **Create** button provided at the bottom of the screen, as shown in the previous screenshot.

We are done!!! Now sit back and relax, and your stream will be created in a few seconds, which can be further seen on the admin page of the Kinesis stream:

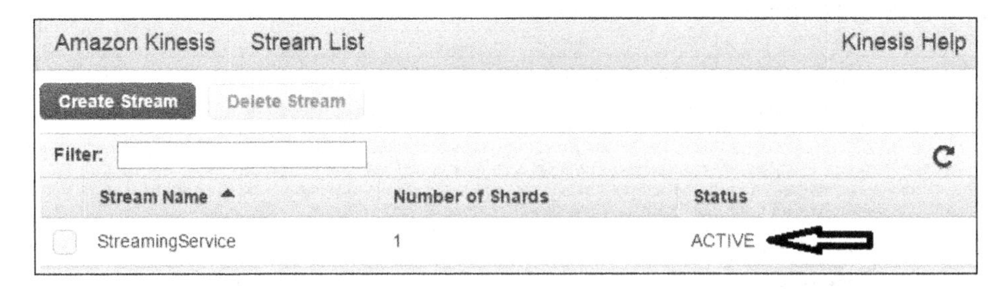

The preceding screenshot shows the admin page of Kinesis streams where it lists all the active or inactive Kinesis streams. We can also click on the name of a stream and see the detailed analysis/throughput (read/write/latency) for each stream.

Our streams are ready to consume the data provided by the producers and deliver it to the consumer for further analysis. Let's also see the steps required to create and manage streams using AWS SDK.

Perform the following steps to create Kinesis streams using AWS SDK:

1. Open your Eclipse project `RealTimeAnalytics-Kinesis` and create a Java class named `ManageKinesisStreams.java` within the `chapter.five.kinesis.admin` package.
2. Edit `ManageKinesisStreams.java` and add the following piece of code into the Java class:

```
package chapter.five.kinesis.admin;

import com.amazonaws.auth.AWSCredentials;
import com.amazonaws.auth.profile.ProfileCredentialsProvider;
import com.amazonaws.services.kinesis.AmazonKinesisClient;
import com.amazonaws.services.kinesis.model.*;

public class ManageKinesisStreams {

  private AmazonKinesisClient kClient;

  /**
   * Constructor which initialize the Kinesis Client for working
with the
   * Kinesis streams.
   */
```

```
  public ManageKinesisStreams() {

    //Initialize the AWSCredentials taken from the profile
configured in the Eclipse
    //replace "kinesisCred" with the profile configured in your
Eclipse or leave blank to sue default.
    //Ensure that Access and Secret key are present in credentials
file
    //Default location of credentials file is $USER_HOME/.aws/
credentials
    AWSCredentials cred = new ProfileCredentialsProvider("kinesisC
red")
        .getCredentials();
    System.out.println("Access Key = "+ cred.getAWSAccessKeyId());
    System.out.println("Secret Key = " + cred.getAWSSecretKey());
    kClient = new AmazonKinesisClient(cred);

  }

  /**
   * Create a Kinesis Stream with the given name and the shards.
   * @param streamName - Name of the Stream
   * @param shards - Number of Shards for the given Stream
   */
  public void createKinesisStream(String streamName, int shards) {

    System.out.println("Creating new Stream = '"+streamName+"',
with Shards = "+shards);
    //Check and create stream only if does not exist.
    if (!checkStreamExists(streamName)) {
      //CreateStreamRequest for creating Kinesis Stream
      CreateStreamRequest createStreamRequest = new
CreateStreamRequest();
      createStreamRequest.setStreamName(streamName);
      createStreamRequest.setShardCount(shards);
      kClient.createStream(createStreamRequest);

      try {
        //Sleep for 30 seconds so that stream is initialized and
created
        Thread.sleep(30000);

      } catch (InterruptedException e) {
        //No need to Print Anything
      }
```

```
        }
      }

      /**
       * Checks and delete a given Kinesis Stream
       *     @param streamName
       *             - Name of the Stream
       */
      public void deleteKinesisStream(String streamName) {

        //Check and delete stream only if exists.
        if (checkStreamExists(streamName)) {
          kClient.deleteStream(streamName);
          System.out.println("Deleted the Kinesis Stream = '" +
    streamName+"'");
          return;
        }

        System.out.println("Stream does not exists = " + streamName);

      }

      /**
       * Utility Method which checks whether a given Kinesis Stream
    Exists or Not
       * @param streamName - Name of the Stream
       * @return - True in case Stream already exists else False
       */
      public boolean checkStreamExists(String streamName) {

        try {
          //DescribeStreamRequest for Describing and checking the
          //existence of given Kinesis Streams.
          DescribeStreamRequest desc = new DescribeStreamRequest();
          desc.setStreamName(streamName);
          DescribeStreamResult result = kClient.describeStream(desc);

          System.out.println("Kinesis Stream '" +streamName+ "'
    already exists...");
          System.out.println("Status of '"+ streamName + "' = "
              + result.getStreamDescription().getStreamStatus());

        } catch (ResourceNotFoundException exception) {
```

```
            System.out.println("Stream '"+streamName+"' does Not
      exists...Need to create One");
            return false;
         }

         return true;   }}
```

The preceding piece of code provides the utility methods for creating and deleting streams. Follow the comments provided in the code itself to understand the functionality and usage of the various methods given. We can also add a `main()` method directly into the preceding code and invoke any of the given methods for creating/deleting Kinesis streams.

> Modification of shards (also known as resharding or merging of shards) is an advanced topic. Please refer to `https://docs.aws.amazon.com/kinesis/latest/dev/kinesis-using-sdk-java-resharding.html` for more information on resharding of streams.

Next, we will create producers that will produce and submit messages to Kinesis streams and we will also create consumers that will consume the messages from Kinesis streams.

Creating Kinesis stream producers

In this section, we will create custom producers using the Kinesis AWS API for producing and submitting messages to the Kinesis streams.

Sample dataset

There are number of free datasets available over the web and we can use any of them for our producers. We will use one such dataset provided by the Research & Development Division of the Chicago Police Department about reported incidents of crime (with the exception of murders where data exists for each victim) that occurred in the City of Chicago from 2001 to the present, minus the most recent in the last seven days. For our use case, we will consider the data for 1 month—August 1, 2015 to August 31, 2015—which can be filtered, extracted, and downloaded from `https://data.cityofchicago.org/Public-Safety/Crimes-2015/vwwp-7yr9`. Alternatively, you can also download the filtered dataset from `http://tinyurl.com/qgxjbej`. Store the Chicago crimes dataset for August 2015 in a local directory and let's refer to the file as `<$CRIME_DATA>`.

Please refer to `http://tinyurl.com/onul54u` to understand the metadata of the crimes dataset.

Use case

Our use case will be to create Kinesis producers which will consume the crimes dataset and submit it to Kinesis streams. In the next section, we will create consumers who will consume the data from Kinesis streams and will generate alerts based on some preconfigured criteria.

In real production scenarios, Kinesis producers can directly connect and consume data from live streams or feeds that publish the crime reports and further submit to Kinesis streams.

Let's perform the following steps for creating producers using APIs provided by the AWS SDK:

1. Open your Eclipse project `RealTimeAnalytics-Kinesis` and add a Java class named `AWSChicagoCrimesProducers.java` within the `chapter.five.kinesis.producers` package.
2. Edit `AWSChicagoCrimesProducers.java` and add following piece of code:

```
package chapter.five.kinesis.producers;

import java.io.*;
import java.nio.ByteBuffer;
import java.util.ArrayList;

import com.amazonaws.auth.AWSCredentials;
import com.amazonaws.auth.profile.ProfileCredentialsProvider;
import com.amazonaws.services.kinesis.AmazonKinesisClient;
import com.amazonaws.services.kinesis.model.*;

public class AWSChicagoCrimesProducers{

private AmazonKinesisClient kClient;

//Location of the file from where we need to read the data
private String filePath="ChicagoCrimes-Aug-2015.csv";

/**
```

```
 * Constructor which initialize the Kinesis Client for working
with the
 * Kinesis streams.
   */
public AWSChicagoCrimesProducers() {
// Initialize the AWSCredentials taken from the profile configured
in
// the Eclipse replace "kinesisCred" with the profile //configured
in your Eclipse or leave blank to use default.
// Ensure that Access and Secret key are present in credentials
file
// Default location of credentials file is $USER_HOME/.aws/
credentials
AWSCredentials cred = new ProfileCredentialsProvider("kinesisCr
ed")
        .getCredentials();
  kClient = new AmazonKinesisClient(cred);
  }

  /**
   * Read Each record of the input file and Submit each record to
Amazon Kinesis Streams.
   * @param streamName - Name of the Stream.
   */
  public void readSingleRecordAndSubmit(String streamName) {

    String data = "";
try (BufferedReader br = new BufferedReader(
      new FileReader(new File(filePath)))) {
      //Skipping first line as it has headers;
      br.readLine();
      //Read Complete file - Line by Line
      while ((data = br.readLine()) != null) {
        //Create Record Request
        PutRecordRequest putRecordRequest = new
PutRecordRequest();
        putRecordRequest.setStreamName(streamName);
        putRecordRequest.setData(ByteBuffer.wrap((data.
getBytes())));
        //Data would be partitioned by the IUCR Codes, which is 5
column in the record
        String IUCRcode = (data.split(","))[4];
        putRecordRequest.setPartitionKey(IUCRcode);
//Finally Submit the records with Kinesis Client Object
System.out.println("Submitting Record = "+data);
```

```
kClient.putRecord(putRecordRequest);
//Sleep for half a second before we read and submit next record.
    Thread.sleep(500);
  }
} catch (Exception e) {
  //Print exceptions, in case any
  e.printStackTrace();
    }

  }

  /**
   * Read Data line by line by Submit to Kinesis Streams in the
Batches.
   * @param streamName - Name of Stream
   * @param batchSize - Batch Size
   */
  public void readAndSubmitBatch(String streamName, int batchSize)
{

    String data = "";
    try (BufferedReader br = new BufferedReader(
        new FileReader(new File(filePath)))) {

    //Skipping first line as it has headers;
    br.readLine();
  //Counter to keep track of size of Batch
  int counter = 0;
  //Collection which will contain the batch of records
      ArrayList<PutRecordsRequestEntry> recordRequestEntryList =
new ArrayList<PutRecordsRequestEntry>();
      while ((data = br.readLine()) != null) {
//Read Data and Create Object of PutRecordsRequestEntry
PutRecordsRequestEntry entry = new PutRecordsRequestEntry();
        entry.setData(ByteBuffer.wrap((data.getBytes())));
        //Data would be partitioned by the IUCR Codes, which is 5
column in the record
        String IUCRcode = (data.split(","))[4];
        entry.setPartitionKey(IUCRcode);
        //Add the record the Collection
        recordRequestEntryList.add(entry);
        //Increment the Counter
        counter++;
```

```
            //Submit Records in case Batch size is reached.
            if (counter == batchSize) {
              PutRecordsRequest putRecordsRequest = new
PutRecordsRequest();
              putRecordsRequest.setRecords(recordRequestEntryList);
              putRecordsRequest.setStreamName(streamName);
              //Finally Submit the records with Kinesis Client Object
              System.out.println("Submitting Records =
"+recordRequestEntryList.size());
              kClient.putRecords(putRecordsRequest);
              //Reset the collection and Counter/Batch
              recordRequestEntryList = new ArrayList<PutRecordsRequest
Entry>();
              counter = 0;
              //Sleep for half a second before processing another
batch
              Thread.sleep(500);
            }
          }
        } catch (Exception e) {
          //Print all exceptions
          e.printStackTrace();
        }
      }
    }
```

This piece of code defines one constructor and two methods. In the constructor, we create a connection to the AWS and then we can use either of the two methods, `readSingleRecordAndSubmit(...)` or `readAndSubmitBatch(...)`, for reading and posting data to Kinesis streams. The difference between the two methods is that the former reads and submits data line by line, but the latter reads the data and then creates and submits data in batches to the Kinesis streams. We can follow the comments within the code to understand each line of code for `AWSChicagoCrimesProducers`.

Please refer to `http://docs.aws.amazon.com/kinesis/latest/dev/developing-producers-with-sdk.html` for more information on the AWS API for creating Kinesis producers.

And we are done with our producers. Now, let's move forward and create consumers that will consume the data published by the Kinesis producers and raise some real-time alerts.

Creating Kinesis stream consumers

In this section, we will create custom consumers using the Kinesis AWS API for consuming the messages from Kinesis streams. Our consumers will consume the messages, but at the same time, consumers will also check for specific crime codes that need special attention and will raise alerts.

Let's perform the following steps for creating consumers using APIs provided by the AWS SDK:

1. Open the Eclipse project `RealTimeAnalytics-Kinesis` and add a Java class named `AWSChicagoCrimesConsumers.java` within the `chapter.five.kinesis.consumers` package. This consumer will use the AWS API to consume and analyze the data from the Kinesis streams, and then generate alerts whenever they encounter specific crime codes appearing in the messages.
2. The complete code for `AWSChicagoCrimesConsumers.java` can be downloaded along with the code samples provided with this book, or you can also download it from `https://drive.google.com/folderview?id=0B5oLQERok6YHUlNQdjFxWXF6WWc&usp=sharing`.

AWS APIs provide the pull model for receiving the messages from the streams, so our consumers will poll the Kinesis streams every 1 second and pull the crime data from the Kinesis streams.

Refer to `http://docs.aws.amazon.com/kinesis/latest/dev/developing-consumers-with-sdk.html` for more information on AWS APIs for developing Kinesis consumers.

Generating and consuming crime alerts

In this section, we will discuss the final set of steps required for running Kinesis producers and Kinesis consumers.

Perform the following steps to execute producers and consumers:

1. Open the Eclipse project `RealTimeAnalytics-Kinesis` and add `MainRunConsumers.java` for running consumers and `MainRunProducers.java` for running producers into the `chapter.five.kinesis` package.
2. Next, add the following piece of code into `MainRunConsumers.java`:

```
package chapter.five.kinesis;

import chapter.five.kinesis.admin.ManageKinesisStreams;
```

```
import chapter.five.kinesis.consumers.*;

public class MainRunConsumers {

//This Stream will be used by the producers/consumers using AWS
SDK
public static String streamNameAWS = "AWSStreamingService";

  public static void main(String[] args) {

    //Using AWS Native API's
    AWSChicagoCrimesConsumers consumers = new
AWSChicagoCrimesConsumers();
    consumers.consumeAndAlert(streamNameAWS);

//Enable only when you want to Delete the streams
ManageKinesisStreams streams = new ManageKinesisStreams();
    //streams.deleteKinesisStream(streamNameAWS);
    //streams.deleteKinesisStream(streamName);
}}
```

3. Add the following piece of code into `MainRunProducers.java`:

```
package chapter.five.kinesis;

import chapter.five.kinesis.admin.ManageKinesisStreams;
import chapter.five.kinesis.producers.*;

public class MainRunProducers {

//This Stream will be used by the producers/consumers using AWS
SDK
  public static String streamNameAWS = "AWSStreamingService";

public static void main(String[] args) {
ManageKinesisStreams streams = new ManageKinesisStreams();
streams.createKinesisStream(streamNameAWS, 1);
//Using AWS Native API's
AWSChicagoCrimesProducers producers = new
AWSChicagoCrimesProducers();

//Read and Submit record by record
//producers.readSingleRecordAndSubmit(streamName);
//Submit the records in Batches of 10
producers.readAndSubmitBatch(streamNameAWS, 10);
```

```
//Enable only when you want to Delete the streams
//streams.deleteKinesisStream(streamNameAWS);
}}
```

4. From Eclipse, execute `MainRunProducers.java` and you will see log messages appearing on the console, which will be similar to the following screenshot:

```
Access Key = AKIAIUXS255DIZ56GO4A
Secret Key = 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
Creating new Stream = 'AWSStreamingService', with Shards = 1
Stream 'AWSStreamingService' does Not exists...Need to create One
Access Key = AKIAIUXS255DIZ56GO4A
Secret Key = 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
Submitting Records = 10
Submitting Records = 10
Submitting Records = 10
Submitting Records = 10
Submitting Records = 10
```

5. Next, we will execute `MainRunConsumers.java` from Eclipse. As soon as you run the consumer, you will see the consumer will start receiving the messages and will log the same on the console, which will be similar to the following screenshot:

```
Data = 10217131,HY403974,08/30/2015 09:30:00 PM,030XX S UNION AVE,0620,BURGLARY,UNLAWFUL ENTRY,RESIDENCE-GARAGE,false,false,
Partition Key = 1320
Sequence Number = 49554892388652275725592564809323220430288270925903167490
Data = 10217163,HY404026,08/30/2015 09:30:00 PM,061XX N WINTHROP AVE,1320,CRIMINAL DAMAGE,TO VEHICLE,RESIDENCE-GARAGE,false,
ALERT!!!!!!!!! IMMEDIATE ACTION REQUIRED !!!!!!
Partition Key = 1305
Sequence Number = 49554892388652275725592564809324429356107885555077873666
Data = 10218049,HY404369,08/30/2015 09:30:00 PM,045XX S WOOD ST,1305,CRIMINAL DAMAGE,CRIMINAL DEFACEMENT,RESIDENCE,false,fal
Partition Key = 3760
Sequence Number = 49554892388652275725592564809325638281927500184252579842
Data = 10217066,HY403883,08/30/2015 09:29:00 PM,057XX W MADISON ST,3760,INTERFERENCE WITH PUBLIC OFFICER,OBSTRUCTING SERVICE
```

We can also enhance our consumers to store all these messages in an RDBMS or NoSQL, which can be further used for performing deep analytics. There are endless possibilities once you have scalable architecture for capturing real-time data feeds.

Remember to clean up, that is, delete, the Kinesis streams and Dynamo tables as soon as you are finished with the processing of the feeds, or you can also invoke the `ManageKinesisStreams.deleteKinesisStream(...)` method to delete the streams and Dynamo tables.

Kinesis producers and consumers can also be developed using KPL (`http://docs.aws.amazon.com/kinesis/latest/dev/developing-producers-with-kpl.html`) and KCL (`http://docs.aws.amazon.com/kinesis/latest/dev/developing-consumers-with-kcl.html`). These libraries are high-level APIs that internally leverage AWS APIs and provide proven design patterns that not only help in expediting the overall development but also help in the development of a robust and stable architecture.

We have skipped the development of producers and consumers, but the sample code provided with this book contains producers and consumers using KPL and KCL. Refer to `chapter.five.kinesis.prducers.KPLChicagoCrimesProducers.java` and `chapter.five.kinesis.consumers.KCLChicagoCrimesConsumers.java` for producers and consumers within the provided samples.

> KPL requires the dependencies for SLF4J (`http://www.slf4j.org/`) and Commons IO (`https://commons.apache.org/proper/commons-io/`). For KCL, we need Amazon Kinesis Client 1.6.0 (`https://github.com/awslabs/amazon-kinesis-client`). Apart from the individual websites, these libraries can be downloaded from `https://drive.google.com/open?id=0B5oLQERok6YHTWs5dEJUaHVDNU0`.

In this section, we have created a Kinesis streaming service that accepts the Chicago crime records as they are available in the given file, and at the same time the consumers also consume the records and generate alerts for specific crime codes as they appear in the data received from the Kinesis streams.

Summary

In this chapter, we have discussed the architecture of Kinesis for processing real-time data feeds. We have explored/developed producers and consumers of Kinesis streams using the AWS APIs. At the end, we also talked about the higher level APIs, such as KPL and KCL, as recommended mechanisms for creating Kinesis producers and consumers, along with their samples.

In the next chapter, we will talk about Apache Spark, which has revolutionized the industry by introducing a new paradigm for batch and real-time data processing.

6
Getting Acquainted with Spark

It is all about data! Isn't it?

One of the most critical objectives of most enterprises is to churn/analyze and mashup the variety of data received from different channels, such as CRM, portals, and so on, and uncover the truth that can help them formulate business/marketing strategies, informed decisions, predictions, recommendations, and so on. Now what matters is how efficiently, effectively, and quickly you can uncover the hidden patterns in the data.

The sooner you can, the better it will be!

Distributed computing (`https://en.wikipedia.org/wiki/Distributed_computing`) or the paradigm of parallel computing/processing played a pivotal role in achieving the key objectives of enterprises. Distributed computing helped enterprises to process large datasets on multiple nodes that were connected to each other, which may be geographically distributed. All these nodes interact with each other and work toward achieving the common goal.

One of the most popular examples of distributed computing is Apache Hadoop (`https://hadoop.apache.org/`), which introduced the framework to execute map/reduce programs in a distributed mode.

Initially, distributed systems were referred to as batch processes where SLAs were not strict and jobs could take hours. Soon this misconception was corrected when enterprises introduced the need for real-time or near real-time data processing where SLAs were strict (milliseconds or seconds).

It was an entirely different world, but it was one of the branches of distributed computing. Soon systems such as Apache Storm (`https://storm.apache.org/`) were introduced, which also helped meet the need of enterprises for real-time or near real-time data processing but to an extent.

It was not too late when enterprises realized that they cannot use two different sets of technologies for processing the same datasets.

They needed a one-stop solution for all of their data processing needs and the answer was: Apache Spark!

Let's move forward and understand more about Apache Spark and its various features.

This chapter will cover the following topics, which will help us understand the overall architecture, components, and use cases of Spark:

- An overview of Spark
- The architecture of Spark
- Resilient Distributed Datasets (RDDs)
- Writing and executing our first Spark program

An overview of Spark

In this section, we will talk about Spark and its emergence as one of the leading frameworks for various kinds of Big Data use cases. We will also talk about the various features of Spark and its applicability in different scenarios.

Another distributed framework for crunching large data? Another version of Hadoop?

This is the first statement that comes to mind when we hear about *Spark* for the first time, but this is not true and neither is there any essence. We will soon talk more about this statement, but before that, let's first understand batch processing and real-time data processing.

Batch data processing

Batch data processing is a process of defining a series of jobs that are executed one after another or in parallel in order to achieve a common goal. Mostly, these jobs are automated and there is no manual intervention. These jobs collect the input data and process the data in *batches* where the size of each batch can vary. It can range from a few GBs to TBs/PBs. These jobs are executed on the set of nodes that are interconnected with each other, resulting in a cluster or farm of nodes.

Another characteristic of batch processes is that they have **relaxed SLAs**. This does not mean that there are no SLAs; of course, there are SLAs, but the batch processes are executed in the off business hours where we do not have any workload from our online users/systems. In other words, the batch processes are provided a *batch window*, which is a period of less-intensive online activity, for example, 9:00 PM to 5:00 AM (off business hours), and all batch processes need to be triggered and completed within this time window itself.

Let's discuss a few use cases for batch data processing:

- **Log analysis/analytics**: This is one of the most popular use cases where application logs are collected over a period of time (day/week/month/year) and stored in Hadoop/HDFS. These log files are further analyzed to derive certain **KPIs** (**Key Performance Indicators**), which can help improve the overall behavior of the application (`https://en.wikipedia.org/wiki/Log_analysis`).
- **Predictive maintenance**: This is another popular use case in the manufacturing industry where we need to analyze the logs/events produced by the equipments to determine their present state and predict when maintenance should be performed. This maintenance requires a considerable amount of investment, and if we know well in advance about the maintenance time frame, then sufficient funds can be reserved/allocated.
- **Faster claim processing**: This is one of the most frequently talked about use cases in the healthcare/insurance sector. Claim processing requires a lot of data to be processed before any claim is approved. Data needs to be collected from multiple sources (maybe in different formats/structures), then verified for the validity of the claim, and finally, processed. Manual processing of claims may involve significant delays (days/months) and sometimes may involve human errors as well.
- **Pricing analytics**: Pricing analytics is again a popular use case in the e-commerce industry where business analysts need to derive the pricing of new products based on the past trends. This process is known as deriving the *price elasticity* of the existing products prevailing in the market over a period of time, which may be based on various factors, such as social/economic conditions, government policies, and many more.

And the list goes on.

All the preceding use cases are very critical and important to the business. They can really change the way in which an organization works and help them in effective planning, understanding past trends, and planning for future. In a nutshell, all the preceding use cases can help the business to take effective and informed decisions with the known or low risk of failures.

These are not new use cases and CEOs/CTOs/entrepreneurs know these problems for years. If this is true, then you may be wondering why it was not implemented yet?

It is not simple and there are challenges, which are as follows:

- **Large data**: Data is really huge (terabytes/petabytes). It requires a considerable amount of hardware resources to churn this data, and it comes with a cost.
- **Distributed processing**: Everything cannot fit into one single machine. We need distributed or parallel processing of the data where we can utilize multiple nodes/machines to process the different parts of the data but work towards the common goal. We certainly need a framework that can provide horizontal and vertical scalability (`https://en.wikipedia.org/wiki/Scalability`).
- **SLAs**: Yes, there are relaxed SLAs, but there are SLAs. All batch processes need to produce the results within the SLAs itself, which if not done, sometimes can incur losses or may leave a negative customer experience.
- **Fault tolerant**: Batch processes churn a huge amount of data and it also takes time. Failures are bound to happen and should not be considered as exceptional scenarios. The processes/hardware/frameworks should be fault tolerant in such a manner that if in case something fails, they should be able to continue with the other available resources from where it failed and not from the beginning (`https://en.wikipedia.org/wiki/Fault_tolerance`).

The preceding use cases and challenges should be sufficient enough to understand the importance, nature, and complexity involved in architecting/designing batch jobs.

It is definitely not simple and easy. It requires an efficient, effective, scalable, performance efficient, fault-tolerant, and distributed architecture. We will soon discuss how Spark will help us solve all these challenges and also why we need to use only Spark and not anything else, but first, let's quickly understand real-time data processing.

Real-time data processing

Real-time data processing systems are those systems that require continuous consumption of data and produce logically correct results instantly (seconds or milliseconds).

Real-time (**RT**) systems are also referred to as the **near real-time** (**NRT**) systems because of the *latency* introduced from the time when data was consumed and results are processed. RT or NRT systems enable the organizations to act and respond quickly in those scenarios where decisions are required to be made instantly, and if not done, it can have an adverse impact on consumer experience, or in certain cases, it could be fatal or catastrophic. These systems have strict SLAs, and under no circumstances, can they afford to break the SLAs. Here are a few examples of RT or NRT use cases:

- **The Internet of Things (IoT)**: IoT, in short, collects the data emitted from the various sensors embedded within various network or hardware devices and then enables the interaction between these devices. For example, the anti-theft devices installed in your car will generate alerts and send these alerts to the owner of the car and also to the nearest police station for an immediate action (`https://en.wikipedia.org/wiki/Internet_of_Things`).
- **Online trading systems**: This is one of the most critical use cases of the finance industry where consumers can purchase goods or services instantly, within seconds. This may include products, such as stocks, bonds, currencies, commodities, derivatives, and many more (`https://en.wikipedia.org/wiki/Electronic_trading_platform`).
- **Online publishing**: This is an example of providing or publishing NRT updates to the users where critical and trending news about various topics, such as politics, breaking news, sports, tech, entertainment, and so on are provided instantly to the users/subscribers (`https://en.wikipedia.org/wiki/Electronic_publishing`).
- **Assembly lines**: These consume, analyze, and process the machine generated data in real time. Appropriate actions taken can save the overall cost of the production which could otherwise have produced low quality or faulty products.
- **Online gaming systems**: Adapting to the behavior of the user and then acting or taking decisions in real time is one of the most popular strategies for online gaming systems.

And it does not stops here, the list goes on.

All the preceding use cases require instant responses to be sent to the users and this introduces some salient features or challenges for an RT or NRT system:

- **Strict SLAs**: RT or NRT systems need to consume and process the data in seconds or milliseconds. The analysis can be pretty simple; for example, finding some predefined patterns in the messages, or it can be a complex one, for example, producing real-time recommendations for the users.

- **Recovering from failures**: NRT systems should be robust enough so that they can recover from failures without having an impact on the response time or SLAs defined by the external systems; and of course, there should be no impact on the integrity of the data.
- **Scalable**: NRT systems need to have a scale-out architecture so that they can meet the ever growing demand of data just by increasing the computational resources without rearchitecting the complete solution.
- **All in-memory**: Any system that reads the data from a persistent storage such as a hard disk would definitely produce additional latency, and in case of NRT systems, we just cannot afford this. So, to minimize the latency and enable quick responses to the users, everything is consumed and processed from the system memory itself. We need to ensure that at any point of time, NRT systems have sufficient memory to consume and process the data.
- **Asynchronous**: Another critical architectural feature of any NRT system is to consume and process the data in an asynchronous manner so that any issues arising in one process do not impact the SLAs defined for the other process.

The preceding use cases and challenges should be sufficient enough to understand that, like batch processing, designing/architecting, RT or NRT systems are not so simple. A high level of expertise and good amount of resources are required to design an efficient, effective, and scalable RT/NRT system.

Now that we have learned about the complexities of batch and real-time data processing, let's move forward and see where does Spark fit the best and also discuss why only Spark and nothing else.

Apache Spark – a one-stop solution

In this section, we will discuss the emergence of Spark as a framework for all our data processing requirements, which either can be batch or NRT.

The frameworks such as Apache Hadoop (`https://hadoop.apache.org/`) or Storm (`https://storm.apache.org/`) were available for designing robust batch or real-time systems, but the real challenge was that the programming paradigm for both these systems were different, and architects/developers need to have two different architectures: one for batch that is deployed on frameworks, such as Hadoop, and the other for RT or NRT systems using frameworks, such as Apache Storm.

It was still acceptable for the systems, which were developed either for batch or for real-time data processing, but considering the requirements of modern enterprises, the data is received from multiple and varied data sources, which is analyzed in real time and batch using the common set of algorithms. The only difference is the volume of data, which can be processed by the system, considering the latency, throughput, and fault-tolerance requirements imposed by the use cases. The objective is to use batch processing to provide comprehensive and accurate views of batch data, while simultaneously using real-time stream processing to provide views of online data. It can be further enhanced where the two view outputs can be joined before a presentation.

This is where architects/developers felt the need for a new architecture paradigm to fulfill the needs of batch and real-time data processing by a single framework.

As we always say, necessity is the mother of invention, and that's what happened.

Apache Spark was developed as a next generation framework and a one-stop solution for all use cases irrespective of the fact of whether they needed to be processed in batches or real time.

Apache Spark started out as a project of AMPLab in 2009 at the University of California at Berkeley before joining the Apache Incubator and ultimately graduated as a top-level project in February 2014. Spark is more of a general-purpose distributed computing platform, which supports both batch as well as near real-time data processing.

Let's discuss a few features of Spark as compared to Apache Hadoop (MapReduce) and Apache Storm:

Feature	Apache Spark	Apache Hadoop	Apache Storm
Data storage	In-memory and backed-up by the configurable distributed filesystem. It can be HDFS or multiple folders on local disks or Tachyon (`http://tachyon-project.org/`).	HDFS—Hadoop Distributed File System.	In-memory.
Use cases	Batch (micro batching), real-time data processing, and iterative and interactive analytics.	Batch processing.	Real time (processes each message as it arrives.)

Feature	Apache Spark	Apache Hadoop	Apache Storm
Fault-tolerance	Captures the computations applied to the raw data to achieve the current state, and in the event of any failures, it applies the same set of computations to the raw data. It is also known as **Data lineage**.	Maintains multiple copies of the same datasets on different nodes.	Storm supports *transactional topologies*, which enables fully fault-tolerant *exactly-once* messaging semantics. For more details, refer to `http://tinyurl.com/o4ex43o`.
Programming languages	Java, Scala, Python, and R.	Java.	Defines the Thrift interface, which can be implemented in any language to define and submit topologies (`http://tinyurl.com/oocmyac`).
Hardware	Commodity hardware.	Commodity hardware.	Commodity hardware.
Management	Easy management as all real-time or batch processing use cases can be deployed in a single framework.	This is suitable only for batch processing use cases.	This is suitable only for near real-time uses cases.
Deployment	Spark is a general-purpose cluster computing framework, which can be deployed in standalone mode and also on a variety of other frameworks, such as YARN or Mesos.	Apache Hadoop has its own deployment model. It cannot be deployed on any other distributed cluster computing frameworks.	Storm has its own deployment model. It cannot be deployed on any other distributed cluster computing frameworks.
Efficiency	10 x faster than Hadoop as data is read/write from/to the memory itself.	Slower as data is read/write from/to the HDFS.	Capable of processing messages in seconds and milliseconds as data is read/write from/to the memory itself.

Feature	Apache Spark	Apache Hadoop	Apache Storm
Distributed caching	Ensures lower latency computations by caching the partial results across the memory of distributed workers.	Completely disk oriented.	Storm does not have any distributed caching capabilities but frameworks such as Memcached or Redis can be used.
Ease of use	Supports functional languages, such as Scala and Python, which produce compact code.	Supports only Java, and hence, MapReduce is lengthy and complex.	Supports a variety of languages.
High-level operations	Provides common operations, such as map, reduce, flatmap, group, sort, union, intersection, aggregation, Cartesian, and so on.	Does not provide any predefined operations except map and reduce.	Storm core framework does not provide any operations but Trident (*Extension* to *Storm*) can be used to perform operations such as joins, aggregation, grouping, and so on (`http://tinyurl.com/o2z5w5j`).
API and extensions	Provides well-defined abstraction over the core APIs, which can be extended to develop extensions/libraries over Core Spark such as Streaming, GraphX, and so on.	Provides a strict API that doesn't allow much versatility.	Storm is a framework used for near real-time processing, which can be extended to develop extensions. For example, Trident (`http://tinyurl.com/o2z5w5j`) is one such framework developed on Storm.
Security	Provides basic security for authentication via a shared secret key (`http://tinyurl.com/q9aro45`).	Apache Hadoop has its own robust and mature security framework, which uses Kerberos and LDAP for authentication and authorization.	Storm 0.10+ provides a pluggable authentication and authorization framework (`http://tinyurl.com/nwlxsxy`).

We will talk about the previously mentioned features of Spark in the upcoming sections, but the preceding comparison should be enough to understand that Spark is a framework, which provides all the features of Hadoop and Storm. It can process the messages in near real-time, and at the same time, it can also provide the batch processing capabilities. The best part is that it provides the common programming paradigm, which can be either applied to batch or near real-time data processing, depending on the needs of the enterprises.

I am sure that now we are convinced that Apache Spark is really a next generation framework and a one-stop solution for all our use cases, which may require processing in real time or in batches.

Let's move on to the next section and also discuss a few of the practical use cases of Apache Spark.

When to use Spark – practical use cases

In this section, we will talk about the various use cases where we can leverage Apache Spark as a distributed computing framework.

Apache Spark is developed as a general-purpose cluster computing framework, which works for a variety of use cases. There are a few use cases where it works the best, and for others, it may work but would not be an ideal choice.

Here are a few of the broad categories of the use cases where Apache Spark works best and would be an ideal choice:

- **Batch processing**: Spark is a general-purpose cluster computing framework that is well suited for most of the batch processing use cases. Use cases such as log analytics, pricing analysis, and claim processing are a few of the examples where Apache Spark can be leveraged.
- **Streaming**: Processing streaming data requires a different perspective where SLAs are strict, and unlike batch processing, results are expected to be delivered in seconds/milliseconds. Processing streaming data is similar to real-time or near real-time data processing. Spark Streaming (`http://spark.apache.org/docs/latest/streaming-programming-guide.html`) is an extension that is developed over the core Spark framework and can be leveraged to implement streaming use cases. Real-time or near real-time use cases, such as IoT, online publishing, and many more, are a few examples where we can leverage Spark and Spark Streaming.

- **Data mining**: This (`https://en.wikipedia.org/wiki/Data_mining`) is a specialized branch or subfield in computer science, which involves identification of hidden patterns in the provided data. It involves the implementation of various iterative and machine learning algorithms for clustering, classifications, recommendations, and many more. Spark provides another extension.
- **MLlib**: This (`http://spark.apache.org/docs/latest/mllib-guide.html`) is developed over the core Spark framework and provides the distributed implementation of varied machine learning algorithms. The Spark machine learning library can be leveraged to develop applications that provide predictive intelligence, customer segmentation for marketing purposes, recommendation engine, and sentiment analysis.
- **Graph computing**: This is another specialized field in computer science where the focus is on the relationship between different entities. The structure is in the form of vertices and edges where vertices are entities themselves and edges are the relationships between these entities. Graph computing is useful in modeling various real-world use cases where data is continuously evolving, such as social networks, network management, public transport links and road maps, and many more. Spark provides another extension.
- **GraphX**: This is used (`http://spark.apache.org/docs/latest/graphx-programming-guide.html`) for modeling and structuring the data in the form of vertices and edges and provides the graph-parallel computation. It also provides the implementation of various graph algorithms.
- **Interactive analysis**: This is a process of collecting historical data across the industry and making it available at the fingertips of engineers for interactive analysis. Ad hoc queries have become increasingly important; not just because the storage is cheaper but because there is a real need for a faster response time for quick, fast, and qualitative decisions. Performing interactive data analysis at scale, demands a high degree of parallelism. Spark provides another extension Spark SQL (`http://spark.apache.org/docs/latest/sql-programming-guide.html`), which facilitates the structuring of the data in rows and columns and further provides the distributed query engine for ad hoc and interactive data analysis.

Spark is still evolving and efforts have been made to develop more and more extensions/libraries over the Core Spark framework so that a variety of business use cases can be solved using Spark and its extensions. In the subsequent sections and chapters, we will talk more about the Spark programming model and its extension.

Let's move on to the next section and dive deep into the architecture of Spark and its various other components, and then in the subsequent chapters, we will also talk about its various extensions.

The architecture of Spark

In this section, we will discuss the architecture of Spark and its various components in detail. We will also briefly talk about the various extensions/libraries of Spark, which are developed over the core Spark framework.

Spark is a general-purpose computing engine that initially focused to provide solutions to the iterative and interactive computations and workloads. For example, machine learning algorithms, which reuse intermediate or working datasets across multiple parallel operations.

The real challenge with iterative computations is the dependency of the intermediate data/steps on the overall job. This intermediate data needs to be cached in the memory itself for faster computations because flushing and reading from a disk is an overhead, which, in turn, makes the overall process unacceptably slow.

The creators of Apache Spark not only provided scalability, fault tolerance, performance, and distributed data processing, but also provided in-memory processing of distributed data over the cluster of nodes.

To achieve this, a new layer abstraction of distributed datasets that is partitioned over the set of machines (cluster) was introduced, which can be cached in the memory to reduce the latency. This new layer of abstraction is known as **resilient distributed datasets** (**RDD**).

RDD, by definition, is an immutable (read-only) collection of objects partitioned across a set of machines that can be rebuilt if a partition is lost.

It is important to note that Spark is capable of performing in-memory operations, but at the same time, it can also work on the data stored on the disk.

We will read more about RDDs in the next section, but let's move forward and discuss the components and architecture of Spark.

High-level architecture

Spark provides a well-defined and layered architecture where all its layers and components are loosely coupled and integration with external components/libraries/extensions is performed using well-defined contracts.

Here is the high-level architecture of Spark 1.5.1 and its various components/layers:

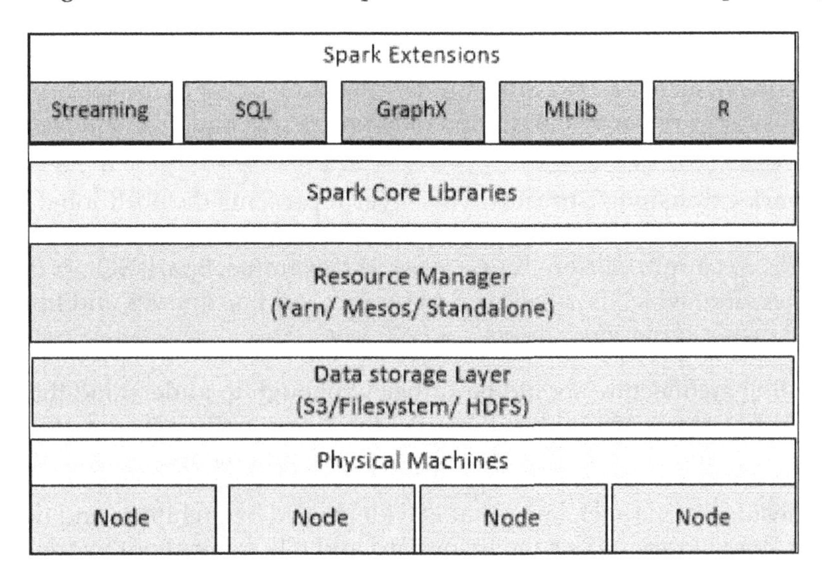

The preceding diagram shows the high-level architecture of Spark. Let's discuss the roles and usage of each of the architecture components:

- **Physical machines**: This layer represents the physical or virtual machines/nodes on which Spark jobs are executed. These nodes collectively represent the total capacity of the cluster with respect to the CPU, memory, and data storage.
- **Data storage layer**: This layer provides the APIs to store and retrieve the data from the persistent storage area to Spark jobs/applications. This layer is used by Spark workers to dump data on the persistent storage whenever the cluster memory is not sufficient to hold the data. Spark is extensible and capable of using any kind of filesystem. RDD, which hold the data, are agnostic to the underlying storage layer and can persist the data in various persistent storage areas, such as local filesystems, HDFS, or any other NoSQL database such as HBase, Cassandra, MongoDB, S3, and Elasticsearch.

- **Resource manager**: The architecture of Spark abstracts out the deployment of the Spark framework and its associated applications. Spark applications can leverage cluster managers such as YARN (`http://tinyurl.com/pcymnnf`) and Mesos (`http://mesos.apache.org/`) for the allocation and deallocation of various physical resources, such as the CPU and memory for the client jobs. The resource manager layer provides the APIs that are used to request for the allocation and deallocation of available resource across the cluster.
- **Spark core libraries**: The Spark core library represents the Spark Core engine, which is responsible for the execution of the Spark jobs. It contains APIs for in-memory distributed data processing and a generalized execution model that supports a wide variety of applications and languages.
- **Spark extensions/libraries**: This layer represents the additional frameworks/APIs/libraries developed by extending the Spark core APIs to support different use cases. For example, Spark SQL is one such extension, which is developed to perform ad hoc queries and interactive analysis over large datasets.

The preceding architecture should be sufficient enough to understand the various layers of abstraction provided by Spark. All the layers are loosely coupled, and if required, can be replaced or extended as per the requirements.

Spark extensions is one such layer that is widely used by architects and developers to develop custom libraries. Let's move forward and talk more about Spark extensions, which are available for developing custom applications/jobs.

Spark extensions/libraries

In this section, we will briefly discuss the usage of various Spark extensions/libraries that are available for different use cases.

The following are the extensions/libraries available with Spark 1.5.1:

- **Spark Streaming**: Spark Streaming, as an extension, is developed over the core Spark API. It enables scalable, high-throughput, and fault-tolerant stream processing of live data streams. Spark Streaming enables the ingestion of data from various sources, such as Kafka, Flume, Kinesis, or TCP sockets. Once the data is ingested, it can be further processed using complex algorithms that are expressed with high-level functions, such as map, reduce, join, and window. Finally, the processed data can be pushed out to filesystems, databases, and live dashboards. In fact, Spark Streaming also facilitates the Spark's machine learning and graph processing algorithms on data streams. For more information, refer to `http://spark.apache.org/docs/latest/streaming-programming-guide.html`.

- **Spark MLlib**: Spark MLlib is another extension that provides the distributed implementation of various machine learning algorithms. Its goal is to make practical machine learning library scalable and easy to use. It provides implementation of various common machine learning algorithms used for classification, regression, clustering, and many more. For more information, refer to `http://spark.apache.org/docs/latest/mllib-guide.html`.
- **Spark GraphX**: GraphX provides the API to create a directed multigraph with properties attached to each vertex and edges. It also provides the various common operators used for the aggregation and distributed implementation of various graph algorithms, such as PageRank and triangle counting. For more information, refer to `http://spark.apache.org/docs/latest/graphx-programming-guide.html`.
- **Spark SQL**: Spark SQL provides the distributed processing of structured data and facilitates the execution of relational queries, which are expressed in a structured query language. (`http://en.wikipedia.org/wiki/SQL`). It provides the high level of abstraction known as **DataFrames**, which is a distributed collection of data organized into named columns. For more information, refer to `http://spark.apache.org/docs/latest/sql-programming-guide.html`.
- **SparkR**: R (`https://en.wikipedia.org/wiki/R_(programming_language`) is a popular programming language used for statistical computing and performing machine learning tasks. However, the execution of the R language is single threaded, which makes it difficult to leverage in order to process large data (TBs or PBs). R can only process the data that fits into the memory of a single machine. In order to overcome the limitations of R, Spark introduced a new extension: **SparkR**. SparkR provides an interface to invoke and leverage Spark distributed execution engine from R, which allows us to run large-scale data analysis from the R shell. For more information, refer to `http://spark.apache.org/docs/latest/sparkr.html`.

All the previously listed Spark extension/libraries are part of the standard Spark distribution. Once we install and configure Spark, we can start using APIs that are exposed by the extensions.

Apart from the earlier extensions, Spark also provides various other external packages that are developed and provided by the open source community. These packages are not distributed with the standard Spark distribution, but they can be searched and downloaded from `http://spark-packages.org/`. Spark packages provide libraries/packages for integration with various data sources, management tools, higher level domain-specific libraries, machine learning algorithms, code samples, and other Spark content.

Let's move on to the next section where we will dive deep into the Spark packaging structure and execution model, and we will also talk about various other Spark components.

Spark packaging structure and core APIs

In this section, we will briefly talk about the packaging structure of the Spark code base. We will also discuss core packages and APIs, which will be frequently used by the architects and developers to develop custom applications with Spark.

Spark is written in Scala (`http://www.scala-lang.org/`), but for interoperability, it also provides the equivalent APIs in Java and Python as well.

For brevity, we will only talk about the Scala and Java APIs, and for Python APIs, users can refer to `https://spark.apache.org/docs/1.5.1/api/python/index.html`.

A high-level Spark code base is divided into the following two packages:

- **Spark extensions**: All APIs for a particular extension is packaged in its own package structure. For example, all APIs for Spark Streaming are packaged in the `org.apache.spark.streaming.*` package, and the same packaging structure goes for other extensions: Spark MLlib—`org.apache.spark.mllib.*`, Spark SQL—`org.apcahe.spark.sql.*`, Spark GraphX—`org.apache.spark.graphx.*`.

For more information, refer to `http://tinyurl.com/q2wgar8` for Scala APIs and `http://tinyurl.com/nc4qu51` for Java APIs.

- **Spark Core**: Spark Core is the heart of Spark and provides two basic components: `SparkContext` and `SparkConfig`. Both of these components are used by each and every standard or customized Spark job or Spark library and extension. The terms/concepts `Context` and `Config` are not new and more or less they have now become a standard architectural pattern. By definition, a `Context` is an entry point of the application that provides access to various resources/features exposed by the framework, whereas a `Config` contains the application configurations, which helps define the environment of the application.

Let's move on to the nitty-gritty of the Scala APIs exposed by Spark Core:

- `org.apache.spark`: This is the base package for all Spark APIs that contains a functionality to create/distribute/submit Spark jobs on the cluster.
- `org.apache.spark.SparkContext`: This is the first statement in any Spark job/application. It defines the `SparkContext` and then further defines the custom business logic that is provided in the job/application. The entry point for accessing any of the Spark features that we may want to use or leverage is `SparkContext`, for example, connecting to the Spark cluster, submitting jobs, and so on. Even the references to all Spark extensions are provided by `SparkContext`. There can be only one `SparkContext` per JVM, which needs to be stopped if we want to create a new one. The `SparkContext` is immutable, which means that it cannot be changed or modified once it is started.
- `org.apache.spark.rdd.RDD.scala`: This is another important component of Spark that represents the distributed collection of datasets. It exposes various operations that can be executed in parallel over the cluster. The `SparkContext` exposes various methods to load the data from HDFS or the local filesystem or Scala collections, and finally, create an RDD on which various operations such as map, filter, join, and persist can be invoked. RDD also defines some useful child classes within the `org.apache.spark.rdd.*` package such as `PairRDDFunctions` to work with key/value pairs, `SequenceFileRDDFunctions` to work with Hadoop sequence files, and `DoubleRDDFunctions` to work with RDDs of doubles. We will read more about RDD in the subsequent sections.
- `org.apache.spark.annotation`: This package contains the annotations, which are used within the Spark API. This is the internal Spark package, and it is recommended that you do not to use the annotations defined in this package while developing custom Spark jobs. The three main annotations defined within this package are as follows:
    - `DeveloperAPI`: All those APIs/methods, which are marked with `DeveloperAPI`, are for advance usage where users are free to extend and modify the default functionality. These methods may be changed or removed in the next minor or major releases of Spark.
    - `Experimental`: All functions/APIs marked as `Experimental` are officially not adopted by Spark but are introduced temporarily in a specific release. These methods may be changed or removed in the next minor or major releases.

    - AlphaComponent: The functions/APIs, which are still being tested by the Spark community, are marked as AlphaComponent. These are not recommended for production use and may be changed or removed in the next minor or major releases.

- org.apache.spark.broadcast: This is one of the most important packages, which is frequently used by developers in their custom Spark jobs. It provides the API for sharing the read-only variables across the Spark jobs. Once the variables are defined and broadcast, they cannot be changed. Broadcasting the variables and data across the cluster is a complex task, and we need to ensure that an efficient mechanism is used so that it improves the overall performance of the Spark job and does not become an overhead.
- Spark provides two different types of implementations of broadcasts—HttpBroadcast and TorrentBroadcast. The HttpBroadcast broadcast leverages the HTTP server to fetch/retrieve the data from the Spark driver. In this mechanism, the broadcast data is fetched through an HTTP Server running at the driver itself and further stored in the executor block manager for faster accesses. The TorrentBroadcast broadcast, which is also the default implementation of the broadcast, maintains its own block manager. The first request to access the data makes the call to its own block manager, and if not found, the data is fetched in chunks from the executor or driver. It works on the principle of BitTorrent and ensures that the driver is not the bottleneck in fetching the shared variables and data. Spark also provides accumulators, which work like broadcast, but provide updatable variables shared across the Spark jobs but with some limitations. You can refer to https://spark.apache.org/docs/1.5.1/api/scala/index.html#org.apache.spark.Accumulator.
- org.apache.spark.io: This provides implementation of various compression libraries, which can be used at block storage level. This whole package is marked as Developer API, so developers can extend and provide their own custom implementations. By default, it provides three implementations: LZ4, LZF, and Snappy.
- org.apache.spark.scheduler: This provides various scheduler libraries, which help in job scheduling, tracking, and monitoring. It defines the **directed acyclic graph** (**DAG**) scheduler (http://en.wikipedia.org/wiki/Directed_acyclic_graph). The Spark DAG scheduler defines the stage-oriented scheduling where it keeps track of the completion of each RDD and the output of each stage and then computes DAG, which is further submitted to the underlying org.apache.spark.scheduler.TaskScheduler API that executes them on the cluster.

- `org.apache.spark.storage`: This provides APIs for structuring, managing, and finally, persisting the data stored in RDD within blocks. It also keeps tracks of data and ensures that it is either stored in memory, or if the memory is full, it is flushed to the underlying persistent storage area.
- `org.apache.spark.util`: These are the utility classes used to perform common functions across the Spark APIs. For example, it defines `MutablePair`, which can be used as an alternative to Scala's Tuple2 with the difference that `MutablePair` is updatable while Scala's Tuple2 is not. It helps in optimizing memory and minimizing object allocations.

Let's move on to the next section where we will dive deep into the Spark execution model, and we will also talk about various other Spark components.

The Spark execution model – master-worker view

Spark essentially enables the distributed in-memory execution of a given piece of code. We discussed the Spark architecture and its various layers in the previous section. Let's also discuss its major components, which are used to configure the Spark cluster, and at the same time, they will be used to submit and execute our Spark jobs.

The following are the high-level components involved in setting up the Spark cluster or submitting a Spark job:

- **Spark driver**: This is the client program, which defines `SparkContext`. The entry point for any job that defines the environment/configuration and the dependencies of the submitted job is `SparkContext`. It connects to the cluster manager and requests resources for further execution of the jobs.
- **Cluster manager/resource manager/Spark master**: The cluster manager manages and allocates the required system resources to the Spark jobs. Furthermore, it coordinates and keeps track of the live/dead nodes in a cluster. It enables the execution of jobs submitted by the driver on the worker nodes (also called Spark workers) and finally tracks and shows the status of various jobs running by the worker nodes.
- **Spark worker/executors**: A worker actually executes the business logic submitted by the Spark driver. Spark workers are abstracted and are allocated dynamically by the cluster manager to the Spark driver for the execution of submitted jobs.

The following diagram shows the high-level components and the master-worker view of Spark:

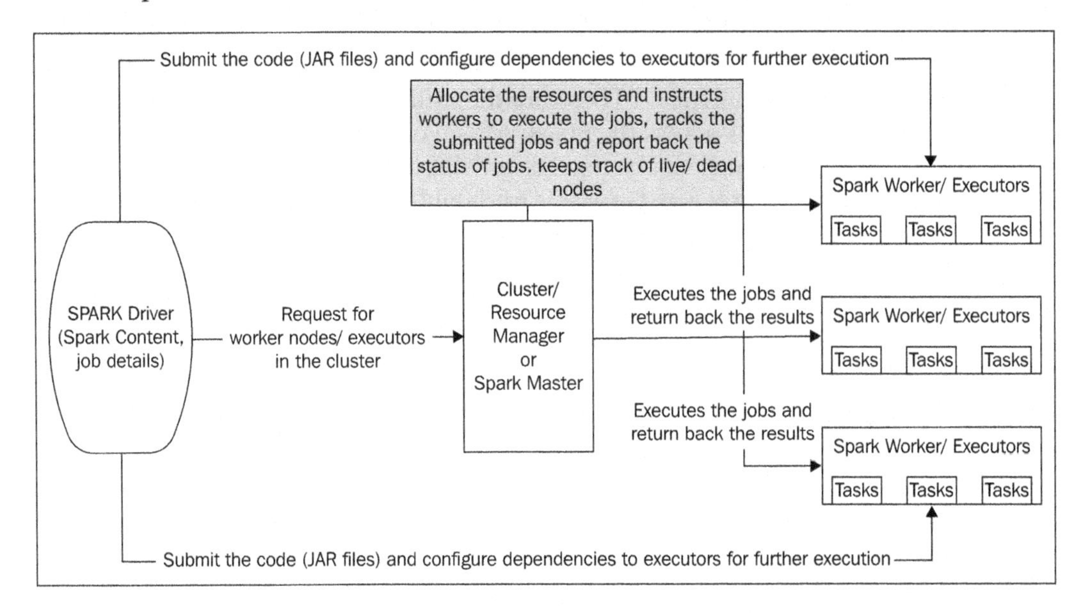

The preceding diagram depicts the various components involved in setting up the Spark cluster, and the same components are also responsible for the execution of the Spark job.

Although all the components are important, let's briefly discuss the cluster/resource manager, as it defines the deployment model and allocation of resources to our submitted jobs.

Spark enables and provides flexibility to choose our resource manager. As of Spark 1.5.1, the following are the resource managers or deployment models that are supported by Spark:

- **Apache Mesos**: Apache Mesos (`http://mesos.apache.org/`) is a cluster manager that provides efficient resource isolation and sharing across distributed applications or frameworks. It can run Hadoop, MPI, Hypertable, Spark, and other frameworks on a dynamically shared pool of nodes. Apache Mesos and Spark are closely related to each other (but they are not the same). The story started way back in 2009 when Mesos was ready and there were talks going on about the ideas/frameworks that can be developed on top of Mesos, and that's exactly how Spark was born.

[Refer to `http://spark.apache.org/docs/latest/running-on-mesos.html` for more information on running Spark jobs on Apache Mesos.]

- **Hadoop YARN**: Hadoop 2.0 (`http://tinyurl.com/lsk4uat`), also known as YARN, was a complete change in the architecture. It was introduced as a generic cluster computing framework that was entrusted with the responsibility of allocating and managing the resources required to execute the varied jobs or applications. It introduced new daemon services, such as the **resource manager** (**RM**), **node manager** (**NM**), and **application master** (**AM**), which are responsible for managing cluster resources, individual nodes, and respective applications. YARN also introduced specific interfaces/guidelines for application developers where they can implement/follow and submit or execute their custom applications on the YARN cluster. The Spark framework implements the interfaces exposed by YARN and provides the flexibility of executing the Spark applications on YARN. Spark applications can be executed in the following two different modes in YARN:
    - **YARN client mode**: In this mode, the Spark driver executes on the client machine (the machine used for submitting the job), and the YARN application master is just used for requesting the resources from YARN. All our logs and sysouts (`println`) are printed on the same console, which is used to submit the job.
    - **YARN cluster mode**: In this mode, the Spark driver runs inside the YARN application master process, which is further managed by YARN on the cluster, and the client can go away just after submitting the application. Now as our Spark driver is executed on the YARN cluster, our application logs/sysouts (`println`) are also written in the log files maintained by YARN and not on the machine that is used to submit our Spark job.

[For more information on executing Spark applications on YARN, refer to `http://spark.apache.org/docs/latest/running-on-yarn.html`.]

- **Standalone mode**: The Core Spark distribution contains the required APIs to create an independent, distributed, and fault tolerant cluster without any external or third-party libraries or dependencies.
- **Local mode**: Local mode should not be confused with standalone mode. In local mode, Spark jobs can be executed on a local machine without any special cluster setup by just passing `local[N]` as the master URL, where `N` is the number of parallel threads.

We will soon implement the same execution model, but before that, let's move on to the next section and understand one of the most important components of Spark: **resilient distributed datasets** (RDD).

Resilient distributed datasets (RDD)

In this section, we will talk about the architecture, motivation, features, and other important concepts related to RDD. We will also briefly talk about the implementation methodology adopted by Spark and various APIs/functions exposed by RDDs.

Frameworks such as Hadoop and MapReduce are widely adopted for parallel and distributed data processing. There is no doubt that these frameworks introduce a new paradigm for distributed data processing and that too in a fault-tolerant manner (without losing a single byte). However, these frameworks do have some limitations; for example, Hadoop is not suited for the problem statements where we need iterative data processing as in recursive functions or machine learning algorithms because this kind of use cases data needs to be in-memory for the computations.

For all these scenarios, a new paradigm, RDD, was introduced that contains all the features of Hadoop-like systems, such as distributed processing, fault-tolerant, and so on, but essentially keeps data in the memory providing distributed in-memory data processing over a cluster of nodes.

RDD – by definition

RDD is a core component of the Spark framework. It is an independent concept, which was developed by the University of California, Berkeley, and was first implemented in systems, such as Spark, to show its real usage and power.

RDD provides an in-memory representation of immutable datasets for parallel and distributed data processing. RDD is an abstract layer and agnostic of the underlying data store, providing the core functionality of in-memory data representation for storing and retrieving data objects. RDDs are further extended to capture various kinds of data structures, such as graphs or relational structures or streaming data.

Let's move on and discuss the important features of RDDs.

Fault tolerance

Fault tolerance is not a new concept and is already been implemented in various distributed processing systems such as Hadoop, key/value stores, and so on. These system leveraged the strategy of data replication to achieve the fault tolerance. They replicate and maintain multiple copies of the same dataset over the various nodes in the cluster, or maintain the log of updates happening over the original datasets, and instantly apply the same over the machines/nodes. This kind of architecture/process is good for disk-based systems but the same mechanism is inefficient for data-intensive workloads or memory-based systems because first they require copying large amounts of data over the cluster network, whose bandwidth is far lower than that of RAM, and second, they incur substantial storage overheads.

The objective of an RDD was to solve the existing challenges and also provide an efficient fault-tolerance mechanism for the datasets, which are already loaded and processed in the memory.

RDD introduced a new concept for fault-tolerance and provided a coarse-grained interface based on transformations. Now instead of replicating data or keeping logs of updates, RDDs keep track of the transformations (such as a map, reduce, join, and so on) applied to the particular dataset, which is also called a *data lineage*.

This allows an efficient mechanism for fault-tolerance where, in the event of loss of any partition, RDD has enough information to derive the same partition by applying the same set of transformations to the original dataset. Moreover, this computation is parallel and involves processing on multiple nodes, so the recomputation is very fast and efficient as well, in contrast to costly replication used by other distributed data processing frameworks.

Storage

The architecture/design of RDD facilitates the data to be distributed and partitioned over clusters of nodes. RDDs are kept in the system's memory, but they also provide operations, which can be used to store RDD on disks or to an external system. Spark and its core packages, by default, provide the API to work with the data residing in local filesystems and HDFS. There are other vendors and open source communities, which provide the appropriate packages and APIs for storage of RDDs in external storage systems such as MongoDB, DataStax, Elasticsearch, and so on.

The following are a few of the functions, which can be used to store RDDs:

- `saveAsTextFile(path)`: This writes the elements of RDD to a text file in a local filesystem or HDFS or any other mapped or mounted network drive.

- `saveAsSequenceFile(path)`: This writes the elements of RDD as a Hadoop sequence file in a local filesystem or HDFS or any other mapped or mounted network drive. This is available on RDDs of key/value pairs that implement Hadoop's writable interface.
- `saveAsObjectFile(path)`: This writes the elements of the dataset to a given path using the Java serialization mechanism, which can then be loaded using `SparkContext.objectFile(path)`.

You can refer to `http://spark.apache.org/docs/latest/api/scala/index.html#org.apache.spark.rdd.RDD` (Scala version) or `http://spark.apache.org/docs/latest/api/scala/index.html#org.apache.spark.api.java.JavaRDD` (Java version) for more information on the APIs exposed by RDD.

Persistence

Persistence in RDD is also called caching of RDD. It can simply be done by invoking `<RDD>.persist(StorageLevel)` or `<RDD>.cache()`. By default, RDD is persisted in memory (default for `cache()`), but it also provides the persistence on disks or any other external systems, which are defined and provided by the `persist(...)` function and its parameter of the `StorageLevel` class (`https://spark.apache.org/docs/latest/api/scala/index.html#org.apache.spark.storage.StorageLevel$`).

The `StorageLevel` class is annotated as `DeveloperApi()`, which can be extended to provide the custom implementation of persistence.

Caching or persistence is a key tool used for iterative algorithms and fast interactive use. Whenever `persist(...)` is invoked on `RDD`, each node stores its associated partitions and computes in memory and further reuses them in other actions on the computed datasets. This, in turn, also enables the future actions to be much faster.

Shuffling

Shuffling is another important concept in Spark. It redistributes data across clusters so that it is grouped differently across the partitions. It is a costly operation as it involves the following activities:

- Copying data across executors and nodes
- Creating new partitions
- Redistributing the newly created partitions across the cluster

There are certain transformation operations defined in `org.apache.spark.rdd.RDD` and `org.apache.spark.rdd.PairRDDFunctions`, which initiate the shuffling process. These operations include the following:

- `RDD.repartition(...)`: This repartitions the existing dataset across the cluster of nodes
- `RDD.coalesce(...)`: This repartitions the existing dataset into a smaller number of given partitions
- All the operations that end with `ByKey` (except count operations) such as `PairRDDFunctions.reducebyKey()` or `groupByKey`
- All the join operations such as `PairRDDFunctions.join(...)` or `PairRDDFunctions.cogroup(...)` operations

The shuffle is an expensive operation since it involves disk I/O, data serialization, and network I/O, but there are certain configurations, which can help in tuning and performance optimizations. Refer to `https://spark.apache.org/docs/latest/configuration.html#shuffle-behavior` for a complete list of parameters, which can be used to optimize the shuffle operations.

Refer to `https://www.cs.berkeley.edu/~matei/papers/2012/nsdi_spark.pdf` for more information on RDDs.

Writing and executing our first Spark program

In this section, we will install/configure and write our first Spark program in Java and Scala.

Hardware requirements

Spark supports a variety of hardware and software platforms. It can be deployed on commodity hardware and also supports deployments on high-end servers. Spark clusters can be provisioned either on cloud or on-premises. Though there is no single configuration or standard, which can guide us through the requirements of Spark, to create and execute Spark examples provided in this book, it would be good to have a laptop/desktop/server with the following configuration:

- **RAM**: 8 GB.
- **CPU**: Dual core or Quad core.

- **DISK**: SATA drives with a capacity of 300 GB to 500 GB with 15 k RPM.
- **Operating system**: Spark supports a variety of platforms that include various flavors of Linux (Ubuntu, HP-UX, RHEL, and many more) and Windows. For our examples, we will recommend that you use Ubuntu for the deployment and execution of examples.

Spark core is coded in Scala, but it offers several development APIs in different languages, such as Scala, Java, and Python, so that developers can choose their preferred weapon for coding. The dependent software may vary based on the programming languages but still there are common sets of software for configuring the Spark cluster and then language-specific software for developing Spark jobs.

In the next section, we will discuss the software installation steps required to write/execute Spark jobs in Scala and Java on Ubuntu as the operating system.

Installation of the basic software

In this section, we will discuss the various steps required to install the basic software, which will help us in the development and execution of our Spark jobs.

Spark

Perform the following steps to install Spark:

1. Download the Spark compressed tarball from `http://d3kbcqa49mib13.cloudfront.net/spark-1.5.1-bin-hadoop2.4.tgz`.
2. Create a new directory `spark-1.5.1` on your local filesystem and extract the Spark tarball into this directory.
3. Execute the following command on your Linux shell in order to set `SPARK_HOME` as an environment variable:

   ```
   export SPARK_HOME=<Path of Spark install Dir>
   ```

4. Now, browse your `SPARK_HOME` directory and it should look similar to the following screenshot:

```
sumit@localhost $ ls -ltr
total 1060
drwxr-xr-x 2 ec2-user ec2-user   4096 Sep 24 06:12 sbin
-rw-r--r-- 1 ec2-user ec2-user    120 Sep 24 06:12 RELEASE
drwxr-xr-x 3 ec2-user ec2-user   4096 Sep 24 06:12 R
drwxr-xr-x 6 ec2-user ec2-user   4096 Sep 24 06:12 python
-rw-r--r-- 1 ec2-user ec2-user  22559 Sep 24 06:12 NOTICE
drwxr-xr-x 3 ec2-user ec2-user   4096 Sep 24 06:12 examples
drwxr-xr-x 3 ec2-user ec2-user   4096 Sep 24 06:12 data
-rw-r--r-- 1 ec2-user ec2-user 960539 Sep 24 06:12 CHANGES.txt
-rw-r--r-- 1 ec2-user ec2-user   3593 Sep 24 06:12 README.md
-rw-r--r-- 1 ec2-user ec2-user  50972 Sep 24 06:12 LICENSE
drwxr-xr-x 2 ec2-user ec2-user   4096 Sep 24 06:12 lib
drwxr-xr-x 3 ec2-user ec2-user   4096 Sep 24 06:12 ec2
drwxr-xr-x 2 ec2-user ec2-user   4096 Sep 24 06:12 conf
drwxr-xr-x 2 ec2-user ec2-user   4096 Sep 24 06:12 bin
sumit@localhost $
```

Java

Perform the following steps to install Java:

1. Download and install Oracle Java 7 from `http://www.oracle.com/technetwork/java/javase/install-linux-self-extracting-138783.html`.
2. Execute the following command on your Linux shell to set `JAVA_HOME` as an environment variable:

```
export JAVA_HOME=<Path of Java install Dir>
```

Scala

Perform the following steps to install Scala:

1. Download the Scala 2.10.5 compressed tarball from `http://downloads.typesafe.com/scala/2.10.5/scala-2.10.5.tgz?_ga=1.7758962.1104547853.1428884173`.
2. Create a new directory, Scala 2.10.5, on your local filesystem and extract the Scala tarball into this directory.
3. Execute the following commands on your Linux shell to set `SCALA_HOME` as an environment variable, and add the Scala compiler to the `$PATH` system:

```
export SCALA_HOME=<Path of Scala install Dir>
export PATH = $PATH:$SCALA_HOME/bin
```

4. Next, execute the command in the following screenshot to ensure that the Scala runtime and Scala compiler is available and the version is 2.10.x:

```
sumit@local : scala -version
Scala code runner version 2.10.5 -- Copyright 2002-2013, LAMP/EPFL
sumit@local : scalac -version
Scala compiler version 2.10.5 -- Copyright 2002-2013, LAMP/EPFL
sumit@local :
```

Spark 1.5.1 supports the 2.10.5 version of Scala, so it is advisable to use the same version to avoid any runtime exceptions due to mismatch of libraries.

Eclipse

Perform the following steps to install Eclipse:

1. Based on your hardware configuration, download Eclipse Luna (4.4) from `http://www.eclipse.org/downloads/packages/eclipse-ide-java-ee-developers/lunasr2`:

2. Next, install the IDE for Scala in Eclipse itself so that we can write and compile our Scala code inside Eclipse (http://scala-ide.org/download/current.html).

We are now done with the installation of all the required software. Let's move on and configure our Spark cluster.

Configuring the Spark cluster

The first step to configure the Spark cluster is to identify the appropriate resource manager. We discussed the various resource managers in *The Spark execution model - master-worker view* section (Yarn, Mesos, and Standalone). Standalone is the most preferred resource manager for development because it is simple/quick and does not require installation of any other component or software.

We will also configure the **Standalone** resource manager for all our Spark examples, and for more information on Yarn and Mesos, refer to *The Spark execution model - master-worker view* section.

Perform the following steps to bring up an independent cluster using Spark binaries:

1. The first step to set up the Spark cluster is to bring up the master node, which will track and allocate the system's resources. Open your Linux shell and execute the following command:

```
$SPARK_HOME/sbin/start-master.sh
```

2. The preceding command will bring up your master node, and it will also enable a UI, the Spark UI to monitor the nodes/jobs in the Spark cluster, http://<host>:8080/. The <host> is the domain name of the machine on which the master is running.
3. Next, let's bring up our worker node, which will execute our Spark jobs. Execute the following command on the same Linux shell:

```
$SPARK_HOME/bin/spark-class org.apache.spark.deploy.worker.Worker
<Spark-Master> &
```

4. In the preceding command, replace the `<Spark-Master>` with the Spark URL, which is shown at the top of the Spark UI, just beside Spark master at. The preceding command will start the Spark worker process in the background and the same will also be reported in the Spark UI.

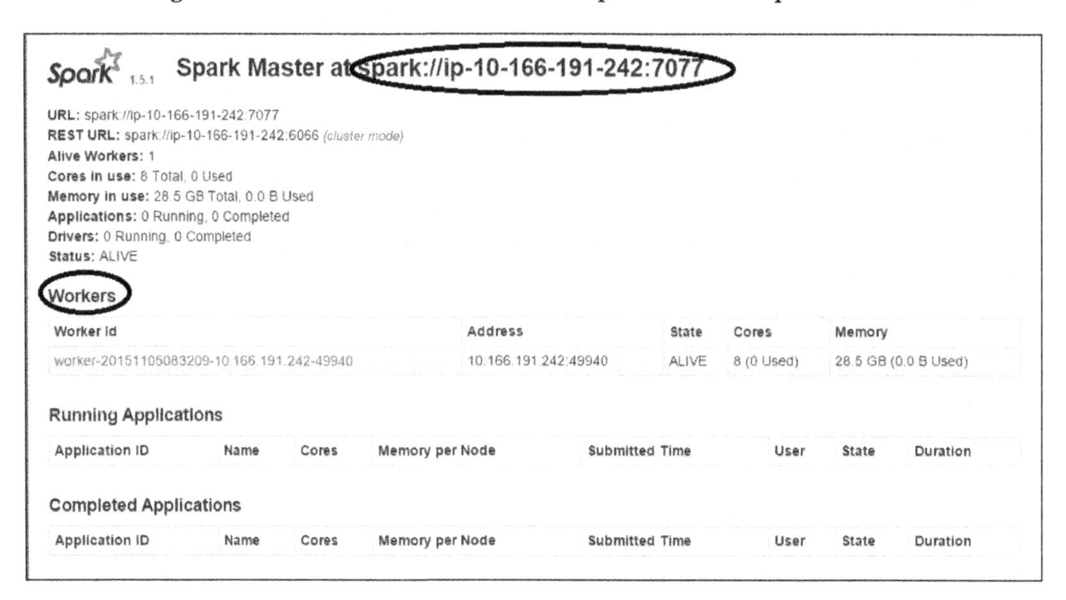

The Spark UI shown in the preceding screenshot shows the three different sections, providing the following information:

- **Workers**: This reports the health of a worker node, which is alive or dead and also provides drill-down to query the status and details logs of the various jobs executed by that specific worker node
- **Running applications**: This shows the applications that are currently being executed in the cluster and also provides drill-down and enables viewing of application logs
- **Completed application**: This is the same functionality as running applications; the only difference being that it shows the jobs, which are finished

We are done!!! Our Spark cluster is up and running and ready to execute our Spark jobs with one worker node. Let's move on and write our first Spark application in Scala and Java and further execute it on our newly created cluster.

Coding a Spark job in Scala

In this section, we will code our first Spark job in Scala, and we will also execute the same job on our newly created Spark cluster and will further analyze the results.

This is our first Spark job, so we will keep it simple. We will use the same Chicago crimes dataset for August 2015, which we described in the *Creating Kinesis stream producers* section in *Chapter 5, Getting Acquainted with Kinesis*, and will count the number of crimes reported in August 2015.

Perform the following steps to code the Spark job in Scala for aggregating the number of crimes in August 2015:

1. Open Eclipse and create a Scala project called `Spark-Examples`.
2. Expand your newly created project and modify the version of the Scala library container to 2.10. This is done to ensure that the version of Scala libraries used by Spark and the custom jobs developed/deployed are the same.

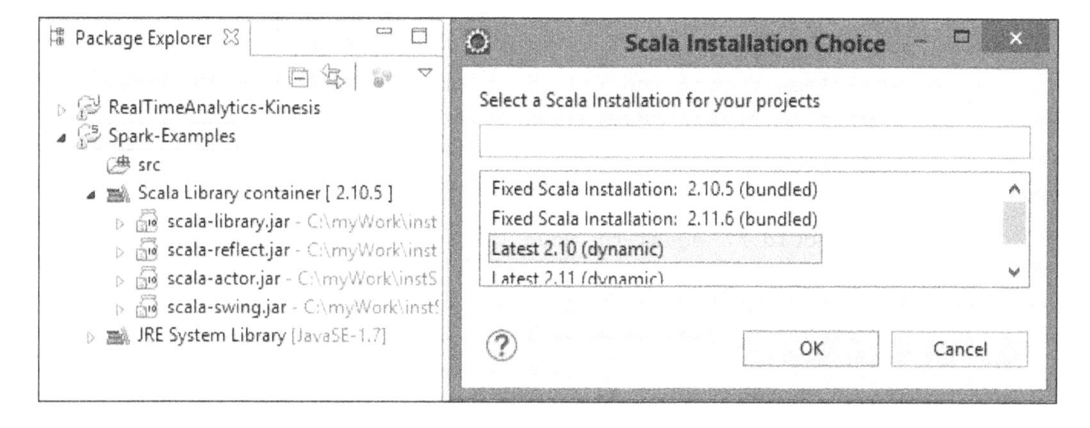

3. Next, open the properties of your project `Spark-Examples` and add the dependencies for the all libraries packaged with the Spark distribution, which can be found at `$SPARK_HOME/lib`.
4. Next, create a `chapter.six` Scala package, and in this package, define a new Scala object by the name of `ScalaFirstSparkJob`.
5. Define a main method in the Scala object and also import `SparkConf` and `SparkContext`.

6. Now, add the following code to the main method of `ScalaFirstSparkJob`:

```
object ScalaFirstSparkJob {

  def main(args: Array[String]) {
    println("Creating Spark Configuration")
   //Create an Object of Spark Configuration
   val conf = new SparkConf()
   //Set the logical and user defined Name of this Application
   conf.setAppName("My First Spark Scala Application")
   println("Creating Spark Context")
   //Create a Spark Context and provide previously created
   //Object of SparkConf as an reference.
   val ctx = new SparkContext(conf)
   //Define the location of the file containing the Crime Data
   val file = "file:///home/ec2-user/softwares/crime-data/
     Crimes_-Aug-2015.csv";
   println("Loading the Dataset and will further process it")
   //Loading the Text file from the local file system or HDFS
   //and converting it into RDD.
   //SparkContext.textFile(..) - It uses the Hadoop's
   //TextInputFormat and file is broken by New line Character.
   //Refer to http://hadoop.apache.org/docs/r2.6.0/api/org/
     apache/hadoop/mapred/TextInputFormat.html
   //The Second Argument is the Partitions which specify the
     parallelism.
   //It should be equal or more then number of Cores in the
     cluster.

   val logData = ctx.textFile(file, 2)

   //Invoking Filter operation on the RDD, and counting the
     number of lines in the Data loaded in RDD.
   //Simply returning true as "TextInputFormat" have already
     divided the data by "\n"
   //So each RDD will have only 1 line.
   val numLines = logData.filter(line => true).count()
   //Finally Printing the Number of lines.
   println("Number of Crimes reported in Aug-2015 = " +
     numLines)
  }

}
```

We are now done with the coding! Our first Spark job in Scala is ready for execution.

Follow the comments provided in the code to understand the functionality. The same style has been used for all other code examples given in this book.

7. Now, from Eclipse itself, export your project as a `.jar` file, name it `spark-examples.jar`, and save this `.jar` file in the root of `$SPARK_HOME`.
8. Next, open your Linux console, go to `$SPARK_HOME`, and execute the following command:

    ```
    $SPARK_HOME/bin/spark-submit --class chapter.six.
    ScalaFirstSparkJob --master spark://ip-10-166-191-242:7077 spark-
    examples.jar
    ```

    In the preceding command, ensure that the value given to `--master` parameter is the same as it is shown on your Spark UI.

The `Spark-submit` is a utility script, which is used to submit the Spark jobs to the cluster.

9. As soon as you click on *Enter* and execute the preceding command, you will see lot of activity (log messages) on the console, and finally, you will see the output of your job at the end:

```
15/11/05 09:57:40 INFO BlockManagerMaster: Registered BlockManager
15/11/05 09:57:40 INFO SparkDeploySchedulerBackend: SchedulerBackend is ready for scheduling beginning after reached minRegisteredResourcesRatio: 0.0
Loading the Dataset and will further process it
15/11/05 09:57:41 INFO MemoryStore: ensureFreeSpace(143968) called with curMem=0, maxMem=555684986
15/11/05 09:57:41 INFO MemoryStore: Block broadcast_0 stored as values in memory (estimated size 140.6 KB, free 529.8 MB)
15/11/05 09:57:41 INFO MemoryStore: ensureFreeSpace(12803) called with curMem=143968, maxMem=555684986
15/11/05 09:57:41 INFO MemoryStore: Block broadcast_0_piece0 stored as bytes in memory (estimated size 12.5 KB, free 529.8 MB)
15/11/05 09:57:41 INFO BlockManagerInfo: Added broadcast_0_piece0 in memory on 10.166.191.242:55264 (size: 12.5 KB, free: 529.9 MB)
15/11/05 09:57:41 INFO SparkContext: Created broadcast 0 from textFile at ScalaFirstSparkJob.scala:31
15/11/05 09:57:41 INFO FileInputFormat: Total input paths to process : 1
15/11/05 09:57:41 INFO SparkContext: Starting job: count at ScalaFirstSparkJob.scala:36
15/11/05 09:57:41 INFO DAGScheduler: Got job 0 (count at ScalaFirstSparkJob.scala:36) with 2 output partitions
15/11/05 09:57:41 INFO DAGScheduler: Final stage: ResultStage 0(count at ScalaFirstSparkJob.scala:36)
15/11/05 09:57:41 INFO DAGScheduler: Parents of final stage: List()
15/11/05 09:57:41 INFO DAGScheduler: Missing parents: List()
15/11/05 09:57:41 INFO DAGScheduler: Submitting ResultStage 0 (MapPartitionsRDD[2] at filter at ScalaFirstSparkJob.scala:36), which has no missing parents
15/11/05 09:57:41 INFO MemoryStore: ensureFreeSpace(3232) called with curMem=156771, maxMem=555684986
15/11/05 09:57:41 INFO MemoryStore: Block broadcast_1 stored as values in memory (estimated size 3.2 KB, free 529.8 MB)
15/11/05 09:57:41 INFO MemoryStore: ensureFreeSpace(1927) called with curMem=160003, maxMem=555684986
15/11/05 09:57:41 INFO MemoryStore: Block broadcast_1_piece0 stored as bytes in memory (estimated size 1927.0 B, free 529.8 MB)
15/11/05 09:57:41 INFO BlockManagerInfo: Added broadcast_1_piece0 in memory on 10.166.191.242:55264 (size: 1927.0 B, free: 529.9 MB)
15/11/05 09:57:41 INFO SparkContext: Created broadcast 1 from broadcast at DAGScheduler.scala:861
15/11/05 09:57:41 INFO DAGScheduler: Submitting 2 missing tasks from ResultStage 0 (MapPartitionsRDD[2] at filter at ScalaFirstSparkJob.scala:36)
15/11/05 09:57:41 INFO TaskSchedulerImpl: Adding task set 0.0 with 2 tasks
15/11/05 09:57:42 INFO SparkDeploySchedulerBackend: Registered executor: AkkaRpcEndpointRef(Actor[akka.tcp://sparkExecutor@10.166.191.242:54159/user/Executor#669136232]
) with ID 0
15/11/05 09:57:42 INFO TaskSetManager: Starting task 0.0 in stage 0.0 (TID 0, 10.166.191.242, PROCESS_LOCAL, 2231 bytes)
15/11/05 09:57:42 INFO TaskSetManager: Starting task 1.0 in stage 0.0 (TID 1, 10.166.191.242, PROCESS_LOCAL, 2231 bytes)
15/11/05 09:57:42 INFO BlockManagerMasterEndpoint: Registering block manager 10.166.191.242:43245 with 529.9 MB RAM, BlockManagerId(0, 10.166.191.242, 43245)
15/11/05 09:57:43 INFO BlockManagerInfo: Added broadcast_1_piece0 in memory on 10.166.191.242:43245 (size: 1927.0 B, free: 529.9 MB)
15/11/05 09:57:43 INFO BlockManagerInfo: Added broadcast_0_piece0 in memory on 10.166.191.242:43245 (size: 12.5 KB, free: 529.9 MB)
15/11/05 09:57:44 INFO TaskSetManager: Finished task 1.0 in stage 0.0 (TID 1) in 1238 ms on 10.166.191.242 (1/2)
15/11/05 09:57:44 INFO TaskSetManager: Finished task 0.0 in stage 0.0 (TID 0) in 1266 ms on 10.166.191.242 (2/2)
15/11/05 09:57:44 INFO TaskSchedulerImpl: Removed TaskSet 0.0, whose tasks have all completed, from pool
15/11/05 09:57:44 INFO DAGScheduler: ResultStage 0 (count at ScalaFirstSparkJob.scala:36) finished in 2.266 s
15/11/05 09:57:44 INFO DAGScheduler: Job 0 finished: count at ScalaFirstSparkJob.scala:36, took 2.370001 s
Number of Crimes reported in Aug-2015 = 23227
15/11/05 09:57:44 INFO SparkContext: Invoking stop() from shutdown hook
15/11/05 09:57:44 INFO SparkUI: Stopped Spark web UI at http://10.166.191.242:4040
15/11/05 09:57:44 INFO DAGScheduler: Stopping DAGScheduler
15/11/05 09:57:44 INFO SparkDeploySchedulerBackend: Shutting down all executors
15/11/05 09:57:44 INFO SparkDeploySchedulerBackend: Asking each executor to shut down
15/11/05 09:57:44 INFO MapOutputTrackerMasterEndpoint: MapOutputTrackerMasterEndpoint stopped!
15/11/05 09:57:44 INFO MemoryStore: MemoryStore cleared
15/11/05 09:57:44 INFO BlockManager: BlockManager stopped
15/11/05 09:57:44 INFO BlockManagerMaster: BlockManagerMaster stopped
15/11/05 09:57:44 INFO OutputCommitCoordinator$OutputCommitCoordinatorEndpoint: OutputCommitCoordinator stopped!
15/11/05 09:57:44 INFO SparkContext: Successfully stopped SparkContext
15/11/05 09:57:44 INFO ShutdownHookManager: Shutdown hook called
15/11/05 09:57:44 INFO ShutdownHookManager: Deleting directory /tmp/spark-41861078-7c3a-43c5-9b13-7c50642fff3f
15/11/05 09:57:44 INFO RemoteActorRefProvider$RemotingTerminator: Shutting down remote daemon.
sumit@localhost $
```

Isn't that simple! As we move forward and discuss about Spark, you will appreciate the ease of coding and simplicity provided by Spark for creating, deploying, and running jobs in a distributed framework.

Your completed job will also be available for viewing at the Spark UI:

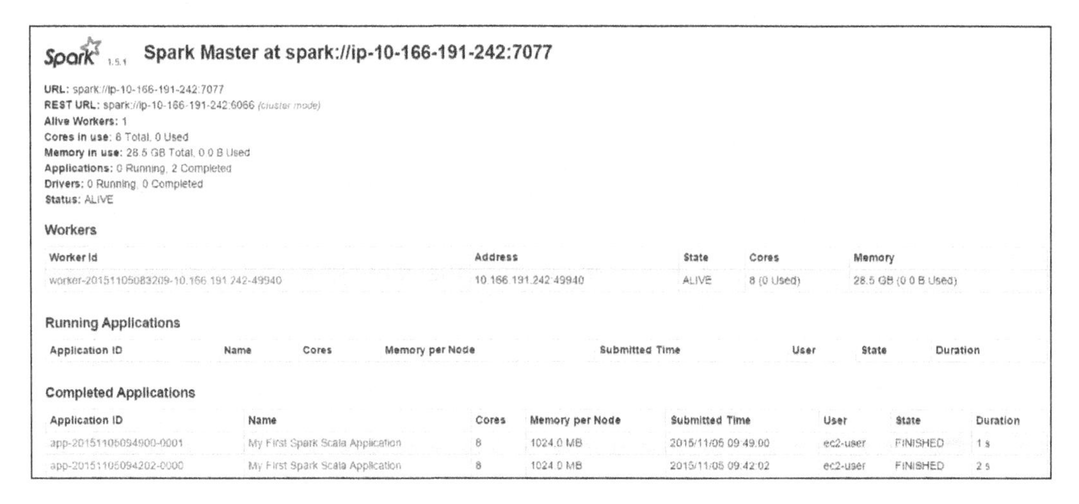

The preceding image shows the status of our first Scala job on the UI. Now let's move forward and develop the same job using Spark Java APIs.

Coding a Spark job in Java

Perform the following steps to code the Spark job in Java for aggregating the number of crimes in August 2015:

1. Open your `Spark-Examples` Eclipse project (created in the previous section).
2. Add a new `chapter.six.JavaFirstSparkJob` Java file, and add the following code snippet:

```
import org.apache.spark.SparkConf;
import org.apache.spark.api.java.JavaRDD;
import org.apache.spark.api.java.JavaSparkContext;
import org.apache.spark.api.java.function.Function;


public class JavaFirstSparkJob {

  public static void main(String[] args) {
    System.out.println("Creating Spark Configuration");
```

```
        // Create an Object of Spark Configuration
        SparkConf javaConf = new SparkConf();
        // Set the logical and user defined Name of this Application
        javaConf.setAppName("My First Spark Java Application");
        System.out.println("Creating Spark Context");
        // Create a Spark Context and provide previously created
        //Objectx of SparkConf as an reference.
        JavaSparkContext javaCtx = new JavaSparkContext(javaConf);
        System.out.println("Loading the Crime Dataset and will
    further process it");

        String file = "file:///home/ec2-user/softwares/crime-data/
    Crimes_-Aug-2015.csv";
        JavaRDD<String> logData = javaCtx.textFile(file);
        //Invoking Filter operation on the RDD.
        //And counting the number of lines in the Data loaded
        //in RDD.
        //Simply returning true as "TextInputFormat" have already
    divided the data by "\n"
        //So each RDD will have only 1 line.
        long numLines = logData.filter(new Function<String,
    Boolean>() {
        public Boolean call(String s) {
        return true;
        }
        }).count();
        //Finally Printing the Number of lines
        System.out.println("Number of Crimes reported in Aug-2015 =
    "+numLines);
        javaCtx.close();

      }
    }
```

3. Next, compile the preceding `JavaFirstSparkJob` from Eclipse itself and perform steps 7, 8, and 9 of the previous section in which we executed the Spark Scala job.

We are done! Analyze the output on the console; it should be the same as the output of the Scala job, which we executed in the previous section.

Troubleshooting – tips and tricks

In this section, we will talk about troubleshooting tips and tricks, which are helpful in solving the most common errors encountered while working with Spark.

Port numbers used by Spark

Spark binds various network ports for communication within the cluster/nodes and also exposes the monitoring information of jobs to developers and administrators. There may be instances where the default ports used by Spark may not be available or may be blocked by the network firewall which in turn will result in modifying the default Spark ports for master/worker or driver. Here is a list of all the ports utilized by Spark and their associated parameters, which need to be configured for any changes (`http://spark.apache.org/docs/latest/security.html#configuring-ports-for-network-security`).

Classpath issues – class not found exception

Classpath is the most common issue and it occurs frequently in distributed applications.

Spark and its associated jobs run in a distributed mode on a cluster. So, if your Spark job is dependent upon external libraries, then we need to ensure that we package them into a single JAR fie and place it in a common location or the default classpath of all worker nodes or define the path of the JAR file within `SparkConf` itself:

```
val sparkConf = new SparkConf().setAppName("myapp").setJars(<path of
Jar file>))
```

Other common exceptions

In this section, we will talk about a few of the common errors/issues/exceptions encountered by architects/developers when they set up Spark or execute Spark jobs:

- **Too many open files**: This increases the `ulimit` on your Linux OS by executing `sudo ulimit -n 20000`.
- **Version of Scala**: Spark 1.5.1 supports Scala 2.10, so if you have multiple versions of Scala deployed on your box, then ensure that all versions are the same, that is, Scala 2.10.
- **Out of memory on workers in standalone mode**: This configures `SPARK_WORKER_MEMORY` in `$SPARK_HOME/conf/spark-env.sh`. By default, it provides a total memory of 1 G to workers, but at the same time, you should analyze and ensure that you are not loading or caching too much data on worker nodes.

- **Out of memory in applications executed on worker nodes**: This configures `spark.executor.memory` in your `SparkConf`, as follows:

```
val sparkConf = new SparkConf().setAppName("myapp")
  .set("spark.executor.memory", "1g")
```

The preceding tips will help you solve basic issues in setting up Spark clusters, but as you move ahead, there could be more complex issues, which are beyond the basic setup, and for all those issues, post your queries at `http://stackoverflow.com/questions/tagged/apache-spark` or mail at `user@spark.apache.org`.

Summary

In this chapter, we discussed the architecture of Spark and its various components. We also talked about a few of the core components of the Spark framework, such as RDDs. We discussed the packaging structure of Spark and its various core APIs, and we also configured our Spark cluster and executed our first Spark job in Scala and Java.

In the next chapter, we talk about the various functions/APIs exposed by Spark RDDs in detail.

7
Programming with RDDs

Analyzing historical data and uncovering the hidden pattern is one of the key objectives of modern enterprises. Data scientists/architects/developers are striving hard to implement various data analysis strategies that can help them in analyzing the data and uncovering the value in the shortest possible time.

Data analysis itself is a complex and multistep process. It is a process of examining each component of the provided data using analytical and logical reasoning, and deriving value out of it. Data from various sources are collected, reviewed, and then analyzed by leveraging variety of data analysis methods like data mining, text analysis, and many more with an objective of discovering useful information, suggesting conclusions, and supporting decision making.

Transformation is a most critical and important step in the data analysis process. It requires deep understanding of various techniques and functions available in a language that can help convert data or information from one format to another, usually from the format of the source system into the required format of the new destination system.

Transformation is very subjective and, depending on the end goal, can perform a variety of functions. Some examples of the common functions involved in the transformation process are aggregations (sum, avg, min, and max), sorting, joining data from multiple sources, disaggregations, deriving new values, and so on.

In this chapter, we will discuss the different transformation functions provided by Spark and **Resilient Distributed Dataset** (**RDD**) APIs. We will also talk about the various strategies for persisting transformed datasets.

This chapter will cover the following points:

- Understanding Spark transformations and actions
- Programming Spark transformations and actions
- Handling persistence in Spark

Understanding Spark transformations and actions

In this section, we will discuss and talk about various transformation and action operations provided by Spark RDD APIs. We will also discuss about the different forms of RDD APIs.

RDD or **Resilient Distributed Dataset** is the core component of Spark. All operations for performing transformations on the raw data are provided in the different RDD APIs. We discussed RDD APIs and its features in the *Resilient distributed datasets (RDD)* section in *Chapter 6, Getting Acquainted with Spark,* but it is important to mention again that there is no API for accessing the raw dataset. The data in Spark can only be accessed by various operations exposed by the RDD APIs. RDDs are immutable datasets, so any transformation applied on the raw dataset, generates a new RDD without any modifications to the datasets/RDD on which transformation operations are invoked. Transformations in RDD are lazy, which means invocation of any transformation is not applied immediately to the underlying dataset. Transformations are only applied when any action is invoked or it requires a result to be returned to the driver program. This process helps the Spark framework to work more efficiently and effectively. The process of keeping track of all the transformation applied (in the same sequence) on the original datasets is known as *data lineage*. Each RDD remembers the way it has been constructed, that means it keeps the track of the transformations applied to the previous RDD which have brought it into existence. At a high level, every RDD API provides the following functionality:

- **Partitions**: One of the primary functions of any RDD is to remember the list of partitions represented by that RDD. Partitions are the logical components that divide the data into pieces so that it can be distributed over clusters to achieve parallelism. To elaborate more, Spark jobs collect and buffer data that is further divided into various stages of execution to form the execution pipeline. Each byte in the dataset is represented by RDD and the execution pipeline is called a **Direct Acyclic Graph** (**DAG**). The dataset involved in each stage of the execution pipeline is further stored in the data blocks of equal sizes, which is nothing more than the partitions represented by the RDD. Lastly, for each partition, we have exactly one task allocated or executed. So the parallelism of our job directly depends on the number of partitions configured for our jobs.
- **Splits**: This function is used to split the provided dataset. For example, we used Hadoop's `TextInputFormat` (`http://tinyurl.com/nq3t2eo`) in the example provided in the *Writing and executing our first Spark program* section in *Chapter 6, Getting Acquainted with Spark*, which uses the new line character (`\n`) for splitting the provided dataset.

- **Dependencies**: This is a list of dependencies on the other RDDs.
- **Partitioner**: This is the type of partitioner used to partition the RDD of key/value pairs. This is optional and will be applicable only if RDD contains the data which is in the form of key/value.
- **Location of splits**: RDD also stores the list of preferred locations to compute each split, for example, block locations for an HDFS file.

Let's move forward and discuss the various RDD APIs provided by Spark, and then we will also talk about their applicability along with the appropriate examples.

RDD APIs

The implementation of all Scala RDD APIs are packaged within the `org.apache.spark.rdd.*` package. Internally, Scala is also compiled into `.class` files, so mostly it is compatible with Java but at some places it may not be, like inline or lambda functions/expressions. For all those scenarios, the corresponding Java implementation is provided by Spark in the `org.apache.spark.api.java.*` package.

The naming convention followed by Spark for Java classes is to prefix the class names with keyword *java* for all Scala classes and remove the keyword *function* in case it is provided in the name of Scala classes, for example, the corresponding implementation of `RDD.Scala` is `JavaRDD.java` or `PairRDDFunctions.scala` is `JavaPairRDD.java`.

Here are a few important RDD APIs provided by the Spark:

- `RDD.scala`: This is the base abstract class for all RDD implementations providing basic operations, for example filter, map, flatmap, foreach, and many more. Refer to `http://tinyurl.com/nqkxgwk` for more information on the operations provided by RDD APIs.
- `DoubleRDDFunctions.scala`: This contains the various numerical and statistical functions for the RDD that only contains values in the form of doubles (`http://www.scala-lang.org/api/2.10.5/index.html#scala.Double`). For example, `mean()`, `stdev()`, `variance()`, and `stats()` are some of the statistical functions provided by the `DoubleRDDFunctions`. Refer to `http://tinyurl.com/ou35u4p` for information on the type of operations provided by `DoubleRDDFunctions.scala`.

- `HadoopRDD`: This provides the utility functions to read the source data from HDFS, HBASE, or S3. It uses the older MapReduce API (`org.apache.hadoop.mapred`) to read the data. There is another API by the name of `NewHadoopRDD` that leverages newer MapReduce APIs (`org.apache.hadoop.mapreduce`) to read the data. `HadoopRDD` and `NewHadoopRDD` are annotated with `@DeveloperAPI`, which means that developers can extend and enhance this API as per their needs or convenience. It is also recommended to use `SparkContext.hadoopRDD()` or `SparkContext.newAPIHadoopRDD()` to get the reference for this API and never instantiate it directly. For more information, refer to `http://tinyurl.com/nctlley` or `http://tinyurl.com/oduzulh` for operations exposed by `HadoopRDD` or `NewHadoopRDD`.
- `JdbcRDD`: This API exposes the operations that can be used to execute the SQL queries to fetch the data from RDBMS and then create RDD from the results. For example, let's assume that we have the RDBMS (for example, Apache Derby) with an EMP table with columns as ID, name, and age, and we want to print the ID of all employees for the age group of 20 to 30. The following piece of code meets this requirement and prints the name and age of the qualified employees on the driver console:

```
//Define the Configuration
val conf = new SparkConf();
//Define Context
val ctx = new SparkContext(conf)
//Define JDBC RDD
val rdd = new JdbcRDD(
ctx,
() => { DriverManager.getConnection("jdbc:derby:temp/Jdbc-
RDDExample")
},
 "SELECT EMP_ID,Name FROM EMP WHERE Age > = ? AND ID <= ?",20,
30, 3,
 (r: ResultSet) => { r.getInt(1); r.getString(2) } ).cache()
//Print only first Column in the ResultSet
System.out.println(rdd.first)
```

For more information, refer to `http://tinyurl.com/pd697q3` for operations exposed by `JdbcRDD`.

- `PairRDDFunctions`: This API provides the operations which can be applied on the RDD of key/value pairs. This API contains similar operations as the RDD but it overrides some of the functions of RDD that cannot be applied to the key/value. For example, RDD provides an `aggregate(...)` operation, which aggregates the elements of each partition and then aggregates the results for all the partitions using a given combine function. The same operation cannot be applied to the key/value, so `PairRDDFunctions` introduced `aggregateByKey(...)` that aggregates the data based on the value of the key. For more information, refer to `http://tinyurl.com/po5vpxb` for operations exposed by `PairRDDFunctions`.
- `OrderedRDDFunctions`: This API is similar to the `PairRDDFunctions` API, with the difference that it works on any type of key that is sortable and has implicit conversion. This API provides the implicit ordering of all primitive types and also provides the flexibility to provide the custom ordering of elements/objects. For example, assume that in an RDD of a key/value pair, the key is a type of string, then the two keys are compared and the dataset is sorted as follows:

  ```
  Key1.toLowerCase.compare(Key2.toLowerCase)
  ```

For more information, refer to `http://tinyurl.com/qhxxv3c` for operations exposed by `OrderedRDDFunctions`.

- `SequenceFileRDDFunctions`: This contains extra functions to convert the RDD of a key/value pair to Hadoop sequence files using an implicit conversion mechanism. This API converts the RDD into the implementation of the Hadoop `Writable` interface (`http://tinyurl.com/qddpbv2`). For more information, refer to `http://tinyurl.com/ph4q6sf` for operations exposed by `SequenceFileRDDFunctions`.

Let's move forward and discuss some of the important transformation and action operations provided by the defined RDD APIs.

RDD transformation operations

In this section, we will discuss some of the important and widely used transformation operations provided by the different types of RDD APIs.

RDD APIs expose a variety of operations that range from simple filtering of dataset to partitioning and repartitioning of datasets. Let's talk about some of the operations exposed by RDD APIs:

- `filter(filterFunc)`: This applies the provided function to all the elements of RDD and generates the RDD only for those elements that return true.
- `map(mapFunc)`: This applies a given function to all elements of RDD and generates a new RDD.
- `flatMap(flatMapFunc)`: This is similar to the `map(...)` operation, but it flattens the results and then generates a new RDD and returns the final result set.
- `mapPartitions(mapPartFunc, preservePartitioning)`: These return a new RDD by applying the provided function once to each partition of the invoking RDD. The custom function must return another `Iterator[U]` and the combined result of all partitions (all `Iterators`) are converted into a new RDD. The second parameter indicates whether we need to preserve the partitioner or not. It should be false unless the RDD contains the key/value and the provided function does not modify or change the keys.
- `distinct()`: This generates the new RDD containing the distinct elements of the invoking RDD.
- `union(otherDataset)`: This operation combines the provided dataset (RDD) and the invoking RDD. The common elements in both the datasets will not be discarded and it will appear in the final RDD. In case we need to discard the duplicate elements, then we need to use the `distinct()` operation.
- `intersection(otherDataset)`: This generates a new RDD of common elements found in the invoking and the provided RDD. This operation does not produce any duplicates. It also performs shuffling and a hash partition across the cluster.
- `groupByKey([numTasks])`: This operation only works with the RDD of key/value pairs. It performs the grouping on the key and provides the `Iterable` values `RDD<Key, Iterable<Value>>`.

- `reduceByKey(func, [numTasks])`: This operation also works on the RDD of key/value pairs. When invoked, it produces the aggregated values of each by applying the provided function. The provided function must perform the aggregation like sum, average, subtract, and so on. It is advised to use `reduceByKey(…)` instead of `groupByKey(…)` whenever the datasets are joined for the sole purpose of performing aggregation, because the performance of `reduceByKey` is better than `groupByKey(…)`.
- `coalesce(numPartitions)`: This decreases the number of partitions in the RDD to `numPartitions`. It is useful for running operations more efficiently after filtering down a large dataset into the smaller number of partitions.
- `sortBy (f,[ascending], [numTasks])`: This performs the sorting and returns the new RDD with sorted elements. The sorting is performed by applying the provided function. This operation also helps in customizing the behavior of sorting where we can implement custom sorting on the user-defined or custom objects.
- `sortByKey([ascending], [numTasks])`: This operation is available on the RDD of the key/value pair and can be invoked only when the key has the implicit `Ordering[Key]` in scope. Though the ordering of all primitive types already exists, we can also customize the behavior of ordering and define custom sorting/ordering of elements. In case of implicit ordering, the closest scope will be used. The output RDD is a shuffled RDD because it stores data that is output by a reducer that has been shuffled. The implementation of this function first uses a range partitioner to partition the data in ranges within the shuffled RDD. Then, it sorts these ranges individually with `mapPartitions` using a standard sort mechanism.
- `repartition(numPartitions)`: This function generates a new RDD that contains a reduced or increased number of partitions based on the number provided as the argument.
- `join(otherDataset, [numTasks])`: This operation works on the RDD of key/value pairs. It joins the data for the keys of the invoking as well as provided RDD and creates a new RDD. For example, the RDD of K and V when joined with RDD of K and V1 will generate a new RDD of (K, (V,V1)). It applies an inner join on the keys of both RDDs and it is mandatory that keys should be comparable. The API also provides other variants of the same operations, such as `leftOuterJoin`, `rightOuterJoin`, and `fullOuterJoin` for supporting left, right, and full outer joins.

The preceding operations are just a glimpse of the variety of transformation operations provided by the RDD APIs. There are many other variants of the previously explained operations which can be found in the API documentation.

Let's move forward and also understand the operations exposed by RDD APIs for performing actions and then we will analyze our Chicago crime data using these transformations and actions.

RDD action operations

In this section, we will discuss some of the important and widely used action operations provide by the RDD APIs.

RDD APIs expose a variety of operations for performing actions, which range from simple printing elements on the driver console to persisting data in HDFS. Let's talk about some of these operations exposed by RDD APIs:

- `reduce(func)`: This operation aggregates the elements of the RDD by applying the provided function. It provides the well-known and popular `reduce` functionality (`https://en.wikipedia.org/wiki/MapReduce`), so the provided function should be commutative and associative so that results can be computed correctly in parallel.
- `collect()`: This collects all the elements of the RDD, converts it into a Scala array, and finally returns the results. There is another variant of the same operation that accepts a *function*, which (if provided) is applied to all elements before they are added to the final Scala array.
- `count()`: This simply counts the number of elements in the RDD.
- `countApproxDistinct(relativeSD: Double = 0.05)`: As the name suggests, this operation returns the approximate number of distinct elements in the RDD. It leverages the algorithm based on the streamlib implementation of *HyperLogLog in Practice: Algorithmic Engineering of a State of the Art Cardinality Estimation Algorithm* (`http://dx.doi.org/10.1145/2452376.2452456`). This operation is efficient and is used in scenarios where large RDDs are spread across the nodes. This operation is generally faster than the other counting methods. The second parameter controls the accuracy of the computation, which must be greater than 0.000017. There are other variants of the same operation which work on the RDD of key/value pairs like `countApproxDistinctByKey`, which compute the approximate number of distinct values for each distinct key.
- `countByKey()`: This operation is only available on RDDs of type key/value. It simply counts the number of keys and returns a `HashMap` of (K, C) pairs, where K is the key and C is the count of each key.
- `first()`: This extracts the first element of the dataset and returns it to the user.

- `take(n)`: This extracts the first *n* elements from the RDD and returns it to the user. The implementation of this operation is tricky as it involves the searching of multiple partitions.
- `takeSample(withReplacement, num, [seed])`: This returns an array with a random sample of `num` elements of the dataset, with or without replacement, optionally specifying a random number generator seeds beforehand.
- `takeOrdered(Int:num)`: This operation first sorts the elements of the RDD by specified implicit `Ordering[T]` in ascending order and then returns the specified number of elements in the form of array.
- `saveAsTextFile (path: String)`: This persists the RDD as a text file using the string representation of the RDD elements on the provided location.
- `saveAsSequenceFile (path: String)`: This operation implements the Hadoop `org.apache.hadoop.io.Writable` interface, converts the RDD of elements into the Hadoop sequence files, and then further persists on the provided HDFS location.
- `saveAsObjectFile (path: String)`: This persists the RDD as a sequence file of serialized objects on the provided location.

The preceding operations are again just a glimpse of the variety of action operations provided by the RDD APIs. There are variants of the previous operations that can be found in the API documentation.

We discussed a lot about the transformation and action operation, so let's move forward towards the next section where we will use these operations to transform and analyze our Chicago crime dataset.

Programming Spark transformations and actions

In this section, we will leverage the various functions exposed by RDD APIs and analyze our Chicago crime dataset. We will start with simple operations and move on to the complex transformations. First, let's create/define some base classes and then we will develop our transformation logic.

Perform the following steps to write the basic building blocks:

1. We will extend our `Spark-Examples` projects and create a new Scala class by the name of `chapter.seven.ScalaCrimeUtil.scala`. This class will contain some utility functions that will be utilized by our *main transformation* job.

2. Open and edit `ScalaCrimeUtil.scala` and add the following piece of code:

```
package chapter.seven

class ScalaCrimeUtil extends Serializable{

   /**
   * Create a Map of the data which is extracted by applying
Regular expression.
   */
  def createDataMap(data:String): Map[String, String] = {

    //Replacing Empty columns with the blank Spaces,
    //so that split function always produce same size Array
    val crimeData = data.replaceAll(",,,", ", , , ")
    //Splitting the Single Crime record
    val array = crimeData.split(",")
    //Creating the Map of values
    val dataMap = Map[String, String](
    ("ID" -> array(0)),
    ("Case Number" -> array(1)),
    ("Date" -> array(2)),
    ("Block" -> array(3)),
    ("IUCR" -> array(4)),
    ("Primary Type" -> array(5)),
    ("Description" -> array(6)),
    ("Location Description" -> array(7)),
    ("Arrest" -> array(8)),
    ("Domestic" -> array(9)),
    ("Beat" -> array(10)),
    ("District" -> array(11)),
    ("Ward" -> array(12)),
    ("Community Area" -> array(13)),
    ("FBI Code" -> array(14)),
    ("X Coordinate" -> array(15)),
    ("Y Coordinate" -> array(16)),
    ("Year" -> array(17)),
    ("Updated On" -> array(18)),
    ("Latitude" -> array(19)),
    ("Longitude" -> array(20).concat(array(21)))

  )
  //Finally returning it to the invoking program
```

```
    return dataMap
    }

  }
```

The preceding code defines a utility function `createDataMap(data:String)` that converts a single line of crime dataset into key/value pairs.

3. Next, we will create our transformation job. Create a new Scala object by the name of `chapter.seven.ScalaTransformCrimeData.scala` and add the following code:

```
package chapter.seven

import org.apache.spark.{ SparkConf, SparkContext }
import org.apache.spark.rdd._
import org.apache.hadoop._
import org.apache.hadoop.mapred.JobConf
import org.apache.hadoop.io._
import org.apache.hadoop.mapreduce._

/**
 * Transformation Job for showcasing different transformations on
the Crime Dataset.
 * @author Sumit Gupta
 *
 */
object ScalaTransformCrimeData {

  def main(args: Array[String]) {
    println("Creating Spark Configuration")
    //Create an Object of Spark Configuration
    val conf = new SparkConf()
    //Set the logical and user defined Name of this Application
    conf.setAppName("Scala - Transforming Crime Dataset")
    println("Creating Spark Context")
    //Create a Spark Context and provide previously created
    //Object of SparkConf as an reference.
    val ctx = new SparkContext(conf)
    //Define the location of the file containing the Crime Data
    val file = "file:///home/ec2-user/softwares/crime-data/
Crimes_-Aug-2015.csv";
    println("Loading the Dataset and will further process it")
    //Loading the Text file from the local file system or HDFS
    //and converting it into RDD.
```

```
    //SparkContext.textFile(..) - It uses the Hadoop's
    //TextInputFormat and file is broken by New line Character.
    //Refer to http://hadoop.apache.org/docs/r2.6.0/api/org/
apache/hadoop/mapred/TextInputFormat.html
    //The Second Argument is the Partitions which specify the
parallelism.
    //It should be equal or more then number of Cores in the
cluster.
    val logData = ctx.textFile(file, 2)

    //Now Perform the Transformations on the Data Loaded by Spark
    executeTransformations(ctx, logData)
   //Stop the Context for Graceful Shutdown
   ctx.stop()

  }

  /**
   * Main Function for invoking all kind of Transformation on
Crime Data
   */
  def executeTransformations(ctx: SparkContext, crimeData:
RDD[String]) {  }
}
```

The preceding code loads the crime dataset and then defines/invokes a new method, `executeTransformations`. This method is the central point for invoking or executing any transformations applied to our Chicago crime dataset. It accepts the dataset loaded by Spark in the form of `RDD[String]` and further analysis is performed to find the answer to the questions asked by the businesses, customers, market analysts, and others. We will also define some questions/scenarios and provide the answers/solution to the same by leveraging various Spark transformations and actions.

Scenario 1

How do we find the total count of the crime registered in the month of August 2015, grouped by the type of crime?

Solution 1

The solution is simple. We first need to convert the data into a key/value pair, filter the data based on the column, **Primary Type**, and then finally aggregate the data based on the column **Primary Type**. The result would be the RDD of a key/value pair where the key will be the type of crime and the value as the count.

Let's define a new function by the name of `findCrimeCountByPrimaryType` just before the closing braces of the Scala object `ScalaTransformCrimeData` and add the following piece of code:

```
/**    * Provide the Count of All Crimes by its "Primary Type"
   */

  def findCrimeCountByPrimaryType(ctx: SparkContext, crimeData:
RDD[String]) {

    //Utility class for Transforming Crime Data
    val analyzer = new ScalaCrimeUtil()

    //Flattening the Crime Data by converting into Map of Key/ Value
Pair
    val crimeMap = crimeData.flatMap(x => analyzer.createDataMap(x))

    //Performing 3 Steps:
    //1. Filtering the Data and fetching data only for "Primary Type"
    //2. Creating a Map of Key Value Pair
    //3. Applying reduce function for getting count of each key
    val results = crimeMap.filter(f => f._1.equals("Primary Type")).
      map(x => (x._2, 1)).reduceByKey(_ + _)

    //Printing the unsorted results on the Console
    println("Printing the Count by the Type of Crime")
    results.collect().foreach(f => println(f._1 + "=" + f._2))
  }
```

Next, invoke the previous function from the `executeTransformations(...)` method and we are done. For executing the job, perform the following steps:

1. Leverage your IDE (Eclipse) and export your project as a `.jar` file, name it `spark-examples.jar`, and save this `.jar` file in the root of `$SPARK_HOME`.
2. Open your Linux console, browse to `$SPARK_HOME`, and execute the following command:

   ```
   $SPARK_HOME/bin/spark-submit --class chapter.seven.
   ScalaTransformCrimeData --master spark://ip-10-166-191-242:7077
   spark-examples.jar
   ```

In the preceding command, ensure that the value given to parameter `--master` is the same as it is shown on your Spark UI.

As soon as you execute the following command, Spark will execute the provided transformation functions and finally print the results on the driver console, which would be similar to the following screenshot:

```
sumit@localhost $ $SPARK_HOME/bin/spark-submit --class chapterseven.ScalaTransformCrimeData --master spark://ip-10-138-152-216:7077 spark-examples.jar
Creating Spark Configuration
Creating Spark Context
15/11/11 06:38:11 WARN NativeCodeLoader: Unable to load native-hadoop library for your platform... using builtin-java classes where applicable
15/11/11 06:38:12 WARN MetricsSystem: Using default name DAGScheduler for source because spark.app.id is not set.
Loading the Dataset and will further process it
Printing the Count by the Type of Crime
CRIM SEXUAL ASSAULT=115
WEAPONS VIOLATION=307
PROSTITUTION=130
Primary Type=1
NARCOTICS=1786
MOTOR VEHICLE THEFT=950
BURGLARY=1198
OTHER OFFENSE=1554
CRIMINAL TRESPASS=564
SEX OFFENSE=72
DECEPTIVE PRACTICE=990
OBSCENITY=1
CRIMINAL DAMAGE=2599
HOMICIDE=47
PUBLIC PEACE VIOLATION=194
ROBBERY=911
HUMAN TRAFFICKING=1
GAMBLING=62
NON - CRIMINAL=2
KIDNAPPING=23
INTIMIDATION=13
NON-CRIMINAL=2
LIQUOR LAW VIOLATION=35
OFFENSE INVOLVING CHILDREN=173
INTERFERENCE WITH PUBLIC OFFICER=129
BATTERY=4468
STALKING=12
ASSAULT=1539
THEFT=5312
ARSON=37
```

Easy isn't it? Let's move to next scenario and perform some real analysis!

Follow the comments provided in the code to understand each statement and transformation performed. The same style is used to explain all other scenarios. Corresponding Java implementation of the previous problem statement can be found in the code examples provided with this book.

Scenario 2

How to uncover the top five crimes performed in Chicago for August 2015?

Solution 2

The solution is again simple. We need to perform all the steps what we did in Solution 1, then sort the values (count) of the resulting map in descending order, then take the top five, and finally print on the console. Let's define a new function by the name of `findTop5Crime(…)` just before the closing braces of the Scala object `ScalaTransformCrimeData` and add the following piece of code:

```
/**
 * Find the Top 5 Crimes by its "Primary Type"
 */
def findTop5Crime(ctx: SparkContext, crimeData: RDD[String]) {

  //Utility class for Transforming Crime Data
```

```
    val analyzer = new ScalaCrimeUtil()

    //Flattening the Crime Data by converting into Map of Key/ Value
Pair
    val crimeMap = crimeData.flatMap(x => analyzer.createDataMap(x))

    //Performing 3 Steps:
    //1. Filtering the Data and fetching data only for "Primary Type"
    //2. Creating a Map of Key Value Pair
    //3. Applying reduce function for getting count of each key
    val results = crimeMap.filter(f => f._1.equals("Primary Type")).
      map(x => (x._2, 1)).reduceByKey(_ + _)

    //Perform Sort based on the Count
    val sortedResults = results.sortBy(f => f._2, false)
    //Collect the Sorted results and print the Top 5 Crime
    println("Printing Sorted Top 5 Crime based on the Primary Type of
Crime")
    sortedResults.collect().take(5).foreach(f => println(f._1 + "=" +
f._2))

  }
```

Now invoke the preceding function from the `executeTransformations(...)` method and we are done. For executing the job, perform the same steps as we did earlier in Solution 1. As soon as we execute the job, Spark will execute the provided transformation functions and finally print the results on the driver console, which would be similar to the following screenshot:

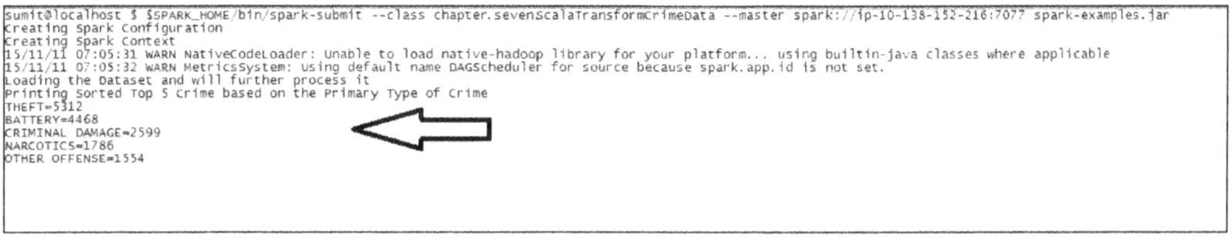

```
sumit@localhost $ $SPARK_HOME/bin/spark-submit --class chapter.sevenScalaTransformCrimeData --master spark://ip-10-138-152-216:7077 spark-examples.jar
Creating Spark Configuration
Creating Spark Context
15/11/11 07:05:31 WARN NativeCodeLoader: Unable to load native-hadoop library for your platform... using builtin-java classes where applicable
15/11/11 07:05:32 WARN MetricsSystem: Using default name DAGScheduler for source because spark.app.id is not set.
Loading the Dataset and will further process it
Printing Sorted Top 5 Crime based on the Primary Type of Crime
THEFT=5312
BATTERY=4468
CRIMINAL DAMAGE=2599
NARCOTICS=1786
OTHER OFFENSE=1554
```

Scenario 3

How to find the total count of the crime in the month of August grouped and sorted by the type of crime (primary type)?

Solution 3

The solution of this scenario is pretty obvious. We need to perform custom sorting on the type of crime. In order to achieve that, we need to perform all the steps what we did in Solution 1 and then perform the custom sorting on the crime type. Let's define a new function by the name of `findCrimeCountByPrimaryType (...)` just before the closing braces of the Scala object `ScalaTransformCrimeData` and add the following piece of code:

```
  /**
   * Provide Custom Sorting on the type of Crime "Primary Type"
   */
  def performSortOnCrimeType(ctx: SparkContext, crimeData:
RDD[String]) {

    //Utility class for Transforming Crime Data
    val analyzer = new ScalaCrimeUtil()

    //Flattening the Crime Data by converting into Map of Key/ Value
Pair
    val crimeMap = crimeData.flatMap(x => analyzer.createDataMap(x))

    //Performing 3 Steps:
    //1. Filtering the Data and fetching data only for "Primary Type"
    //2. Creating a Map of Key Value Pair
    //3. Applying reduce function for getting count of each key
    val results = crimeMap.filter(f => f._1.equals("Primary Type")).
      map(x => (x._2, 1)).reduceByKey(_ + _)

    //Perform Custom Sort based on the Type of Crime (Primary Type)
    import scala.reflect.classTag
    val customSortedResults = results.sortBy(f => createCrimeObj(f._1,
f._2), true)
     (CrimeOrdering, classTag[Crime])
    //Collect the Sorted results and print the Top 5 Crime
    println("Now Printing Sorted Results using Custom
Sorting.............")
    customSortedResults.collect().foreach(f => println(f._1 + "=" +
f._2))

  }

  /**
   * Case Class which defines the Crime Object
```

```
     */
    case class Crime(crimeType: String, count: Int)

    /**
     * Utility Function for creating Object of Class Crime
     */
    val createCrimeObj = (crimeType: String, count: Int) => {
      Crime(crimeType, count)
    }

    /**
     * Custom Ordering function which defines the Sorting behavior.
     */
    implicit val CrimeOrdering = new Ordering[Crime] {
      def compare(a: Crime, b: Crime): Int = a.crimeType.compareTo(b.
  crimeType)
    }
```

Now, invoke the preceding function from the `executeTransformations(...)` method and we are done. For executing the job, perform the same steps we used earlier in Solution 1. As soon as we execute the job, Spark will execute the provided transformation functions and finally print the results on the driver console, which will be similar to the following screenshot:

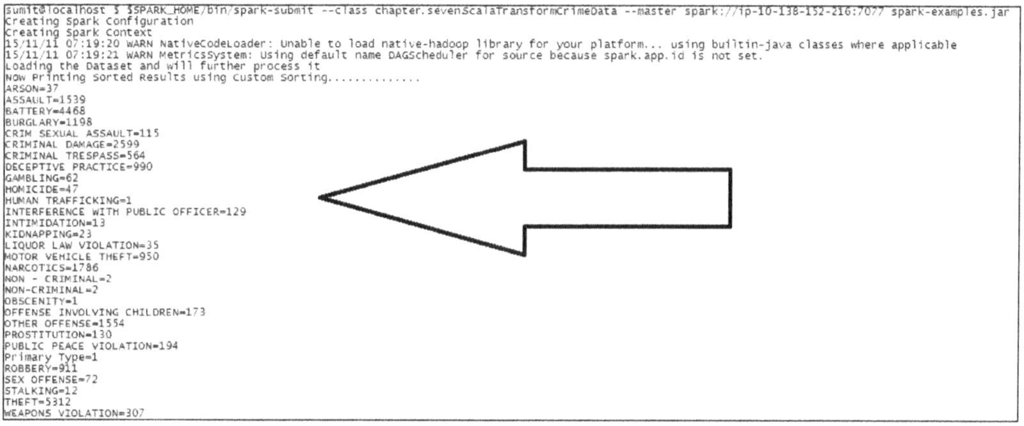

```
sumit@localhost $ $SPARK_HOME/bin/spark-submit --class chapter.sevenScalaTransformCrimeData --master spark://ip-10-138-152-216:7077 spark-examples.jar
Creating Spark Configuration
Creating Spark Context
15/11/11 07:19:20 WARN NativeCodeLoader: Unable to load native-hadoop library for your platform... using builtin-java classes where applicable
15/11/11 07:19:21 WARN MetricsSystem: Using default name DAGScheduler for source because spark.app.id is not set.
Loading the Dataset and will further process it
Now Printing Sorted Results using Custom Sorting.............
ARSON=37
ASSAULT=1539
BATTERY=4468
BURGLARY=1198
CRIM SEXUAL ASSAULT=115
CRIMINAL DAMAGE=2599
CRIMINAL TRESPASS=564
DECEPTIVE PRACTICE=990
GAMBLING=62
HOMICIDE=47
HUMAN TRAFFICKING=1
INTERFERENCE WITH PUBLIC OFFICER=129
INTIMIDATION=13
KIDNAPPING=23
LIQUOR LAW VIOLATION=35
MOTOR VEHICLE THEFT=950
NARCOTICS=1786
NON - CRIMINAL=2
NON-CRIMINAL=2
OBSCENITY=1
OFFENSE INVOLVING CHILDREN=173
OTHER OFFENSE=1554
PROSTITUTION=130
PUBLIC PEACE VIOLATION=194
Primary Type=1
ROBBERY=911
SEX OFFENSE=72
STALKING=12
THEFT=5312
WEAPONS VIOLATION=307
```

Scenario 4

How to persist the filtered crime data map either as the text file or the object file on a local filesystem?

Solution 4

We need to perform all the steps we did in Solution 1 and then invoke `saveAsTextFile(path:String)` and `saveAsObjectFile(path:String)`. Let's define a new function by the name of `persistCrimeData(...)` just before the closing braces of the Scala object `ScalaTransformCrimeData` and add the following piece of code:

```
/**
  * Persist the filtered Crime Data Map into various formats (Text/
Object/ HDFS)
  */
  def persistCrimeData(ctx: SparkContext, crimeData: RDD[String]) {

  //Utility class for Transforming Crime Data
  val analyzer = new ScalaCrimeUtil()

  //Flattening the Crime Data by converting into Map of Key/ Value
Pair
  val crimeMap = crimeData.flatMap(x => analyzer.createDataMap(x))

  //Performing 3 Steps:
  //1. Filtering the Data and fetching data only for "Primary Type"
  //2. Creating a Map of Key Value Pair
  //3. Applying reduce function for getting count of each key
  val results = crimeMap.filter(f => f._1.equals("Primary Type")).
    map(x => (x._2, 1)).reduceByKey(_ + _)

  println("Now Persisting as Text File")
  //Ensure that the Path on local file system exists till "output"
folder.
  results.saveAsTextFile("file:///home/ec2-user/softwares/crime-
data/output/Crime-TextFile"+System.currentTimeMillis())
  println("Now Persisting as Object File")
  //Ensure that the Path on local file system exists till "output"
folder.
  results.saveAsObjectFile("file:///home/ec2-user/softwares/crime-
data/output/Crime-ObjFile"+System.currentTimeMillis())
}
```

Now, invoke the preceding function from the `executeTransformations(...)` method and we are done. For executing the job, perform the same steps as we did earlier in Solution 1.

Scenario 5

How to persist data in Hadoop HDFS?

Solution 5

In order to persist data on Hadoop HDFS, first we need to set up Hadoop. So let's perform the following steps to set up Hadoop and HDFS:

1. Download the Hadoop 2.4.0 distribution from `https://archive.apache.org/dist/hadoop/common/hadoop-2.4.0/hadoop-2.4.0.tar.gz` and extract the archive to any folder of your choice on the same machine where you configured Spark.
2. Open the Linux shell and execute the following command:

   ```
   export HADOOP_PREFIX=<path of your directory where we extracted
   Hadoop>
   ```

3. Follow the steps defined in `http://hadoop.apache.org/docs/r2.5.2/hadoop-project-dist/hadoop-common/SingleCluster.html` for single-node setup. After completing the prerequisites defined in the given link, you can follow the setup instructions defined either for the pseudo-distributed mode or the fully-distributed mode. For us, the pseudo-distributed mode will work but that does not stop you from trying the latter one.
4. Once you have completed the setup, open your Linux shell and execute the following commands:

   ```
   $HADOOP_PREFIX/bin/hdfs namenode -format
   $HADOOP_PREFIX/sbin/start-dfs.sh
   ```

5. The first command will format `namenode` and make the filesystem ready for use. With the second command, we are starting the minimum required Hadoop services that will include `namenode` and secondary `namenode`.
6. Next, let's execute these commands to create a directory structure in HDFS where we will store our data:

   ```
   $HADOOP_PREFIX/bin/hdfs dfs -mkdir /spark
   $HADOOP_PREFIX/bin/hdfs dfs -mkdir /spark/crime-data
   $HADOOP_PREFIX/bin/hdfs dfs -mkdir /spark/ crime-data/oldApi
   $HADOOP_PREFIX/bin/hdfs dfs -mkdir /spark/s crime-data/newApi
   ```

If everything goes right and there are no exceptions then open your browser, browse to `http://localhost:50070/explorer.html#/` and you will be able to see the empty directories created by the preceding commands, as shown in the following screenshot:

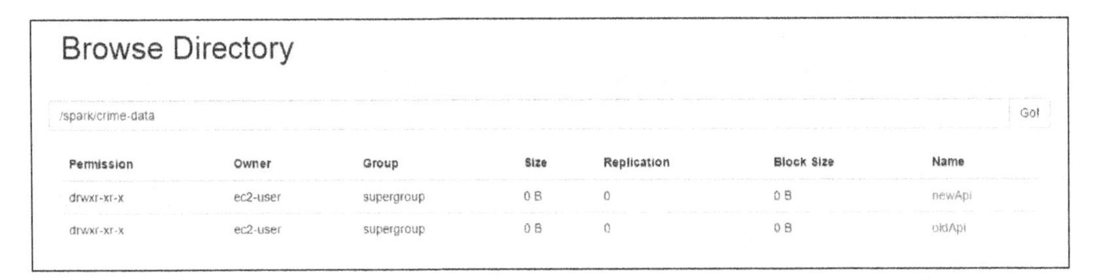

Browse Directory

/spark/crime-data   Go!

Permission	Owner	Group	Size	Replication	Block Size	Name
drwxr-xr-x	ec2-user	supergroup	0 B	0	0 B	newApi
drwxr-xr-x	ec2-user	supergroup	0 B	0	0 B	oldApi

The preceding screenshot shows the HDFS file system explorer where we can browse, view, and download any of the files created by the users using HDFS APIs.

Refer to `http://hadoop.apache.org/` for more information on Hadoop and HDFS.

As we are done with the Hadoop installation, let's modify our existing function `persistCrimeData(...)` and add the following piece of code just before the closing braces:

```
    //Creating an Object of Hadoop Config with default Values
    val hConf = new JobConf(new org.apache.hadoop.conf.Configuration())

    //Defining the TextOutputFormat using old APIs available with
=<0.20
    val oldClassOutput = classOf[org.apache.hadoop.mapred.
TextOutputFormat[Text,Text]]
    //Invoking Output operation to save data in HDFS using old APIs
    //This method accepts the following Parameters:
    //1.Path of the File on HDFS
    //2.Key - Class which can work with the Key
    //3.Value - Class which can work with the Key
    //4.OutputFormat - Class needed for writing the Output in a
specific Format
    //5.HadoopConfig - Object of Hadoop Config
    println("Now Persisting as Hadoop File using in Hadoop's Old APIs")
    results.saveAsHadoopFile("hdfs://localhost:9000/spark/crime-
data/oldApi/Crime-"+System.currentTimeMillis(), classOf[Text],
classOf[Text], oldClassOutput ,hConf )
```

```
    //Defining the TextOutputFormat using new APIs available with >0.20
    val newTextOutputFormat = classOf[org.apache.hadoop.mapreduce.lib.
output.TextOutputFormat[Text, Text]]

    //Invoking Output operation to save data in HDFS using new APIs
    //This method accepts same set of parameters as "saveAsHadoopFile"
    println("Now Persisting as Hadoop File using in Hadoop's New APIs")
    results.saveAsNewAPIHadoopFile("hdfs://localhost:9000/spark/
crime-data/newApi/Crime-"+System.currentTimeMillis(), classOf[Text],
classOf[Text], newTextOutputFormat ,hConf )
```

For executing the job, perform the same steps as we did earlier in Solution 1 and as soon as we execute our job, we will see the data files being generated and persisted in Hadoop HDFS:

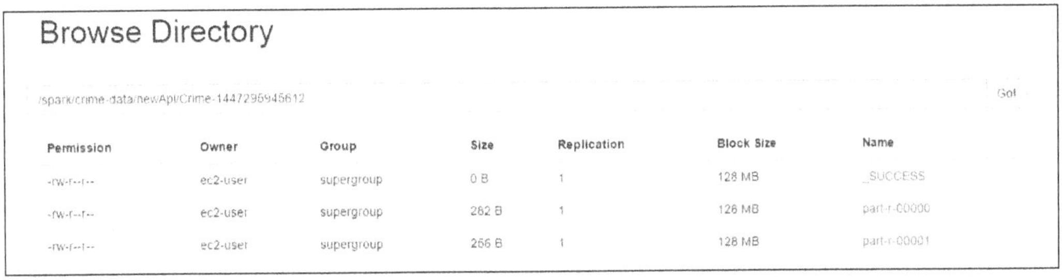

Browse Directory

/spark/crime-data/newApi/Crime-1447295945612 Go!

Permission	Owner	Group	Size	Replication	Block Size	Name
-rw-r--r--	ec2-user	supergroup	0 B	1	128 MB	_SUCCESS
-rw-r--r--	ec2-user	supergroup	262 B	1	128 MB	part-r-00000
-rw-r--r--	ec2-user	supergroup	266 B	1	128 MB	part-r-00001

The preceding screenshot shows the files being generated by our Spark job in HDFS directories.

Scenario 6

How to find the total count of the crime registered in the month of August grouped by the IUCR code names?

Solution 6

IUCR codes or **Illinois Uniform Crime Reporting** (**IUCR**) codes are the standard crime codes given by the Chicago Police Department. They need to be downloaded from `http://data.cityofchicago.org/Public-Safety/Chicago-Police-Department-Illinois-Uniform-Crime-R/c7ck-438e` and stored by the name of `IUCRCodes.txt` in the same directory where we have stored our Chicago crime data. Now the solution to problem would be a two-step process. First, we need to group the crimes based on IUCR codes and second we need to merge the IUCR codes and add/replace them with their real names from `IUCRCodes.txt` file.

Perform the following steps to implement the solution:

1. Define a new function in `ScalaCrimeUtil.scala` by the name of `createIUCRDataMap(…)`. This function will convert the IUCR data files into a map of key/value pairs. Next, add the following code in `createIUCRDataMap(…)`:

```
   /**
   * Create a Map of the data which is extracted by applying
Regular expression.
   */
  def createIUCRDataMap(data:String): Map[String, String] = {

    //Replacing Empty columns with the blank Spaces,
    //so that split function always produce same size Array
    val icurData = data.replaceAll(",,,", ", , , ")
    //Splitting the Single Crime record
    val array = icurData.split(",")
    //Creating the Map of values "IUCR Codes = Values"
    val iucrDataMap = Map[String, String](
    (array(0) -> array(1))
  )
  //Finally returning it to the invoking program
  return iucrDataMap
  }
```

2. Let's define a new function by the name of `findCrimeCountByIUCRCodes(…)` just before the closing braces of the Scala object—`ScalaTransformCrimeData` and add the following piece of code:

```
  /**
   * Find the Crime Count by IUCR Codes and also display the IUCR
Code Names
   */
   def findCrimeCountByIUCRCodes(ctx: SparkContext, crimeData:
RDD[String]) {

         //Utility class for Transforming Crime Data
    val analyzer = new ScalaCrimeUtil()

    //Flattening the Crime Data by converting into Map of Key/
Value Pair
    val crimeMap = crimeData.flatMap(x => analyzer.
createDataMap(x))

    //Performing 3 Steps:
```

```
    //1. Filtering the Data and fetching data only for "Primary
Type"
    //2. Creating a Map of Key Value Pair
    //3. Applying reduce function for getting count of each key
    val results = crimeMap.filter(f => f._1.equals("IUCR")).
      map(x => (x._2, 1)).reduceByKey(_ + _)


    //Loading IUCR Codes File in Spark Memory
    val iucrFile = "file:///home/ec2-user/softwares/crime-data/
IUCRCodes.txt";
    println("Loading the Dataset and will further process it")
    val iucrCodes = ctx.textFile(iucrFile, 2)
    //Convert IUCR Codes into a map of Values
    val iucrCodeMap = iucrCodes.flatMap(x => analyzer.
createIUCRDataMap(x))
    //Apply Left Outer Join to get all results from Crime RDD
    //and matching records from IUCR RDD
    val finalResults = results.leftOuterJoin(iucrCodeMap)

    //Finally Print the results
    finalResults.collect().foreach(f => println(""+f._1 + "=" +
f._2))

  }
```

And we are done. The next step is to execute the preceding piece of code. Perform the same set of steps as we did to execute Solution 1. Once we execute the job, the outcome of the job will be similar to the following screenshot:

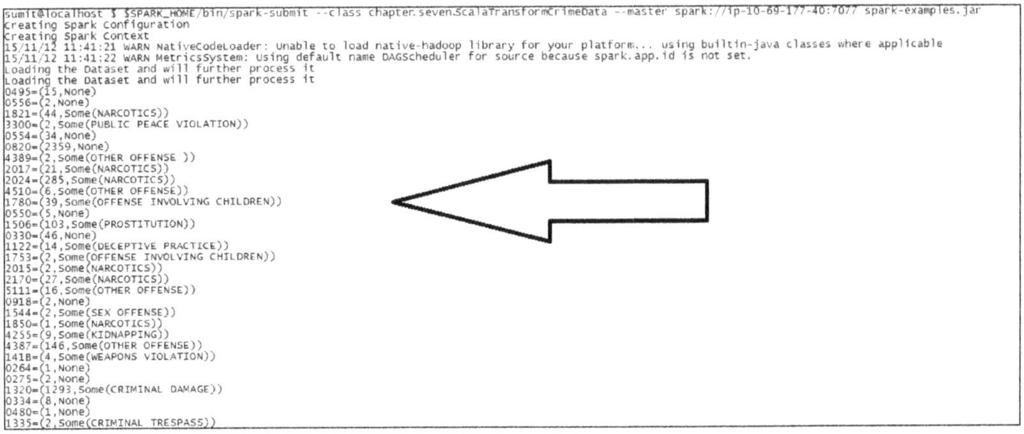

```
sumit@localhost $ $SPARK_HOME/bin/spark-submit --class chapter.seven.ScalaTransformCrimeData --master spark://ip-10-69-177-40:7077 spark-examples.jar
Creating Spark Configuration
Creating Spark Context
15/11/12 11:41:21 WARN NativeCodeLoader: Unable to load native-hadoop library for your platform... using builtin-java classes where applicable
15/11/12 11:41:22 WARN MetricsSystem: Using default name DAGScheduler for source because spark.app.id is not set.
Loading the Dataset and will further process it
Loading the Dataset and will further process it
0495=(15,None)
0556=(2,None)
1821=(44,Some(NARCOTICS))
3300=(2,Some(PUBLIC PEACE VIOLATION))
0554=(34,None)
0820=(2359,None)
4389=(2,Some(OTHER OFFENSE ))
2017=(21,Some(NARCOTICS))
2024=(285,Some(NARCOTICS))
4510=(6,Some(OTHER OFFENSE))
1780=(39,Some(OFFENSE INVOLVING CHILDREN))
0550=(5,None)
1506=(103,Some(PROSTITUTION))
0330=(46,None)
1122=(14,Some(DECEPTIVE PRACTICE))
1753=(2,Some(OFFENSE INVOLVING CHILDREN))
2015=(2,Some(NARCOTICS))
2170=(27,Some(NARCOTICS))
5111=(16,Some(OTHER OFFENSE))
0918=(2,None)
1544=(2,Some(SEX OFFENSE))
1850=(1,Some(NARCOTICS))
4255=(9,Some(KIDNAPPING))
4387=(146,Some(OTHER OFFENSE))
141B=(4,Some(WEAPONS VIOLATION))
0264=(1,None)
0275=(2,None)
1320=(1293,Some(CRIMINAL DAMAGE))
0334=(8,None)
0480=(1,None)
1335=(2,Some(CRIMINAL TRESPASS))
```

The preceding screenshot shows the output of the Spark job which merges two different datasets and then prints the result on the driver console.

> Some of the values of IUCR code names are printed as `None` because there are no matching codes in the IUCR code came file (`IUCRCodes.txt`). As we are using `leftOuterJoin`, all data from the left-hand side dataset (crime records) is considered, while only matching records are taken from right-hand side dataset (IUCR codes) and all unmatched records are marked as `None`.

In this section, we discussed examples for performing transformations and actions to solve real-life problem statements. Let's move forward to the next section where we will discuss persistence in Spark.

Handling persistence in Spark

In this section, we will discuss how the persistence or caching is being handled in Spark. We will talk about various persistence and caching mechanisms provided by Spark along with their significance.

Persistence/caching is one the important components or features of Spark. Earlier, we talked about the computations/transformations are lazy in Spark and the actual computations do not take place unless any action is invoked on the RDD. Though this is a default behavior and provides fault tolerance, sometimes it also impacts the overall performance of the job, especially when we have common datasets that are leveraged and used across the computations.

Persistence/caching helps us in solving this problem by exposing the `persist()` or `cache()` operations in the `RDD`. The `persist()` or `cache()` operations store the computed partition of the invoking RDD in the memory of all nodes and reuses them in other actions on that dataset (or datasets derived from it). This enables the future transformations/actions to be much faster—sometimes more than 10x. Caching/persistence is also a key tool for machine learning and iterative algorithms.

Spark provides different levels of the persistence, which are known as storage levels. They allow us to persist the data only in memory, only on disk, in memory but in compressed form, or maybe use some off heap storage mechanism like Tachyon (`http://tachyon-project.org/`). All these storage levels are defined by `org.apache.spark.storage.StorageLevel`.

Let's discuss the various storage levels provided by Spark and also their appropriate use cases:

- `StorageLevel.MEMORY_ONLY`: This storage level stores the RDD in the Spark cluster memory in the deserialized Java objects. In case memory is not sufficient to store the complete dataset, then some partitions may not be stored and will be recomputed each time it is required. This is the default level and allows the highest level of performance for our Spark jobs. This level should only be considered when we have enough memory to store/persist the computed dataset in the memory.
- `StorageLevel.MEMORY_ONLY_SER`: This is similar to `MEMORY_ONLY` with the difference that it stores the computed data in the form of serialized Java objects that in turn help in saving some space. We need to be cautious that serialization/deserialization mechanisms should not be overhead. In a nutshell, we need to use fast serialization libraries like `https://github.com/EsotericSoftware/kryo`.

Refer to `http://spark.apache.org/docs/latest/tuning.html#data-serialization` for more information on tune and optimize serialization process.

- `StorageLevel.MEMORY_AND_DISK`: This is similar to `MEMORY_ONLY` and the only difference is that it stores the computed partitions on the `DISK` only when memory is not sufficient to store everything. It reads computed partitions from the `DISK` and does not recompute each time data is requested. We need to be cautious while using this level and ensure that reading and writing from disk is really faster than the whole process of recomputation of the dataset.
- `StorageLevel.MEMORY_AND_DISK_SER`: Similar to `MEMORY_AND_DISK` with a difference that it stores the computed partitions in form of serialized Java objects. Similar to `MEMORY_ONLY_SER` level, we need to be careful and use a fast serialization library and ensure that the serialization process is not causing significant latency.
- `StorageLevel.DISK_ONLY`: This stores the computed partitions on the disk only. There is nothing in the memory and the data is read each time it is requested. This is not recommended for the jobs where performance is the criteria for success.

- `StorageLevel.MEMORY_ONLY_2`, `MEMORY_AND_DISK_2`, and so on: All storage levels that end with `_2` provide similar functionality to the previously defined levels with an added capability of replicating the computed partitions to at least two nodes in the cluster. For example, `MEMORY_ONLY_2` is similar to `MEMORY_ONLY` but at the same time it also replicates the computed partitions to two nodes in the cluster.
- `StorageLevel.OFF_HEAP`: This storage level is marked as experimental and is still being tested for the actual production use cases. In `OFF_HEAP`, the data is stored in a serialized format in Tachyon (`http://tachyon-project.org/`). Tachyon is an optimized off heap storage solution which reduces the overhead of garbage collection and allows executors to be smaller and to share a pool of memory, which in turn makes it attractive in environments where we need large heaps for data storage or maybe multiple concurrent applications running in same JVM. Persisting data in off heap storage like Tachyon also has an added benefit that Spark does not have to recompute the data in case Spark executors crash. As cached partitions are stored in off heap memory, Spark executors are used only for executing the Spark jobs and for data storage off heap memory is leveraged. In this mode, the memory in Tachyon can be discarded. Thus, Tachyon does not attempt to reconstruct a block that it evicts from memory.

[Spark provides compatibility with Tachyon. Refer to `http://tachyon-project.org/master/Running-Spark-on-Tachyon.html` for more info on integrating Spark with Tachyon.]

Apart from the different storage levels, Spark provides performance optimization by persisting intermediate data in shuffle operations (for example, `reduceByKey`), even without users explicitly calling persist. This is done to avoid recomputing the entire input if a node fails during the shuffle. It is also important to note that the persistence level can be defined once for an RDD and once it is defined, it cannot be changed during the lifetime of the job execution.

Spark leverages **least-recently-used** (**LRU**) for automatically discarding or flushing the data from the memory (based on storage levels). But we can also explicitly invoke `RDD.unpersist()` for freeing up the Spark memory.

Summary

In this chapter, we discussed various transformation and actions provided by the Spark RDD API. We also discussed various real-life problem statements and solved them by using Spark transformation and actions. At the end, we also discussed the persistence/caching provided by Spark for optimizing the performance.

In the next chapter, we will discuss interactive analytics using Spark SQL.

8

SQL Query Engine for Spark – Spark SQL

Enabling easy access to data and empowering users to perform quick/fast analysis and take informed decision is the key objective for all modern enterprises.

Interactive analytics using **Structured Query Language** (**SQL**) (`https://en.wikipedia.org/wiki/SQL`) is one such option that has always helped to achieve this critical objective of enterprises. It's needless to mention that SQL has always been a preferred language for analysts because of its several advantages (`http://www.moreprocess.com/database/sql/pros-advantages-of-sql-structured-query-language`), but with the emergence of Big Data it was difficult to continue using SQL over RDBMS for interactive analytics. There was an urgent need for a framework that could provide an SQL-like interface over the various Big Data frameworks such as NoSQL databases, Hadoop, and others. This need was soon realized and Apache introduced Apache Hive (`https://hive.apache.org/`), which provided an SQL-like interface along with an *almost* SQL-like syntax and enabled analysts to perform analysis on the data stored in HDFS.

There were no questions or doubts about the capabilities of Hive, but Hive did not meet the primary objective of interactive analytics. Apache Hive extended the principle of Hadoop and MapReduce, which was meant for batch processing and lacks the power of real-time or interactive analysis.

Apache Spark was already an in-memory distributed processing framework, and it soon realized this need and provided another extension/library over its core framework: SPARK SQL (`http://spark.apache.org/sql/`).

In this chapter, we will discuss the architecture of Spark SQL along with its various features that enable analysts to perform interactive analysis/analytics in near real-time on Big Data.

This chapter will cover the following topics:

- The architecture of Spark SQL
- Coding our first Spark SQL job
- Converting RDD to DataFrames
- Working with Parquet
- Working with Hive tables
- Performance tuning and best practices

The architecture of Spark SQL

In this section, we will discuss the overall design, architecture, and various components of Spark SQL. This will help us to understand the varied features and capabilities of Spark SQL.

The emergence of Spark SQL

Storing data in relational structures such as **Relational Database Management Systems (RDBMS)** (such as Oracle, MySQL, and others) and leveraging SQL is a well-known and industry-wide standard for performing analysis over the data collected from various sources such as online portals, surveys, and so on.

It worked fine but only till the time when the data was limited and reasonable in size, that is, not more than a few GBs. As soon as it grew to TBs, it started giving nightmares where SQL queries would take hours, sometimes they would not even complete, and many a times crashed the whole system itself.

That's where Apache Hadoop (`https://en.wikipedia.org/wiki/Apache_Hadoop`) was introduced as a distributed, scalable, fault tolerant, parallel, and batch processing framework for processing terabytes/ petabytes of data on commodity hardware. Hadoop was developed on the popular programming paradigm of MapReduce (`http://tinyurl.com/m5wgezy`). Though Hadoop was meant for hardcore Java programmers who could develop lengthy and complex MapReduce programs using Java, it also introduced frameworks such as Pig (`https://pig.apache.org/`) and Hive (`https://hive.apache.org/`) on top of Hadoop, which were for people from a non-Java background.

Apache Pig was more of a scripting language, while Hive provided the SQL-like syntax where the analyst can write SQL-like queries that were automatically converted into MapReduce jobs, executed over a cluster of nodes, and finally produced results.

Hadoop brought a revolution and its associated frameworks such as Apache Hive soon became popular among analysts as a data analysis framework for TBs/PBs of data. The only drawback with Hive was that it executed the queries in **batch mode** and queries could take minutes to hours, which was against the principle of interactive analytics.

There was a need for a framework that could produce results in seconds or maybe in minutes and not in hours! It was understood that only relational approaches may not be sufficient to work with varied kinds of Big Data applications, and it would require the support to write/execute procedural languages along with declarative queries (the relational approach).

Spark SQL was developed with the same objective of providing the users flexibility of using a mix of relational queries and complex procedural algorithms (such as machine learning algorithms) for performing in-memory analysis, producing results in seconds or minutes. Here are a few of the salient features of Spark SQL:

- Supports merging and combining the data already in Spark memory (RDDs) and external data sources and finally providing relational processing
- Leverages already established DBMS techniques and provides high performance
- Supports new data sources, including semistructured data and external databases amenable to query federation
- Enables extension with advanced analytics algorithms such as graph processing and machine learning

Spark SQL was first released in May 2014, and it's now one of the most actively developed components in Spark. It is battle tested; it has been deployed in large-scale data processing environments, where the size of a cluster was around 8,000 nodes and over 100 PBs of data. Interesting, isn't it?

We will talk more about it and also see some real-world examples, but before that let's move to the next section where we will discuss the overall architecture and components of Spark SQL.

The components of Spark SQL

In this section, we will discuss the various components exposed by Spark SQL. Spark SQL was developed as a separate extension over the core Spark APIs. It introduced two new components to achieve the desired objectives:

- **DataFrame API**: This is the API for performing relational operations on both external data sources and Spark's built-in distributed collections

- **Catalyst optimizer**: This is an extensible optimizer that is used for adding new data sources, optimization rules, and data types for various kinds of domains such as machine learning

We will discuss both these components in detail, but let's see the overall architecture of Spark SQL now:

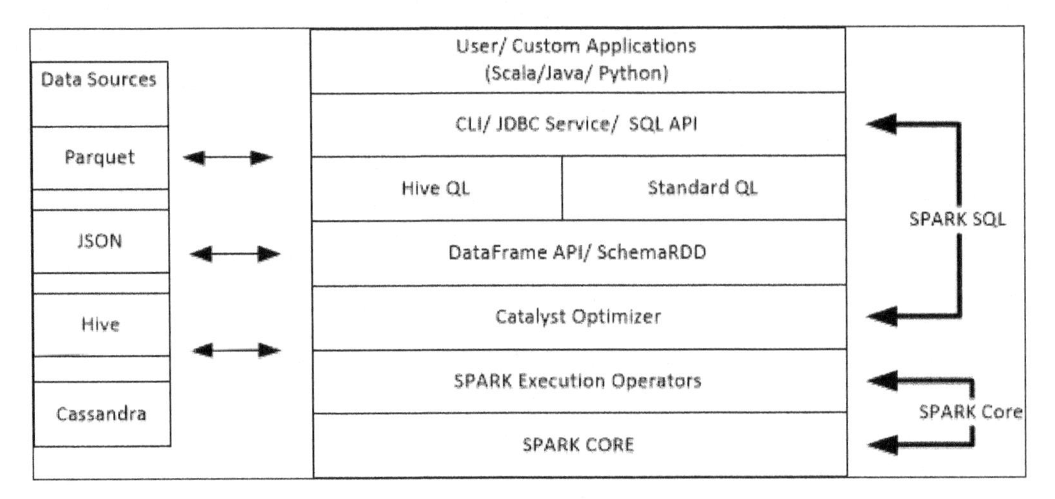

The preceding diagram shows the high-level architecture of Spark SQL and its various components. Let's move forward and discuss the two major components of Spark SQL.

The DataFrame API

DataFrame or SchemaRDD is not a new concept and it has already been implemented in languages in R (`www.r-tutor.com/r-introduction/data-frame`) or Pandas in Python (`http://pandas.pydata.org/pandas-docs/stable/dsintro.html`).

Spark extended and leveraged the same concept and the implemented DataFrames for storing distributed collection of rows with the same schema. It is the main abstraction in Spark SQLs API and is equivalent to a table in a relational database. It can be manipulated in similar ways as we do with Spark Core distributed collections (RDDs). DataFrames keep track of their schema and support various relational operations that lead to more optimized execution. Let us discuss a few features of DataFrames.

DataFrames and RDD

DataFrames are more or less the RDD of row objects which allow users to invoke procedural SPARK API functions such as `map`, `reduce`, and many more. They can be constructed in a variety of ways, directly from tables in relational data stores or JSON or Cassandra or maybe from existing RDDs created by Scala/Java/Python code. Once DataFrames are constructed they can be queried or manipulated using various relational operators such as `Group By`, `Order By`, and so on, which accept the expressions in domain-specific language.

It is important to note that like RDDs, DataFrames are also lazy and no physical execution takes place unless a user invokes any output operation such as `print()` or `count()` on DataFrames. DataFrames such as RDD also cache the data in memory, but they store it in the form of *columnar storage* that helps in reducing memory footprint. They also apply columnar compression schemes such as dictionary encoding and run-length encoding that makes them further better as compared to the caching of native Java/Scala objects in RDD.

User-defined functions

DataFrames also support **user-defined functions** (**UDFs**) that can be applied as inline functions without the complicated packaging and registration process. Once registered, they can also be used via the JDBC/ODBC interface by business intelligence tools. They also provide the flexibility to define UDFs on the entire table and then expose them as advance analytical functions to SQL users.

Here's the basic Scala code to show how DataFrames are constructed from JSON files:

```
val sparkCtx = new SparkContext(new SparkConf())
val sqlCtx = new SQLContext(sparkCtx)
//This will return the DataFrame which can be further queried
val dataFrame = sqlCtx.read.json("/home/ec2-user/softwares/company.
json")
```

DataFrames and SQL

At a high level, DataFrames provide a similar functionality as provided by SQL. Using Spark SQL and DataFrames, it is much easier to perform analysis as compared to relational queries (SQL). DataFrames provide a one-stop solution where users not only can code SQL queries, but also develop and leverage Scala, Java, or Python functions that pass DataFrames between them to build a logical plan and still benefit from optimizations across the whole plan when finally executed. Developers can use control structures like `if` statements and loops to structure their work.

The DataFrame API analyzes logical plans pretty early so that any errors such as missing column names are identified, while developers are coding. However, the actual query is still executed only when an output operation is invoked.

We will discuss the various examples of loading and processing (SQL or Scala code) data from varied data sources (Parquet, Hive, or JSON), but before that let's also understand the other components of Spark SQL.

The Catalyst optimizer

The Catalyst optimizer was specifically designed to optimize a SQL query or code generated by DataFrames for performing data analysis. It is based on functional programming constructs in Scala and supports both rule-based and cost-based optimization. The objective of Catalyst was first to ensure that new optimization techniques and features are added easily to Spark SQL and second, enable community developers to extend and add new data source specific rules to the optimizer, or add new data types without much of a problem. Both the objectives were easily met by leveraging Scala programming constructs. At a high level, the following are the different phases of Catalyst:

- Analysis
- Logical optimization
- Physical planning
- Code generation

Here's the high-level process flows of how all the preceding phases are connected to each other:

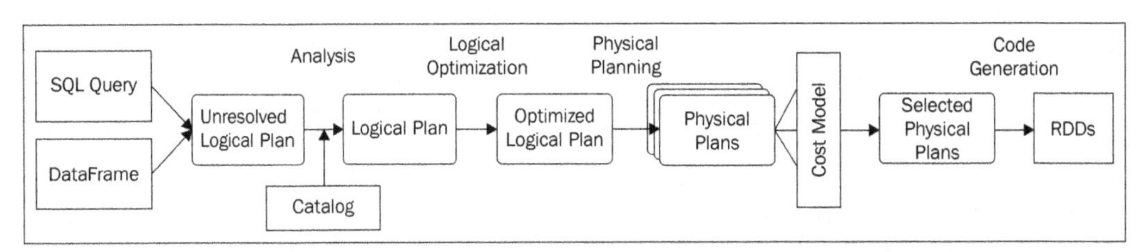

Source: `https://databricks.com/wp-content/uploads/2015/04/Screen-Shot-2015-04-12-at-8.41.26-AM-1024x235.png`

Let's briefly discuss each of these phases of Spark SQL:

- **Analysis**: In this phase, Spark SQL constructs the relationships which are either from AST (short for **Abstract Syntax Tree**) produced by SQL queries, or from DataFrame objects constructed using the Spark SQL API. This phase starts with the creation of unresolved logical plans that have missing relationships, for example, the SQL query `Select name from emp` does not tell whether this query is valid or not (valid column name or table name). It executes Catalyst's rules on the query to convert it into a logical plan. Here are a few examples of the Catalyst rule that are executed over unresolved logical plans:
    - Spark SQL maintains a catalog of all tables and their columns, so the very basic rule is to validate the relationships by looking into the catalog
    - Verifying the mapping of different column and operators applied
    - Validating and resolving subexpressions and the operators used to evaluate subexpressions along with their types
- **Logical optimization**: Once the logical plan is created, the very next step is the logical optimizations phase in which standard **rule based optimizations** are applied to the logical plan. This includes rules such as constant folding, predicate pushdown, projection pruning, null propagation, Boolean expression simplification, and many more. **Cost-based optimization** can also be performed by generating multiple plans using rules, and then computing their costs. In Scala, these kinds of optimizations are much easier to code and provide a richer functionality that is beyond simple pattern-matching. The best example is that the whole code for logical optimization is not more than 700 lines of code.
- **Physical planning**: The next step after logical planning is to generate one or more physical plans using physical operators that match the Spark execution engine. Then, it selects a physical plan using the cost model.

  The physical planner also performs rule-based physical optimizations, such as pipelining projections or filters into one Spark map operation. In addition, it can push operations from the logical plan into data sources that support predicate or projection pushdown.
- **Code generation**: The last and final phase of the whole process is generating byte/binary code that can be executed on all nodes. Spark is essentially all in-memory, which means it is CPU bound and hence Catalyst needs to be extra cautious while generating the final code. Considering all factors, Spark folks decided to leverage a special feature of the Scala language, **quasiquotes** (`http://docs.scala-lang.org/overviews/quasiquotes/intro.html`), to make code generation simpler and more efficient.

Refer to `http://people.csail.mit.edu/matei/papers/2015/sigmod_spark_sql.pdf` for more information about the architecture and components of Spark SQL

SQL and Hive contexts

Apart from DataFrames and Catalyst, Spark SQL exposes another component: `SQLContext`. `SQLContext` encapsulates all relational functionality in Spark and it is the entry point for accessing all Spark SQL functionalities. `SQLContext` is created from the existing `SparkContext`.

`HiveContext` provides a superset of the functionality provided by `SQLContext`. It is used to write queries using the HiveQL parser and read data from Hive tables.

We will soon discuss and use SQL/Hive contexts in various examples provided in subsequent sections. In this section, we discussed the various components and architecture of Spark SQL. Let's move forward and look upon various features of Spark SQL with appropriate examples.

Coding our first Spark SQL job

In this section, we will discuss the basics of writing/coding Spark SQL jobs in Scala and Java. Spark SQL exposes the rich DataFrame API (`http://spark.apache.org/docs/latest/api/scala/index.html#org.apache.spark.sql.DataFrame`) for loading and analyzing datasets in various forms. It not only provides operations for loading/analyzing data from structured formats such as Hive, Parquet, and RDBMS, but also provides flexibility to load data from semistructured formats such as JSON and CSV. In addition to the various explicit operations exposed by the DataFrame API, it also facilitates the execution of SQL queries against the data loaded in the Spark.

Let's move ahead and code our first Spark SQL job in Scala and then we will also look at the corresponding implementation in Java.

Coding a Spark SQL job in Scala

In this section, we will code and execute our first Spark SQL Job using Scala APIs.

It is our first Spark SQL job, so we will make it simple and use some sample data of company, departments, and employees in the JSON format. Consider the following code:

```
[
   {
      "Name":"DEPT_A",
      "No_Of_Emp":10,
      "No_Of_Supervisors":2
   },
   {
      "Name":"DEPT_B",
      "No_Of_Emp":12,
      "No_Of_Supervisors":2
   },
   {
      "Name":"DEPT_C",
      "No_Of_Emp":14,
      "No_Of_Supervisors":3
   }
]
```

We need to copy the preceding JSON data and save it at the same location where we saved our Chicago crime dataset and name it `company.json`.

Next, perform the following steps to process the same data using Scala APIs:

1. Open your `Spark-Examples` project and create a new package and Scala object named `chapter.eight.ScalaFirstSparkSQLJob`.
2. Edit `ScalaFirstSparkSQLJob` and add following code snippet just below the package declaration:

```
import org.apache.spark.sql._
import org.apache.spark._

object ScalaFirstSparkSQLJob {

  def main(args: Array[String]) {
      //Defining/ Creating SparkConf Object
      val conf = new SparkConf()
      //Setting Application/ Job Name
      conf.setAppName("First Spark SQL Job in Scala")
      // Define Spark Context which we will use to initialize our
SQL Context
      val sparkCtx = new SparkContext(conf)
      //Creating SQL Context
      val sqlCtx = new SQLContext(sparkCtx)
```

```
        //Defining path of the JSON file which contains the data in
JSON Format
        val jsonFile = "file:///home/ec2-user/softwares/crime-data/
company.json"

        //Utility method exposed by SQLContext for reading JSON file
        //and create dataFrame
        //Once DataFrame is created all the data names like "Name"
in the JSON file
        //will interpreted as Column Names and their data Types will
be
        //interpreted automatically based on their values
        val dataFrame = sqlCtx.read.json(jsonFile)

        //Defining a function which will execute operations
        //exposed by DataFrame API's
        executeDataFrameOperations(sqlCtx,dataFrame)
        //Defining a function which will execute SQL Queries using
        //DataFrame API's
        executeSQLQueries(sqlCtx,dataFrame)

    }

    /**
     * This function executes various operations exposed by
DataFrame API
     */
    def executeDataFrameOperations(sqlCtx:SQLContext,
dataFrame:DataFrame):Unit = {
        //Invoking various basic operations available with DataFrame
        println("Printing the Schema...")
        dataFrame.printSchema()
        //Printing Total Rows Loaded into DataFrames
        println("Total Rows - "+dataFrame.count())
        //Printing first Row of the DataFrame
        println("Printing All Rows in the Data Frame")
        println(dataFrame.collect().foreach { row => println(row) })
        //Sorting the records and then Printing all Rows again
        //Sorting is based on the DataType of the Column.
        //In our Case it is String, so it be natural order sorting
        println("Here is the Sorted Rows by 'No_Of_Supervisors' -
Descending")
        dataFrame.sort(dataFrame.col("No_Of_Supervisors").desc).
show(10)
```

```
    }

    /**
     * This function registers the DataFrame as SQL Table and
  execute SQL Queries
     */
    def executeSQLQueries(sqlCtx:SQLContext,
  dataFrame:DataFrame):Unit = {

      //The first step is to register the DataFrame as temporary
  table
      //And give it a name. In our Case "Company"
      dataFrame.registerTempTable("Company")
      println("Executing SQL Queries...")
      //Now Execute the SQL Queries and print the results
      //Calculating the total Count of Rows
      val dfCount = sqlCtx.sql("select count(1) from Company")
      println("Calculating total Rows in the Company Table...")
      dfCount.collect().foreach(println)

      //Printing the complete data in the Company table
      val df = sqlCtx.sql("select * from Company")
      println("Dumping the complete Data of Company Table...")
      dataFrame.collect().foreach(println)

      //Printing the complete data in the Company table sorted by
  Supervisors
      val dfSorted = sqlCtx.sql("select * from Company order by No_
  Of_Supervisors desc")
      println("Dumping the complete Data of Company Table, sorted by
  Supervisors - Descending...")
      dfSorted.collect().foreach(println)

    }}
```

The preceding piece of code loads and transforms the JSON data (`company.json`) and then executes a few operations using the DataFrame API and it also performs transformation using SQL queries.

3. Next, we will execute our `ScalaFirstSparkSQLJob` and see the results on the driver console. Assuming that your Spark cluster is up and running, you just need to use the same `spark-submit` utility to submit your job. This is the same as what we did in the *Coding Spark job in Scala* section in *Chapter 6, Getting Acquainted with Spark*. Our `spark-submit` command would look something like this:

```
$SPARK_HOME/bin/spark-submit --class chapter.eight.
ScalaFirstSparkSQLJob --master spark://ip-10-166-191-242:7077
spark-examples.jar
```

As soon as you execute the command, your job will start executing and will produce results similar to the following screenshot:

```
sumit@localhost $ $SPARK_HOME/bin/spark-submit --class chapter.eight.ScalaFirstSparkSQLJob --master spark://ip-10-231-73-237:7077 spark-examples.jar
15/11/19 02:20:03 WARN NativeCodeLoader: Unable to load native-hadoop library for your platform... using builtin-java classes where applicable
15/11/19 02:20:04 WARN MetricsSystem: Using default name DAGScheduler for source because spark.app.id is not set.
Printing the Schema...
root
 |-- Name: string (nullable = true)
 |-- No_Of_Emp: long (nullable = true)
 |-- No_Of_Supervisors: long (nullable = true)

Total Rows - 3
Printing All Rows in the Data Frame
[DEPT_A,10,2]
[DEPT_B,12,2]
[DEPT_C,14,3]
()
Here is the Sorted Rows by 'No_Of_Supervisors' - Descending
+------+---------+-----------------+
|  Name|No_Of_Emp|No_Of_Supervisors|
+------+---------+-----------------+
|DEPT_C|       14|                3|
|DEPT_A|       10|                2|
|DEPT_B|       12|                2|
+------+---------+-----------------+

Executing SQL Queries...
Calcualting total Rows in the Company Table...
[3]
Dumping the complete Data of Company Table...
[DEPT_A,10,2]
[DEPT_B,12,2]
[DEPT_C,14,3]
Dumping the complete Data of Company Table, sorted by Supervisors - Descending...
[DEPT_C,14,3]
[DEPT_A,10,2]
[DEPT_B,12,2]
```

The preceding screenshot shows the output of our first Spark SQL job on the driver console. Let's move towards the next section where we will code the same job using Spark Java APIs.

Coding a Spark SQL job in Java

In this section, we will discuss and write our first Spark SQL job using Spark SQL Java APIs.

Assuming that `company.json`, which we created in the previous section, still exists on your cluster, perform the following steps to process the same data using Scala APIs:

1. Open your `Spark-Examples` project and create a new package and Scala object named `chapter.eight.JavaFirstSparkSQLJob`.
2. Edit `JavaFirstSparkSQLJob` and add the following code snippet just below the package declaration:

   ```
   import org.apache.spark.*;
   import org.apache.spark.sql.*;
   import org.apache.spark.api.java.*;

   public class JavaFirstSparkSQLJob {
   ```

```
  public JavaFirstSparkSQLJob() {
    System.out.println("Creating Spark Configuration");
    // Create an Object of Spark Configuration
    SparkConf javaConf = new SparkConf();
    // Set the logical and user defined Name of this Application
    javaConf.setAppName("First Spark SQL Job in Java");
    System.out.println("Creating Spark Context");
    // Create a Spark Context and provide previously created
    // Object of SparkConf as an reference.
    JavaSparkContext javaCtx = new JavaSparkContext(javaConf);

    // Defining path of the JSON file which contains the data in
JSON Format
    String jsonFile = "file:///home/ec2-user/softwares/crime-data/
company.json";

    // Creating SQL Context
    SQLContext sqlContext = new SQLContext(javaCtx);
    // Utility method exposed by SQLContext for reading JSON file
    // and create dataFrame
    // Once DataFrame is created all the data names like "Name" in
the JSON
    // file will be interpreted as Column Names and their data
Types
    // will be interpreted automatically based on their values
    DataFrame dataFrame = sqlContext.read().json(jsonFile);
    // Defining a function which will execute operations
    // exposed by DataFrame API's
    executeDataFrameOperations(sqlContext, dataFrame);
    // Defining a function which will execute SQL Queries using
    // DataFrame API's
    executeSQLQueries(sqlContext, dataFrame);

    //Closing Context for clean exit
    javaCtx.close();

  }

  /**
   * This function executes various operations exposed by
DataFrame API
   */
  public void executeDataFrameOperations(SQLContext sqlCtx,
      DataFrame dataFrame) {
```

```
    // Invoking various basic operations available with DataFrame
    System.out.println("Printing the Schema...");
    dataFrame.printSchema();
    // Printing Total Rows Loaded into DataFrames
    System.out.println("Total Rows - " + dataFrame.count());
    // Printing first Row of the DataFrame
    System.out.println("Printing All Rows in the Data Frame");
    dataFrame.show();
    // Sorting the records and then Printing all Rows again
    // Sorting is based on the DataType of the Column.
    // In our Case it is String, so it be natural order sorting
    System.out.println("Here is the Sorted Rows by 'No_Of_
Supervisors' - Descending");
    DataFrame sortedDF = dataFrame.sort(dataFrame.col("No_Of_
Supervisors").desc());
    sortedDF.show();

  }

  /**
   * This function registers the DataFrame as SQL Table and
execute SQL
   * Queries
   */
  public void executeSQLQueries(SQLContext sqlCtx, DataFrame
dataFrame) {

    // The first step is to register the DataFrame as temporary
table
    // And give it a name. In our Case "Company"
    dataFrame.registerTempTable("Company");
    System.out.println("Executing SQL Queries...");
    // Now Execute the SQL Queries and print the results
    // Calculating the total Count of Rows
    DataFrame dfCount = sqlCtx
        .sql("select count(1) from Company");
    System.out.println("Calculating total Rows in the Company
Table...");
    dfCount.show();
```

```
    // Printing the complete data in the Company table
    DataFrame df = sqlCtx.sql("select * from Company");
    System.out.println("Dumping the complete Data of Company
Table...");
    df.show();
    // Printing the complete data in the Company table sorted by
Supervisors
    DataFrame dfSorted = sqlCtx
        .sql("select * from Company order by No_Of_Supervisors
desc");
    System.out
        .println("Dumping the complete Data of Company Table,
sorted by Supervisors - Descending...");
    dfSorted.show();

  }
  public static void main(String[] args)
{new JavaFirstSparkSQLJob();}}
```

The preceding piece of code performs a similar function to our Scala job but it leverages Java APIs.

3. Next, we will execute `JavaFirstSparkSQLJob` and see the results on the driver console. Assuming that your Spark cluster is up and running, you just need to use the same `spark-submit` utility to submit your job. This is the same as what we did in the *Coding Spark job in Scala* section in *Chapter 6, Getting Acquainted with Spark*. Your `spark-submit` command would look something like this:

   ```
   $SPARK_HOME/bin/spark-submit --class chapter.eight.
   JavaFirstSparkSQLJob --master spark://ip-10-166-191-242:7077
   spark-examples.jar
   ```

   As soon as you execute the preceding command, your job will start executing and the results will be similar to what we saw for our Scala job.

Finally, we are done with coding and executing our first Spark SQL job using Scala and Java APIs. In the next sections, we will discuss the nitty-gritty of Spark SQL and its various features.

To avoid verbosity, going forward, we will discuss the implementations using Scala APIs.

Converting RDDs to DataFrames

In this section, we will discuss the strategies exposed by Spark SQL for transforming existing RDDs into DataFrames.

In today's enterprise world, data analysis requires the usage of more than one tool or technology. There could be scenarios where we want the Spark batch to initially load and process the data for a few insights and at the same we also want Spark SQL to process the same data to get the rest of the insights. In these kinds of scenarios, data would be loaded only once, either by a Spark batch or Spark SQL, and then it will be further processed by other Spark extensions. We need to consider that loading the data twice will be a waste of memory and time.

In order to solve this problem, Spark SQL (DataFrames) provides the interoperability with Spark batches (RDD). In short, Spark SQL provides APIs that can convert an RDD into a DataFrame and it can be used for data analysis.

Spark SQL provides two different processes for converting an existing RDD into a DataFrame:

- **Automated process**: Using the reflection mechanism, infers the types and objects and also produces concise code. It works well only when we know the type of schema at the time of writing Spark applications.
- **Manual process**: Schema is manually defined and mapped and then data is loaded in Spark.

Let's move ahead and understand each of the processes.

Automated process

Scala APIs, provided by Spark SQL, support the automated process of converting RDD into DataFrames. The objective is to define the Scala case class and then map the columns of the case class to the columns of the RDD. In order to understand it better, let's move ahead and use our crime dataset where data is in form of CSV file (comma separated). We will load this data as an RDD, then convert the same into DataFrames, and finally perform some analysis.

Perform the following steps for converting RDD to DataFrames using the automated process:

1. Open and edit the `Spark-Examples` project and add a new Scala object `ScalaRDDToDFDynamicSchema` within the package `chapter.eight`.

2. Next, edit `ScalaRDDToDFDynamicSchema.scala` and add the following piece of code:

```
package chapter.eight
import org.apache.spark.sql._
import org.apache.spark._

object ScalaRDDToDFDynamicSchema {

  def main(args: Array[String]) {
    //Defining/ Creating SparkConf Object
    val conf = new SparkConf()
    //Setting Application/ Job Name
    conf.setAppName("Spark SQL - RDD To DataFrame - Dynamic
Schema")
    // Define Spark Context which we will use to initialize our
SQL Context
    val sparkCtx = new SparkContext(conf)
    //Creating SQL Context
    val sqlCtx = new SQLContext(sparkCtx)

    //Define path of our Crime Data File which needs to be
processed
    val crimeData = "file:///home/ec2-user/softwares/crime-data/
Crimes_-Aug-2015.csv";

    //this is used to implicitly convert an RDD to a DataFrame.
    import sqlCtx.implicits._

    //Load the data from Text File
    val rawCrimeRDD = sparkCtx.textFile(crimeData)
    //As data is in CSV format so first step is to Split it
    val splitCrimeRDD = rawCrimeRDD.map(_.split(","))
    //Next Map the Split RDD to the Crime Object
    val crimeRDD = splitCrimeRDD.map(c => Crime(c(0),
c(1),c(2),c(3),c(4),c(5),c(6)))
    //Invoking Implicit function to create DataFrame from RDD
    val crimeDF = crimeRDD.toDF()

    //Invoking various DataFrame Functions
    println("Printing the Schema...")
    crimeDF.printSchema()
    //Printing Total Rows Loaded into DataFrames
    println("Total Rows - "+crimeDF.count())
    //Printing first 5 Rows of the DataFrame
    println("Here is the First 5 Row")
    crimeDF.show(5)
    //Sorting the records and then Printing First 5 Rows
    //Sorting is based on the DataType of the Column.
```

```
        //In our Case it is String, so it be natural order sorting.
        //Last parameter of sort() shows the complete data on Console
        //(It does not Truncate anything while printing the results)
        println("Here is the First 5 Sorted Rows by 'Primary Type'")
        crimeDF.sort("primaryType").show(5,false)

    }

    // Define the schema using a case class.
    // Note: Case classes in Scala 2.10 can support only up to 22 
  fields. To work around this limit,
    // you can use custom classes that implement the Product 
  interface.
    //ID,Case Number,Date,Block,IUCR,Primary Type,Description
    case class Crime(id: String, caseNumber:String, date:String, 
  block:String, IUCR:String, primaryType:String, desc:String)
  }
```

3. Once the Scala class is defined, the next step is to use the steps defined in the *Coding Spark job in Scala* section in *Chapter 6, Getting Acquainted with Spark*, and execute our job on a Spark cluster using the `spark-submit` command which looks something like this:

   `$SPARK_HOME/bin/spark-submit --class chapter.eight.ScalaRDDToDFDynamicSchema --master spark://ip-10-166-191-242:7077 spark-examples.jar`

As soon as we submit our job, it will be accepted and Spark executors will start processing it and produce the results, which would be similar to the following screenshot:

```
sumit@localhost $ $SPARK_HOME/bin/spark-submit --class chapter.eightScalaRDDToDFDynamicSchema --master spark://ip-10-144-123-219:7077 spark-examples.jar
15/11/19 10:18:11 WARN NativeCodeLoader: Unable to load native-hadoop library for your platform... using builtin-java classes where applicable
15/11/19 10:18:13 WARN MetricsSystem: Using default name DAGScheduler for source because spark.app.id is not set.
Printing the Schema...
root
 |-- id: string (nullable = true)
 |-- caseNumber: string (nullable = true)
 |-- date: string (nullable = true)
 |-- block: string (nullable = true)
 |-- IUCR: string (nullable = true)
 |-- primaryType: string (nullable = true)
 |-- desc: string (nullable = true)

Total Rows - 23227
Here is the First 5 Row
+--------+----------+--------------------+--------------------+----+---------------+--------------------+
|      id|caseNumber|                date|               block|IUCR|    primaryType|                desc|
+--------+----------+--------------------+--------------------+----+---------------+--------------------+
|      ID|Case Number|                Date|               Block|IUCR|   Primary Type|         Description|
|10217189|  HY404004|08/31/2015 12:00:...|  051XX W ADDISON ST|1320|CRIMINAL DAMAGE|          TO VEHICLE|
|10217252|  HY403984|08/31/2015 12:00:...|083XX S MARYLAND AVE|041A|        BATTERY|AGGRAVATED: HANDGUN|
|10217276|  HY403985|08/31/2015 12:00:...|093XX S LAFAYETTE...|031A|        ROBBERY|     ARMED: HANDGUN|
|10218505|  HY404795|08/31/2015 12:00:...|078XX S CONSTANCE...|1310|CRIMINAL DAMAGE|         TO PROPERTY|
+--------+----------+--------------------+--------------------+----+---------------+--------------------+
only showing top 5 rows

Here is the First 5 Sorted Rows by 'Primary Type'
+--------+----------+----------------------+----------------------+----+-----------+----------+
|id      |caseNumber|date                  |block                 |IUCR|primaryType|desc      |
+--------+----------+----------------------+----------------------+----+-----------+----------+
|10198336|HY385970  |08/15/2015 06:00:00 PM|033XX W 13TH ST       |1020|ARSON      |BY FIRE   |
|10194317|HY381569  |08/14/2015 12:01:00 AM|077XX S CORNELL AVE   |1025|ARSON      |AGGRAVATED|
|10195765|HY382947  |08/15/2015 12:20:00 AM|018XX S KOMENSKY AVE  |1020|ARSON      |BY FIRE   |
|10194917|HY381879  |08/14/2015 09:20:00 AM|002XX S COLUMBUS DR   |1020|ARSON      |BY FIRE   |
|10194330|HY381645  |08/14/2015 02:40:00 AM|005XX N CENTRAL PARK AVE|1020|ARSON      |BY FIRE   |
+--------+----------+----------------------+----------------------+----+-----------+----------+
only showing top 5 rows
```

The preceding screenshot shows the result of the Spark SQL job that loads the data into an RDD, converts the RDD into Spark SQL DataFrame, and then finally performs the data analysis.

The manual process

The manual process is leveraged wherever we cannot define the case classes and we need to infer the structure of the data at the runtime itself. For example, consider the following scenarios:

- The data and the structure is encoded, so we cannot infer the structure and data type of columns/records unless we decode it.
- PII or SPI data (`https://en.wikipedia.org/wiki/Personally_identifiable_information`) is mostly masked and based on the privileges of the users we may or may not show the real values, so the structure and schema needs to be applied only after we know the identity of the user who is requesting the data.

The manual process of defining schema and converting it into DataFrame will involve the following steps:

1. Create an RDD of `Row` objects (`http://spark.apache.org/docs/latest/api/scala/index.html#org.apache.spark.sql.Row`)
2. Define the schema using `StructType` (`http://spark.apache.org/docs/latest/api/scala/index.html#org.apache.spark.sql.types.StructType`)
3. Finally, apply `StructType` to RDD of `Row` objects.

Let's perform the preceding steps and convert our crime data into DataFrames using the manual process. Perform the following steps to convert RDD to DataFrames using the manual process:

1. Open and edit the `Spark-Examples` project and add a new Scala object `ScalaRDDToDFManualSchema.scala`.
2. Next, edit `ScalaRDDToDFManualSchema.scala` and add following code:

```
package chapter.eight

import org.apache.spark.sql._
import org.apache.spark.sql.types._
import org.apache.spark._

object ScalaRDDToDFManualSchema {

  def main(args: Array[String]) {
    //Defining/ Creating SparkConf Object
    val conf = new SparkConf()
    //Setting Application/ Job Name
```

```
    conf.setAppName("Spark SQL - RDD To DataFrame - Dynamic 
Schema")
    // Define Spark Context which we will use to initialize our 
SQL Context
    val sparkCtx = new SparkContext(conf)
    //Creating SQL Context
    val sqlCtx = new SQLContext(sparkCtx)

    //Define path of our Crime Data File which needs to be 
processed
    val crimeDataFile = "file:///home/ec2-user/softwares/crime-
data/Crimes_-Aug-2015.csv";
    // Create an RDD
    val crimeData = sparkCtx.textFile(crimeDataFile)

    //Assuming the Schema needs to be created from the String of 
Columns
    val schema = "ID,CaseNumber,Date,Block,IUCR,PrimaryType,Descri
ption"

    val colArray = schema.split(",")

    val structure = StructType(List(
          StructField(colArray(0), StringType, true),
          StructField(colArray(1), StringType, true),
          StructField(colArray(2), StringType, true),
          StructField(colArray(3), StringType, true),
          StructField(colArray(4), StringType, true),
          StructField(colArray(5), StringType, true),
          StructField(colArray(6), StringType, true)
                ))


    //Convert records of the RDD (Crime Records) to Rows.
    val crimeRowRDD = crimeData.map(_.split(",")).map(p => 
Row(p(0), p(1), p(2), p(3), p(4), p(5), p(6)))

    //Apply the schema to the RDD.
    val crimeDF = sqlCtx.createDataFrame(crimeRowRDD, structure)

    //Invoking various DataFrame Functions
    println("Printing the Schema...")
    crimeDF.printSchema()
    //Printing Total Rows Loaded into DataFrames
    println("Total Rows - "+crimeDF.count())
```

```
        //Printing first 5 Rows of the DataFrame
        println("Here is the First 5 Row")
        crimeDF.show(5)
        //Sorting the records and then Printing First 5 Rows
        //Sorting is based on the DataType of the Column.
        //In our Case it is String, so it be natural order sorting
        println("Here is the First 5 Sorted Rows by 'PrimaryType'")
        crimeDF.sort("PrimaryType").show(5,false)

    }
}
```

And we are done! The final step is to execute the preceding code using the same steps we performed in previous sections using the `spark-submit` command and analyze the results, which would again be similar to the results we saw after executing `ScalaRDDToDFDynamicSchema`.

We need to use a Spark SQL extension (`https://github.com/databricks/spark-csv`) for directly loading CSV formats using `SQLContext`.

Let's go to the next section where we will talk about various other data sources and features supported by Spark SQL.

Working with Parquet

In this section, we will discuss and talk about various operations provided by Spark SQL for working with Parquet data formats with appropriate examples.

Parquet is one of popular columnar data storage format for storing the structured data. Parquet leverages the *record shredding and assembly algorithm* (`http://tinyurl.com/p8kaawg`) as described in the Dremel paper (`http://research.google.com/pubs/pub36632.html`). Parquet supports efficient compression and encoding schemes which is better than just simple flattening of structured tables. Refer to `https://parquet.apache.org/` for more information on the Parquet data format.

The DataFrame API of Spark SQL provides convenience operations for writing and reading data in the Parquet format. We can persist Parquet tables as temporary tables within Spark SQL and perform all other operations provided by the DataFrame API for data manipulation or analysis.

Let's see the example for writing/reading Parquet data formats and then we will also see some advanced features provided by the DataFrame API, specifically for working with Parquet formats.

Perform the following steps for reading/writing our Chicago crime data in the Parquet format:

1. Open your `Spark-Examples` project and create a new package and Scala object named `chapter.eight.ScalaRDDToParquet.scala`.
2. Edit `ScalaRDDToParquet.scala` and add following code snippet just below the package declaration:

```
import org.apache.spark.sql._
import org.apache.spark._
import org.apache.spark.sql.hive._

/**
 * Reading and Writing Parquet Formats using SQLContext and
HiveContext
 */
object ScalaRDDToParquet {

  /**
   * Main Method
   */
  def main(args:Array[String]){

    //Defining/ Creating SparkConf Object
    val conf = new SparkConf()
    //Setting Application/ Job Name
    conf.setAppName("Spark SQL - RDD To Parquet")
    // Define Spark Context which we will use to initialize our
SQL Context
    val sparkCtx = new SparkContext(conf)
    //Works with Parquet using SQLContext
    parquetWithSQLCtx(sparkCtx)

  }
case class Crime(id: String, caseNumber:String, date:String,
block:String, IUCR:String, primaryType:String, desc:String)
}
```

The preceding code snippet defines the `main` method that creates `SparkContext` and invokes a method named `parquetWithSQLCtx(sparkCtx)`. This new method will contain the logic for writing and reading Parquet formats using `SQLContext`. We also define a case class named `Crime` for dynamically converting RDDs to DataFrames. Refer to the *Converting RDD to DataFrames* section for the dynamic conversion of RDD to DataFrames.

3. Continue to edit `ScalaRDDToParquet`. Just before the closing braces of the Scala object, add a new function named `def parquetWithSQLCtx(sparkCtx :SparkContext)` and add the following code in this new function:

```
def parquetWithSQLCtx(sparkCtx:SparkContext){
    //Creating SQL Context
    val sqlCtx = new SQLContext(sparkCtx)

    //Define path of our Crime Data File which needs to be
processed
    val crimeData = "file:///home/ec2-user/softwares/crime-data/
Crimes_-Aug-2015.csv";
    //this is used to implicitly convert an RDD to a DataFrame.
    import sqlCtx.implicits._
    //Load the data from Text File
    val rawCrimeRDD = sparkCtx.textFile(crimeData)
    //As data is in CSV format so first step is to Split it
    val splitCrimeRDD = rawCrimeRDD.map(_.split(","))
    //Next Map the Split RDD to the Crime Object
    val crimeRDD = splitCrimeRDD.map(c => Crime(c(0),
c(1),c(2),c(3),c(4),c(5),c(6)))
    //Invoking Implicit function to create DataFrame from RDD
    val crimeDF = crimeRDD.toDF()

    //Persisting Chicago Crime Data in the Spark SQL Memory by
name of "ChicagoCrime.parquet"
    //In this below operation we are also using "mode" provides
the instruction
    //to Overwrite the data in case it already exist by that name
    crimeDF.write.mode("overwrite").parquet("ChicagoCrime.
parquet")
    //Now Read and print the count of Rows and Structure of
Parquet tables
    val parquetDataFrame = sqlCtx.read.parquet("ChicagoCrime.
parquet")
    println("Count of Rows in Parquet Table = "+parquetDataFrame.
count())
    parquetDataFrame.printSchema()
  }
```

The preceding piece of code first loads the crime data, convert it into a DataFrame and then use utility functions provided by the DataFrame API to write and read the Parquet formats.

Leaving all aside, we need to focus on the following two lines that do all the magic:

```
crimeDF.write.mode("overwrite").parquet("ChicagoCrime.parquet")
val parquetDataFrame = sqlCtx.read.parquet("ChicagoCrime.parquet")
```

The first line writes the DataFrame in the Parquet format in Spark SQL memory and the latter one reads the same data. We have used `mode` in the first statement, which is a utility operation that tells the Spark framework how to deal with the already existing data. It provides the following options:

- `error`: This is the default mode. In this mode, if data already exists, then Spark throws an exception and exits.
- `overwrite`: Replace the existing data/table with the new data.
- `append`: Append the new data to the already existing data in table/path.
- `ignore`: In case data already exists, then do not do anything. Neither save the new data nor modify the existing data. It is an idempotent operation that does not produce any results if data already exists at the specified path/table.

The preceding two magical statements can also be written as follows:

```
crimeDF.write.format("parquet").mode("overwrite").
save("ChicagoCrime.parquet")
val parquetDataFrame = sqlCtx.read.format("parquet").
load("ChicagoCrime.parquet")
```

Spark SQL also supports ORC formats (`http://tinyurl.com/oe3jh45`). ORC formats can be used in a similar fashion as we have used Parquet. In short just replace `parquet` with `orc` and things would work.

4. The last and final step is to execute our job using `spark-submit`, which would produce results similar to the following screenshot:

```
sumit@localhost $ $SPARK_HOME/bin/spark-submit --class chaptereight.ScalaRDDToParquet --master spark://ip-10-81-210-35:7077 spark-examples.jar
15/11/22 01:06:39 WARN NativeCodeLoader: Unable to load native-hadoop library for your platform... using builtin-java classes where applicable
15/11/22 01:06:41 WARN MetricsSystem: Using default name DAGScheduler for source because spark.app.id is not set.
SLF4J: Failed to load class "org.slf4j.impl.StaticLoggerBinder".
SLF4J: Defaulting to no-operation (NOP) logger implementation
SLF4J: See http://www.slf4j.org/codes.html#StaticLoggerBinder for further details.
Count of Rows in Parquet Table = 23227
root
 |-- id: string (nullable = true)
 |-- caseNumber: string (nullable = true)
 |-- date: string (nullable = true)
 |-- block: string (nullable = true)
 |-- IUCR: string (nullable = true)
 |-- primaryType: string (nullable = true)
 |-- desc: string (nullable = true)
```

The preceding screenshot shows the output of the Spark SQL job on the driver console.

Persisting Parquet data in HDFS

In today's modern enterprises, architects and developers are trying to develop centralized systems that would act as a single source of truth for all departments or use cases requesting for data. Now, Parquet is an efficient format and enterprises are focused on developing a system that can store data into Parquet formats that will be available to the all other users/departments within the organization. Spark does not have its own storage, but its integration with HDFS can help in achieving the objective of enterprises.

Spark SQL makes it much easier by directly writing and reading Parquet data formats from persistent storage area such as HDFS. The DataFrame API exposes utility functions/operations that help to automatically store the data in HDFS in Parquet format. Let's move ahead and write/read our Chicago crime data in HDFS.

Perform the following steps to develop a Spark job for writing/reading Parquet data from HDFS:

1. Browse `http://<HOST-NAME>:50070` and ensure that your Hadoop and HDFS is up and running. If the URL does not show up in the NameNode home page, then follow the steps defined in the *Programming Spark transformation and actions* section in *Chapter 7, Programming with RDDs*, to configure Hadoop and HDFS.
2. Once your Hadoop and HDFS is up and running, edit your `Spark-Examples` projects, add a new operation named `def parquetWithHiveCtx(sparkCtx :SparkContext)` within the existing Scala object `ScalaRDDToParquet`, and invoke the same from the `main` method.
3. Next, write the code in `parquetWithHiveCtx(sparkCtx:SparkContext)` to load the crime data and convert it into DataFrame from RDD. Leverage the same code which we wrote in the previous examples with a small change. Instead of creating `SQLContext`, we will create an instance of `org.apache.spark.sql.hive.HiveContext`. `HiveContext` provides all the functionality of `SQLContext` and at the same time it also provides the features to persist the DataFrames in HDFS, which is totally hidden and abstracted from the developers. Developers just need to change the type of context to `HiveContext` and the data would be persisted in HDFS.
4. Next, we will add the following piece of code just after we have converted our RDD to DataFrame:

```
    //Persisting Chicago Crime Data in the HDFS by name of
"ChicagoCrimeParquet" as a Table
    //We are also using "mode" which provides the instruction
    //to "Overwrite" the data in case it already exist by that
name
```

```
    crimeDF.write.mode("overwrite").format("parquet").saveAsTable(
"ChicagoCrimeParquet")
    //Persisting Chicago Crime Data in the HDFS by name of
"ChicagoCrime.parquet" in a
    //path/ directory that already exists on HDFS.
    crimeDF.write.mode("overwrite").format("parquet").save("/
spark/sql/hiveTables/parquet/")

    //Read and print the Parquet tables from the HDFS
    val parquetDFTable = hiveCtx.read.format("parquet").
table("ChicagoCrimeParquet")
    println("Count of Rows in Parquet Table = "+parquetDFTable.
count())
    println("Printing Schema of Parquet Table")
    parquetDFTable.printSchema()

    //Read the Parquet data from the Specified path on HDFS
    val parquetDFPath = hiveCtx.read.format("parquet").load("/
spark/sql/hiveTables/parquet/")
    println("Count of Rows in Parquet Table, Loaded from HDFS Path
= "+parquetDFPath.count())
    println("Printing Schema of Parquet Table, Loaded from HDFS
Path")
    parquetDFPath.printSchema()
```

The preceding piece of code persists our Chicago crime data in HDFS in the form of a table and at the same time it also persists the same data to a HDFS directory (`/spark/sql/hiveTables/parquet/`).

5. Next, we need to create the same directory structure in the HDFS as we have specified in our job. Execute the following commands on your Linux console:

```
$HADOOP_HOME/bin/hdfs dfs -mkdir /spark
$HADOOP_HOME/bin/hdfs dfs -mkdir /spark/sql
$HADOOP_HOME/bin/hdfs dfs -mkdir /spark/sql/hiveTables
$HADOOP_HOME/bin/hdfs dfs -mkdir /spark/sql/hiveTables/parquet
```

6. The last and the final step would be to execute the job using the `spark-submit` command. If there are no errors on the driver console, then your data is persisted in HDFS and can be browsed from the Hadoop UI itself:

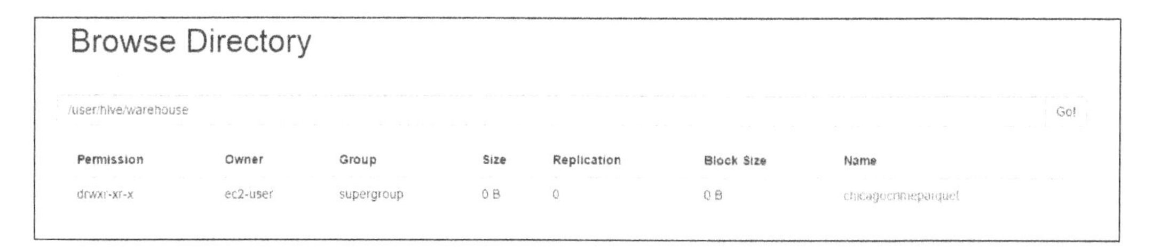

The preceding screenshot shows the Parquet table created by our Spark job in HDFS.

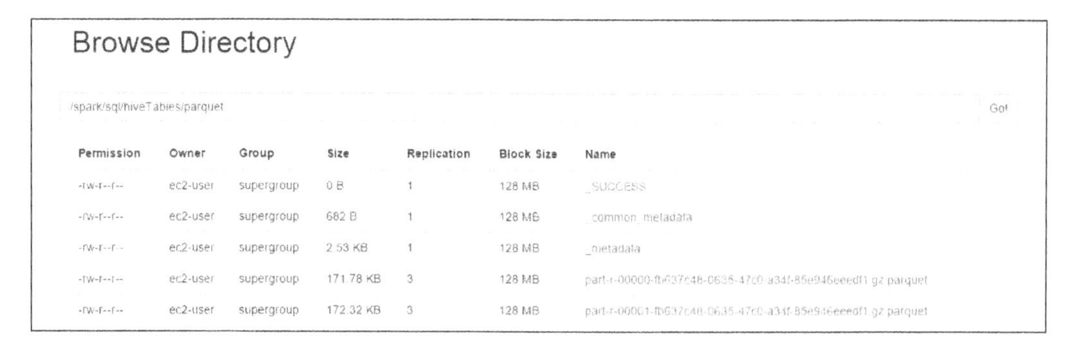

The preceding screenshot shows the Parquet data files created by our Spark job in HDFS at the location specified in our job.

Partitioning and schema evolution or merging

Spark SQL also supports data partitioning and schema merging, which is transparent to the users/developers and not much effort or code needs to be developed to work with both features. Let us briefly talk about both the concepts and how they are being handled with Spark SQL.

Partitioning

Partitioning is a common optimization technique in databases (`https://en.wikipedia.org/wiki/Partition_(database)`). In Hive, the data of the partitioned tables are stored in different directories within HDFS and to load all partitions of the table we just need to provide the base location in HDFS where we have stored our Parquet tables. Our Spark SQL will automatically discover the partitions associated with the table and will load it into the Spark memory. The parameter that enables the automatic discovery of partition is `spark.sql.sources.partitionColumnTypeInference.enabled`. It is enabled by default, so users/developers can work seamlessly without any changes to the code.

Schema evolution/merging

Data in enterprises is never static, it keeps on evolving and hence new parameters, columns, or structures are formed based on the data received from the outside world. Change in the structure of data is inevitable, but it is difficult to keep creating new schemas and loading the same data to these new schemas each time there is a change in the structure. **ProtocolBuffer** (`https://developers.google.com/protocol-buffers/?hl=en`), **Avro** (`https://avro.apache.org/`), **Thrift** (`https://thrift.apache.org/`), and Parquet are a few such data formats that support schema evolution and merging. Spark SQL extends the same concept and provides the implementation for schema merging with Parquet data formats. Again, the complete implementation is abstracted from users/developers and it can be enabled with minimum required code. Schema evolution/merging is an expensive operation, so we need to be careful when we use this feature and hence it is switched off by default.

Developers need to perform either of the following to enable schema evolution/merging:

- Configure the global SQL option `spark.sql.parquet.mergeSchema` to `true` in `SparkConf`.
- Configure `mergeSchema` to `true` while reading the Parquet data:

  ```
  hiveContext.read.option("mergeSchema", "true").parquet("<name of Table>")
  ```

In this section, we discussed the integration and support of Parquet data formats in Spark SQL with appropriate examples. Let's move on to the next section where we will discuss the integration of Spark SQL and Apache Hive.

Working with Hive tables

In this section, we will discuss the integration of Spark SQL with Hive tables. We will see the process of executing the Hive queries in Spark SQL, which will help us in creating and analyzing Hive tables in HDFS.

Spark SQL provides the flexibility of directly executing Hive queries with our Spark SQL codebase. The best part is that the Hive queries are executed on the Spark cluster and we just require the setup of HDFS for reading and storing the Hive tables. In other words, there is no need to set up a complete Hadoop cluster with services like ResourceManager or NodeManager. We just need services of HDFS, which are available as soon as we start NameNode and DataNode.

Perform the following steps for creating Hive tables for our Chicago crime data and at the same time also execute some analytical Hive queries:

1. Open and edit the `Spark-Examples` project and create a Scala object named `chapter.eight.ScalaSparkSQLToHive.scala`.
2. Next, edit `chapter.eight.ScalaSparkSQLToHive.scala` and add the following piece of code in it:

```
import org.apache.spark.sql._
import org.apache.spark._
import org.apache.spark.sql.hive.HiveContext

object ScalaSparkSQLToHive {

  def main(args:Array[String]){

    //Defining/ Creating SparkConf Object
    val conf = new SparkConf()
    //Setting Application/ Job Name
    conf.setAppName("Spark SQL - RDD To Hive")
    // Define Spark Context which we will use to initialize our
SQL Context
    val sparkCtx = new SparkContext(conf)
    //Creating Hive Context
    val hiveCtx = new HiveContext(sparkCtx)
    //Creating a Hive Tables
    println("Creating a new Hive Table -
ChicagoCrimeRecordsAug15")
    hiveCtx.sql("CREATE TABLE IF NOT EXISTS
ChicagoCrimeRecordsAug15(ID STRING,CaseNumber STRING, CrimeDate
STRING,Block STRING,IUCR STRING,PrimaryType STRING,Description
STRING,LocationDescription STRING,Arrest STRING,Domestic
STRING,Beat STRING,District STRING,Ward STRING,CommunityArea
STRING,FBICode STRING,XCoordinate STRING,YCoordinate STRING,Year
STRING,UpdatedOn STRING,Latitude STRING,Longitude STRING) ROW
FORMAT DELIMITED FIELDS TERMINATED BY ',' stored as textfile")
    println("Creating a new Hive Table - iucrCodes")
    hiveCtx.sql("CREATE TABLE IF NOT EXISTS iucrCodes(IUCR
STRING,PRIMARY_DESC STRING ,SECONDARY_DESC STRING,INDEXCODE
STRING) ROW FORMAT DELIMITED FIELDS TERMINATED BY ',' stored as
textfile")
    //Load the Data in Hive Table
    println("Loading Data in Hive Table -
ChicagoCrimeRecordsAug15")
    hiveCtx.sql("LOAD DATA LOCAL INPATH '/home/ec2-user/
softwares/crime-data/Crimes_-Aug-2015.csv' OVERWRITE INTO TABLE
ChicagoCrimeRecordsAug15")
    println("Loading Data in Hive Table - iucrCodes")
```

```
    hiveCtx.sql("LOAD DATA LOCAL INPATH '/home/ec2-user/softwares/
crime-data/IUCRCodes.csv' OVERWRITE INTO TABLE iucrCodes")
    //Quick Check on the number of records loaded in the Hive
Table
    println("Quick Check on the Number of records Loaded in
ChicagoCrimeRecordsAug15")
    hiveCtx.sql("select count(1) from ChicagoCrimeRecordsAug15").
show()
    println("Quick Check on the Number of records Loaded in
iucrCodes")
    hiveCtx.sql("select count(1) from iucrCodes").show()

    println("Now Performing Analysis")
    println("Top 5 Crimes in August Based on IUCR Codes")
    hiveCtx.sql("select B.PRIMARY_DESC, count(A.IUCR) as countIUCR
from ChicagoCrimeRecordsAug15 A,iucrCodes B where A.IUCR=B.IUCR
group by B.PRIMARY_DESC order by countIUCR desc").show(5)

    println("Count of Crimes which are of Type 'Domestic' and
someone is 'Arrested' by the Police")
    hiveCtx.sql("select B.PRIMARY_DESC, count(A.IUCR) as countIUCR
from ChicagoCrimeRecordsAug15 A,iucrCodes B where A.IUCR=B.IUCR
and A.domestic='true' and A.arrest='true' group by B.PRIMARY_DESC
order by countIUCR desc").show()

    println("Find Top 5 Community Areas where Highest number of
Crimes have been Committed in Aug-2015")
    hiveCtx.sql("select CommunityArea, count(CommunityArea) as cnt
from ChicagoCrimeRecordsAug15 group by CommunityArea order by cnt
desc").show(5)

  }
}
```

The preceding piece of code first creates the `HiveContext` and then leverages HiveQL (`https://cwiki.apache.org/confluence/display/Hive/LanguageManual`) for creating Hive tables, loading data in Hive tables, and finally performing various kinds of analysis.

We are done with the coding of our Spark job and now we have to perform the following configurations before we can execute our Spark SQL job:

1. Ensure your Hadoop HDFS is up and running by browsing to `http://<HOST_NAME>:50070/`. It should show up the Hadoop NameNode UI. If the URL does not show the NameNode home page, then follow the steps defined in the *Programming Spark transformation and actions* section in *Chapter 7, Programming with RDDs*, to configure Hadoop and HDFS.

2. The next step is to configure Apache Hive parameters in our Spark installation, which can be easily done by creating a `hive-site.xml` file and placing it in the `$SPARK_HOME/conf` folder. In case you already have Hive installed, then you just need to copy `hive-site.xml` from your Hive installation directory to the `$SPARK_HOME/conf` folder. In case you do not have it, then create a new file in `$SPARK_HOME/conf/hive-site.xml` and add the following content in it:

```
<configuration>

 <property>
    <name>javax.jdo.option.ConnectionURL</name>
    <value>jdbc:derby:;databaseName=/home/ec2-user/softwares/hive-
1.2.1/metastore/metastore_db;create=true</value>
    <description>JDBC connect string for a JDBC metastore</
description>
  </property>

</configuration>
```

   The preceding configuration is the bare minimum configuration required to execute Hive queries. The property defines the location of the Hive metastore DB, which will contain all the metadata about the Hive tables. We need to be careful with this property because if the metastore is deleted, then we cannot access any of the Hive tables.

3. We are done with all configurations and our last and final step is to export our Eclipse project and execute our Spark SQL job using `spark-submit`:

```
$SPARK_HOME/bin/spark-submit --class chapter.eight.
ScalaSparkSQLToHive --master spark://ip-10-184-194-147:7077 spark-
examples.jar
```

As soon as we execute the preceding command on our Linux console, Spark will accept our job, start executing it, and further the results of our analysis on the console. The result will be similar to the following screenshot:

```
Creating a new Hive Table - ChicagoCrimeRecordsAug15
Creating a new Hive Table - icurCodes
Loading Data in Hive Table - ChicagoCrimeRecordsAug15
Loading Data in Hive Table - iucrCodes
Quick Check on the Number of records Loaded in ChicagoCrimeRecordsAug15
+-----+
|  _c0|
+-----+
|23227|
+-----+

Quick Check on the Number of records Loaded in iucrCodes
+---+
|_c0|
+---+
|402|
+---+

Now Performing Analysis
Top 5 Crimes in August Based on IUCR Codes
+------------------+---------+
|      PRIMARY_DESC|countIUCR|
+------------------+---------+
|   CRIMINAL DAMAGE|     2599|
|         NARCOTICS|     1786|
|     OTHER OFFENSE|     1552|
|DECEPTIVE PRACTICE|      990|
| CRIMINAL TRESPASS|      564|
+------------------+---------+
only showing top 5 rows

Count of Crimes which are of Type 'Domestic' and someone is 'Arrested' by the Police
+--------------------+---------+
|        PRIMARY_DESC|countIUCR|
+--------------------+---------+
|       OTHER OFFENSE|       52|
|     CRIMINAL DAMAGE|       31|
|             ASSAULT|       10|
|OFFENSE INVOLVING...|        7|
|   CRIMINAL TRESPASS|        4|
|   WEAPONS VIOLATION|        1|
|          KIDNAPPING|        1|
|               ARSON|        1|
+--------------------+---------+

Find Top 5 Community Areas where Highest number of Crimes have been Comitted in Aug-2015
+-------------+----+
|CommunityArea| cnt|
+-------------+----+
|           25|1534|
|            8| 861|
|           43| 804|
|           32| 757|
|           29| 730|
+-------------+----+
only showing top 5 rows
```

The preceding screenshot shows the output of the Hive queries that we executed in our Spark SQL job on the driver console.

Spark also provides a utility (`$SPARK_HOME/bin/spark-sql`) that can be executed on our Linux console and further we can execute all our Hive queries and see the result on the same console. It helps in quick development of our Hive queries and we can also analyze the performance of our Hive queries by appending the `explain` keyword at the beginning of our Hive queries.

Refer to `https://cwiki.apache.org/confluence/display/Hive/LanguageManual` for more information on the syntax of HiveQL.

It is important to mention that *Hive on Spark* is not same as *Spark on Hive*. We discussed the scenarios where we execute the Hive queries using Spark SQL APIs, which is essentially referred as *Spark on Hive*. *Hive on Spark* is a separate discussion where we discuss adding Spark as a third execution engine (apart from MapReduce and Tez) for Apache Hive. Refer to following links for more information on *Hive on Spark*:

- `https://cwiki.apache.org/confluence/display/Hive/Hive+on+Spark%3A+Getting+Started`
- `https://cwiki.apache.org/confluence/display/Hive/Hive+on+Spark`

In this section, we discussed the integration of Spark SQL with Hive with appropriate examples. Let's move forward towards the next section where we will talk about performance tuning and best practices for Spark SQL.

Performance tuning and best practices

In this section, we will discuss various strategies for optimizing the performance of our Spark jobs. We will also discuss a few best practices with respect to Spark and Spark SQL.

Performance tuning is very subjective and a wide open statement. The very first step in performance tuning is to answer the question, "Do we really need to performance tune our jobs?" Now before we answer this question, we need to consider the following aspects:

- Are our jobs meeting SLAs specified by the business?

  If yes, then no need for performance tuning.

- What do we want to achieve and is it realistic?

  For example, expecting all Spark jobs (irrespective of data size or computations performed) to be completed in milliseconds is unrealistic.

Once we answer and define the need for performance tuning, only then should we move ahead and think of the strategy and start identifying areas where we can performance tune our Spark jobs.

Though there is no standard guide for performance tuning, there are a few common areas that we should consider in our strategy for performance tuning.

Partitioning and parallelism

Spark jobs load the data in the executor's memory that is further divided into various stages of execution to form the execution pipeline. Each byte in the dataset is represented by RDD and the execution pipeline is called as **Direct Acyclic Graph (DAG)**.

The dataset involved in each stage of the execution pipeline is further stored in the data blocks of equal sizes which is nothing but the **partitions** represented by the RDD.

> Refer to the *Programming Spark transformation and actions* section in *Chapter 7, Programming with RDDs*, for more information on partitions.

Lastly, for each partition we have exactly one task allocated/executed. So the parallelism of our job directly depends upon the number of partitions configured for our jobs, which can be controlled by defining `spark.default.parallelism` in `$SPARK_HOME/conf/spark-defaults.conf`. It needs to be configured appropriately so that our Spark job gets sufficient amount of parallelism. The general rule is to configure parallelism at least twice the number of total cores in the cluster but that is a bare minimum value, which gives us a starting point and it may vary for different workloads.

Unless specified by RDDs, Spark by default leverages `org.apache.spark.HashPartitioner` and the default value for the maximum number of partitions will be same as the number of partitions in the largest upstream RDD.

> Refer to `http://www.bigsynapse.com/spark-input-output` for more details on understanding partitioning and parallelism.

Serialization

The data processed by our Spark jobs needs to be moved/shuffled across the cluster nodes and for that the Spark framework serializes and deserializes the datasets. For example, serialization and deserialization is required for shuffling data between worker nodes or when persisting RDDs to disk. Any slowness either in the serialization or deserialization process will impact the overall slowness of our jobs.

By default, Spark utilizes the Java serialization mechanism that is compatible with most of the file formats but at the same time it is slow too.

We can switch to **Kryo serialization** (`https://github.com/EsotericSoftware/kryo`), which is very compact and faster than Java serialization. Though it does not support all serializable types, it is much faster than the Java serialization mechanism for all the compatible file formats. We can configure our jobs to use `KryoSerializer` by configuring `spark.serializer` in our `SparkConf` object:

```
conf.set("spark.serializer", "org.apache.spark.serializer.
KryoSerializer")
```

`KryoSerializer` by default stores the full class names with their associated objects in the Spark executor's memory which again is a waste of memory. To optimize it, it is advisable to register all required classes in advance with `KryoSerializer` so that all objects are mapped to class IDs and not with full class names. This can be done by defining explicit registrations of all required classes using `SparkConf.registerKryoClasses(...)`.

[Refer to the Kryo documentation at `https://github.com/EsotericSoftware/kryo` for more optimization parameters and compatible file formats.]

Caching

We can enable the caching of Spark SQL tables by invoking `sqlContext.cacheTable("tableName")` or `dataFrame.cache()`.

Spark SQL caches all tables in the columnar format which is optimized for scanning. Spark SQL automatically tunes and compresses the cached tables but nevertheless we can free up the memory by removing tables from the cache by invoking `sqlContext.uncacheTable("tableName")`. We can further tune our in-memory caching using the following two parameters:

- `spark.sql.inMemoryColumnarStorage.compressed`: This parameter is used to automatically compress the in-memory data using compression codec available with the Spark framework. The default value is `true`.
- `spark.sql.inMemoryColumnarStorage.batchSize`: The data in Spark SQL is cached in batches. The bigger the batches are, the better would be the performance, but bigger batches can also produce OOM instances, so we need to carefully analyze them before modifying the default value. The default value is 10,000.

Memory tuning

Spark is a JVM-based execution framework, so tuning the JVM for the right kind of workloads can also significantly improve the overall response time of our Spark jobs. To begin with, there are a couple of areas where we should focus:

- **Garbage collection**: As a first step, we need to uncover the current GC behavior and statistics and for that we should configure the following parameters in our `$SPARK_HOME/conf/spark-defaults.conf` file:

  ```
  spark.executor.extraJavaOptions = -XX:+PrintFlagsFinal
  -XX:+PrintReferenceGC -Xloggc:$JAVA_HOME/jvm.
  log -XX:+PrintGCDetails -XX:+PrintGCTimeStamps
  -XX:+PrintAdaptiveSizePolicy
  ```

  Now, our GC details are printed and available in `$JAVA_HOME/jvm.log`. We can further analyze the behavior of our JVM and then apply various optimization techniques.

Refer to `https://databricks.com/blog/2015/05/28/tuning-java-garbage-collection-for-spark-applications.html` for more details on various optimization techniques and tuning GC for Spark applications.

- **Object sizes**: Optimizing the size of the objects which are stored in the memory can also improve the overall performance of our application. Here are a few tips which can help us to improve the memory consumed by our objects:
  - Avoid wrapper objects or pointer based data structures or nested data structures with lot of small objects.
  - Use an array of objects or primitive types in our data structures. For example, we use the **fastutil** library (`http://fastutil.di.unimi.it/`) that provides faster and optimized collection classes.
  - Avoid strings or custom objects and instead use numbers as IDs for the objects.
- **Executor memory**: Another aspect would be to configure the memory of the Spark executors and also decide the appropriate size given in the memory to our Spark jobs for caching the RDDs.

Executor memory can be configured by defining the `spark.executor.memory` property in our `SparkConf` object itself or `$SPARK_HOME/conf/spark-defaults.conf`, or we can also define the same while submitting our jobs, as shown here. We can use this:

```
val conf = new SparkConf().set("spark.executor.memory", "1g")
```

Or this:

```
$SPARK_HOME/bin/spark-submit --executor-memory 1g .....
```

The Spark framework (by default) takes up to 60% of the executor's configured memory for caching RDDs, which leaves only 40% available memory for the execution of your Spark jobs. This may not be sufficient and if you see full GCs or slowness in your tasks or are experiencing *out of memory* situations, then you can reduce the cache size by configuring `spark.storage.memoryFraction` in your `SparkConf` object:

```
val conf = new SparkConf().set("spark.storage.memoryFraction","0.4")
```

This statement reduces the memory allocated for caching RDDs to 40%.

Finally, we can also think about using off heap caching solutions which do not use any JVM such as Tachyon (`http://tachyon-project.org/Running-Spark-on-Tachyon.html`).

For more details on performance aspects, refer to `https://spark.apache.org/docs/1.5.1/tuning.html` and `https://spark.apache.org/docs/1.5.1/configuration.html` for various available configuration parameters.

Spark and Spark extensions are still evolving and with each version we see considerable changes for achieving better performance. Each version of Spark might introduce new or deprecate various configuration parameters. Refer to `http://spark.apache.org/docs/1.5.1/sql-programming-guide.html#other-configuration-options` for other configuration options available for optimizing our Spark SQL jobs for Spark 1.5.0.

In this section, we talked about various aspects of tuning our Spark jobs. No matter how much we discuss, performance is always tricky and there will always be new discoveries which may require expert advice. So for expert advice, do post your queries on the Spark community page (`https://spark.apache.org/community.html`).

Summary

In this chapter, we discussed Spark SQL as a one-stop solution for processing large data using a mix of SQL-like queries and complex procedural algorithms in-memory, producing results in seconds/minutes but not hours.

We started with the various aspects of Spark SQL including its architecture and various components. We also talked about the complete process of writing Spark SQL jobs in Scala and at the same time, we also talked about various methodologies for converting Spark RDDs into DataFrames. Toward the middle of the chapter, we executed various examples of Spark SQL using different data formats such as Hive/Parquet along with important aspects such as schema evolution and schema merging. Finally at the end, we discussed the various aspects of performance tuning our Spark SQL code/queries.

In the next chapter, we will discuss capturing, processing, and analyzing streaming data using Spark Streaming.

9
Analysis of Streaming Data Using Spark Streaming

Enterprises in today's modern era consume data from a variety of data sources. The delivery of data from these sources is not only in different formats (CSV, text, Excel, and so on), but at the same time they may provide different mechanisms for data consumption. For example, some data sources may provide a particular location on the shared filesystem or some may provide data streams (`https://en.wikipedia.org/wiki/Data_stream`) or queuing-based systems.

Though there are tools and technologies to handle the complexities of data consumption, the real challenge is always to have a single solution/platform that can meet and solve all problems. Enterprises have been focusing on developing/deploying a single platform that is flexible and extendable to handle all complexities of data consumption/processing and produce it in a unified format.

Spark with its extensions is emerging as a one-stop solution to meet all the requirements of enterprises. Spark not only performs the consumption and processing of data for batch use cases, but it also provides the consumption and processing of data in near real-time from distributed data streams with the latency in seconds or milliseconds.

Spark Streaming is another extension that provides the consumption and processing of streaming data in near real-time. In this chapter, we will discuss Spark Streaming and its various features that provide the APIs for consuming and processing data in near real-time. We will also talk about its integration with Spark SQL for executing SQL queries in near real-time.

This chapter will cover the following topics:

- High-level architecture
- Coding our first Spark Streaming job

- Querying streaming data in real time
- Deployment and monitoring

High-level architecture

In this section, we will talk about the high-level architecture of Spark Streaming. We will also discuss the important components of Spark Streaming such as Discretized Streams, microbatching, and more. At the end, we will also write our first Spark streaming job for consuming and processing data in near real-time.

Spark Streaming is one of the powerful extensions provided by Spark for consuming and processing the events produced by various data sources in near real-time. Spark Streaming extended the Spark core architecture and produced a new architecture based on *microbatching*, where live/streaming data is received and collected from various data sources and further divided into a series of deterministic microbatches. The size of each microbatch is essentially governed by the batch duration provided by the user. In order to understand it better, let's take an example of an application receiving live/streaming data of 20 events per second where the batch duration provided by the user is 2 seconds. Now, our Spark Streaming will continuously consume the data as it arrives, but it will create microbatches of data received at the end of every 2 seconds (each batch will consists of 40 events) and submit this to the user-defined jobs for further processing. The most important decision here is to define the appropriate number for batch duration. Batch duration is nothing but the acceptable latency agreed upon by the business for a particular use case. It can be in seconds or in milliseconds. In our given example, it is 2 seconds. These microbatches are referred to as **DStreams** or Discretized Streams in Spark Streaming, which is nothing but a series of **Resilient Distributed Datasets** (**RDDs**).

Let's move to the next section where we will discuss the architecture and each of the components of Spark Streaming.

The components of Spark Streaming

In this section, we will deep dive into the architecture and various components of Spark Streaming. The high-level architecture for any Spark Streaming application will be similar to the following diagram:

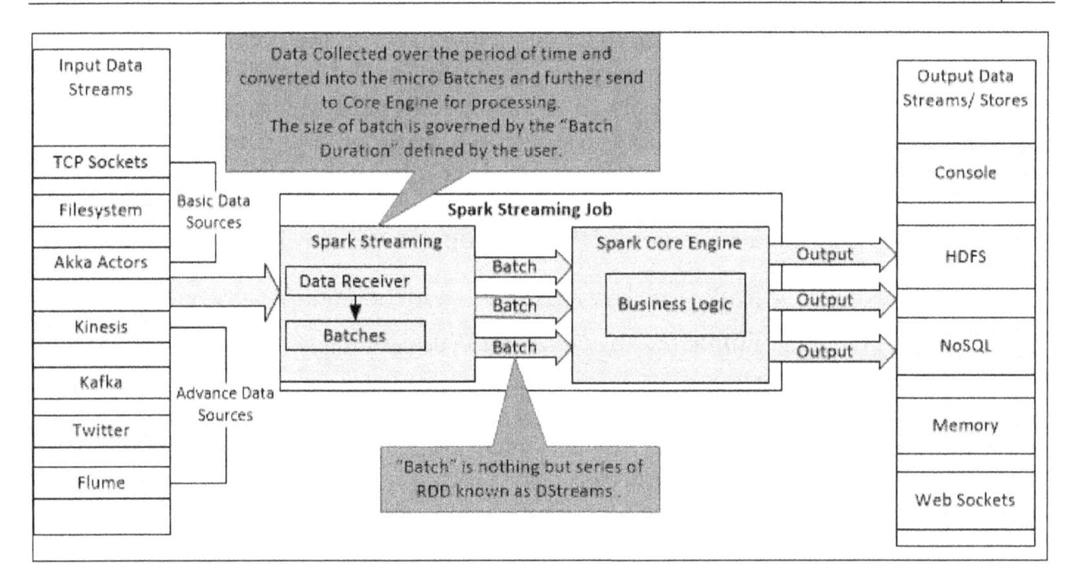

The preceding diagram shows the high-level architecture of any Spark job developed using Spark Streaming. It defines various architecture components such as input data streams, output data streams, and more. Each of the components has their own life cycle and plays a pivotal role in the overall architecture. Let's understand and discuss the role of each of the components:

- **Input data streams**: These are the input data sources; essentially the sources which are emitting the live/streaming data at a very high frequency (seconds or milliseconds). These sources can be a raw socket, filesystem, or even highly scalable queuing products such as Kafka. Spark Streaming jobs connect to input data sources using various available connecters. These connectors might be available with the Spark distribution itself, or we might have to download it separately and configure it in our Spark Streaming job. These input streams are also referred to as input DStreams. Based on the availability of connecters, input data sources are divided into following categories:
    - **Basic data sources**: The connectors and all of their dependencies for the basic data sources are packaged and shipped with the standard distribution of Spark. We do not have to download any other package to make it work.

- **Advance data sources**: The connectors and the dependencies required by these connectors are not available with the standard distribution of Spark. It is simply to avoid the complexity and the version conflicts. We need to download and configure the dependencies for these connectors separately or provide as dependencies in Maven scripts as instructed in the integration guidelines for each of the data sources, as mentioned here:
  - Kafka (`http://tinyurl.com/oew96sg`)
  - Flume (`http://tinyurl.com/o4ntmdz`)
  - Kinesis (`http://tinyurl.com/pdhtgu3`)

  Refer to `http://tinyurl.com/psmtpco` for the list of available advanced data sources.

The Spark community also provides various other connectors that can be directly downloaded from `http://spark-packages.org`. Check out `http://tinyurl.com/okrd34e` for developing custom connectors.

- **Spark Streaming job**: The Spark Streaming job is the custom job developed by the user for consumption and processing of the data feeds in near real-time. It has the following components:
  - **Data receiver**: This is a receiver that is dedicated for receiving/consuming the data produced by the data source. Every data source has its own receiver and cannot be generalized or be common across varied kinds of data sources.
  - **Batches**: This is the collection of messages that is received over the period of time by the receiver. Every batch has specific number of messages or data collected in a specific time interval (batch window) provided by the user. These microbatches are nothing but a series of RDDs known as DStreams.

- **DStreams**: This is a new stream processing model in which computations are structured as a series of stateless, deterministic batch computations at small time intervals. This new stream processing model enables powerful recovery mechanisms (similar to those in batch systems) and outperforms replication and upstream backup. It extends and leverages the concepts of resilient distributed datasets and creates a series of RDDs (of the same type) in one single DStream, which is processed and computed at a user-defined time interval (batch duration). DStreams can be created from input data streams that are connected to varied data sources like sockets, filesystems, and many more, or it can be created by applying high-level operations on other DStreams (similar to the RDDs). There can be multiple DStreams in the Spark Streaming context and each DStream contains a series of RDDs. Each RDD is the snapshot of the data received at a particular point in time from the receiver. Refer to `http://tinyurl.com/nnw4xvk` for more information on DStreams.
- **Streaming contexts**: Spark Streaming extends the Spark context and provides a new context, `StreamingContext`, for accessing all the functionality and features of Spark Streaming. It is the main entry of point and provides methods for initializing DStreams from various input data sources. Refer to `http://tinyurl.com/p5z68gn` for more information on `StreamingContext`.

- **Spark core engine**: This is the core engine that receives the input in the form of RDDs, further processes it as per the user-defined business logic, and finally sends it to the associated output data streams.
- **Output data streams**: The final output of each processed batch is sent to the output streams for further processing. These output data streams can be of varied types, ranging from a raw filesystem, web sockets, NoSQL, and many more.

In this section, we discussed the high-level architecture and various components of Spark Streaming. Let's move forward and also discuss about the various APIs and operations exposed by Spark Streaming and then we will quickly write our first Spark Streaming job.

The packaging structure of Spark Streaming

In this section, we will discuss about the various APIs and operations exposed by Spark Streaming.

Spark Streaming APIs

All Spark Streaming classes are packaged in the `org.apache.spark.streaming.*` package. Spark Streaming defines two core classes that also provide access to all Spark Streaming functionality: `StreamingContext.scala` and `DStream.scala`. Let's examine the functions and roles performed by these classes:

- `org.apache.spark.streaming.StreamingContext`: This is the entry point to Spark Streaming functionality. It defines methods to create the objects of `DStream.scala` and also starts and stops the Spark Streaming jobs.
- `org.apache.spark.streaming.dstream.DStream.scala`: DStream, or Discretized Streams, provides the basic abstraction of Spark Streaming. It provides the sequence of RDDs created from the live data or transforming of existing DStreams. This class defines the global operations that can be performed on all DStreams and a few specific operations that can be applied on specific types of DStreams.

Apart from these defined classes, Spark Streaming also defines various subpackages for exposing functionality for various types of input receivers:

- `org.apache.spark.streaming.kinesis.*`: This provides classes for consuming input data from Kinesis (`http://aws.amazon.com/kinesis/`).
- `org.apache.spark.streaming.flume.*`: This provides classes for consuming input data from Flume (`https://flume.apache.org/`).
- `org.apache.spark.streaming.kafka.*`: This provides classes for consuming input data from Kafka (`http://kafka.apache.org/`).
- `org.apache.spark.streaming.zeromq.*`: This provides classes for consuming input data from ZeroMQ (`http://zeromq.org/`).
- `org.apache.spark.streaming.twitter.*`: This provides classes for consuming input data from Twitter feeds using Twitter4J (`http://twitter4j.org`).

For more information on Spark Streaming APIs, refer to `http://tinyurl.com/qz5bvvb` for Scala APIs and `http://tinyurl.com/nh9wu9d` for Java APIs.

Spark Streaming operations

Spark provides various operations which can be performed over DStreams. All operations are categorized into **transformations** and **output operations**. Let's discuss both these operations.

Transformations are those operations that help in modifying or changing the structure of data in input streams. They are similar and support almost all transformation operations provided by RDDs, for example, `map()`, `flatmap()`, `union()`, and many more. Refer to the DStream API (`http://tinyurl.com/znfgb8a`) for a complete list of transformation operations supported on input streams.

Apart from the regular transformation operation defined by DStreams and similar to RDD, DStreams provides few special transformation operations on streaming data. Let's discuss these operations:

- **Windowing operations**: Windowing is a special type of operation that is provided only by DStreams. Windowing operations group all the records from a sliding window of past time intervals into one RDD. They provide the functionality of defining the scope of data which needs to be analyzed and processed. The DStream API also provides the functionality of incremental aggregation or processing on sliding windows where we can compute an aggregate like a count or max over a sliding window. There are a variety of windowing operations provided by the DStream API. All methods in `DStream.scala` prefixed with `Window` provide incremental aggregations, such as `countByWindow`, `reduceByWindow`, and many more.
- **Transform operations**: Transform operations like `transform(...)` or `transformWith(...)` are special types of operations that provide the flexibility to perform arbitrary RDD to RDD operations. Essentially, they help in performing any RDD operation which is not provided/exposed by the DStream API. This method is also used to merge the two Spark worlds, the batch and the streaming one. We can create RDDs using batch processes and merge with RDDs created using Spark Streaming. It helps in code reusability across Spark batches and streaming, where we may have written functions in Spark batch applications that we now want to use in our Spark Streaming application.
- **updateStateByKey Operation**: Another special operation exposed by the DStream API for stateful processing where the state once computed is continuously updated with the new information. Let's take an example of webserver logs where we need to compute the running count of all GET or POST requests served by the webserver. This type of functionality can be achieved by leveraging the `updateStateByKey` operation.

Refer to `http://tinyurl.com/zh2w6k6` for more information on the various transformation operations performed by Spark Streaming.

- **Output operations**: These operations help in processing the final output produced by applying various transformations. It may be simply printing on the console or persisting in cache or any external systems such as NoSQL databases. Output operations are similar to the actions defined by RDDs and trigger all transformations as defined by the user on DStreams (again similar to RDDs).

  As of Spark 1.5.1, the following output operations are supported on DStreams:

  - `print()`: This is one of the most common operations used by the developers for debugging their jobs. It prints the first 10 elements of every batch of data in a DStream on the console of the driver node running the streaming application.
  - `saveAsTextFiles(prefix, suffix)`: This persists the content of DStreams as text files. The filename of each batch is generated by appending `prefix` and `suffix`.
  - `saveAsObjectFiles(prefix, suffix)`: This persists the content of DStreams as sequence files of serialized Java objects. The filename of each batch is generated by appending `prefix` and `suffix`.
  - `saveAsHadoopFiles(prefix, suffix)`: This persists the content of DStreams as Hadoop files. The filename of each batch is generated by appending `prefix` and `suffix`.
  - `foreachRDD(func)`: This is one of the most important, widely used and generic functions for processing the output. It applies the given function `func` to each RDD generated from the stream. This operation can be used for writing custom business logic for persisting the output in external systems such as saving to NoSQL databases or writing to web sockets. It is important to note that this function is executed at the driver node running the streaming application.

In this section, we discussed the high-level architecture, components, and packaging structure of Spark Streaming. We also talked about the various transformation and output operations as provided by the DStream API. Let's move forward and code our first Spark Streaming job in Scala and Java.

Coding our first Spark Streaming job

In this section, we will code and execute our first Spark Streaming job in Scala. We will also simulate the streaming data by creating a temporary stream.

Creating a stream producer

Perform the following steps to create a stream producer which continuously reads the input data provided by the user from the console and then further submits that data to a socket:

1. Open and edit your `Spark-Examples` project and create a new Scala package and class named `chapter.nine.StreamProducer.java`.
2. Next, edit `StreamProducer.java` and add the following piece of code:

```
import java.net.*;
import java.io.*;

public class StreamProducer {

  public static void main(String[] args) {

    if (args == null || args.length < 1) {
      System.out.println("Usage - java chapter.nine.StreamProducer
<port#>");
      System.exit(0);
    }
    System.out.println("Defining new Socket on " + args[0]);
try (ServerSocket soc = new ServerSocket(Integer.
parseInt(args[0]))) {

System.out.println("Waiting for Incoming Connection on "
          + args[0]);
      Socket clientSocket = soc.accept();
    System.out.println("Connection Received");
    OutputStream outputStream = clientSocket.getOutputStream();
// Keep Reading the data in an Infinite loop and send it over to
the Socket.
      while (true) {
    PrintWriter out = new PrintWriter(outputStream, true);
        BufferedReader read = new BufferedReader(new
InputStreamReader(
            System.in));
```

```
            System.out.println("Waiting for user to input some data");
            String data = read.readLine();
    System.out.println("Data received and now writing it to Socket");
        out.println(data);

      }
        } catch (Exception e) {
          e.printStackTrace();
        }
      }
    }
```

And we are done with our stream producer. It is pretty simple and straightforward. First, it opens the server socket so that clients can connect and then it infinitely waits for the input from the user. As soon as it receives the input, it immediately sends across the same input to the connected clients. The clients can be any consumer, but in our case it will be our Spark Streaming job that we will create in the next section.

Let's move to the next section where we will create our streaming job in Scala and Java for accepting and transforming the data generated by our stream producer.

Writing our Spark Streaming job in Scala

Perform the following steps for writing our first Spark Streaming job in Scala:

1. Create a new Scala object in our `Spark-Examples` project named `chapter.nine.ScalaFirstSparkStreamingJob.scala`.
2. Next, edit `ScalaFirstSparkStreamingJob.scala` and add the following piece of code:

```
package chapter.nine

import org.apache.spark.SparkConf
import org.apache.spark.streaming.StreamingContext
import org.apache.spark.streaming._
import org.apache.spark.storage.StorageLevel._
import org.apache.spark.rdd.RDD
import org.apache.spark.streaming.dstream.DStream
import org.apache.spark.streaming.dstream.ForEachDStream


object ScalaFirstSparkStreamingJob {

  def main(args:Array[String]){
```

```
    println("Creating Spark Configuration")
    //Create an Object of Spark Configuration
    val conf = new SparkConf()
    //Set the logical and user defined Name of this Application
    conf.setAppName("Our First Spark Streaming Application in
Scala")

    println("Retrieving Streaming Context from Spark Conf")
    //Retrieving Streaming Context from SparkConf Object.
    //Second parameter is the time interval at which streaming
data will be divided into batches
    val streamCtx = new StreamingContext(conf, Seconds(2))

    //Define the type of Stream. Here we are using TCP Socket as
text stream,
    //It will keep watching for the incoming data from a specific
machine (localhost) and port (provided as argument)
    //Once the data is retrieved it will be saved in the memory
and in case memory
    //is not sufficient, then it will store it on the Disk
    //It will further read the Data and convert it into DStream
    val lines = streamCtx.socketTextStream("localhost", args(0).
toInt, MEMORY_AND_DISK_SER_2)

    //Apply the Split() function to all elements of DStream
    //which will further generate multiple new records from each
record in Source Stream
    //And then use flatmap to consolidate all records and create a
new DStream.
    val words = lines.flatMap(x => x.split(" "))

    //Now, we will count these words by applying a using map()
    //map() helps in applying a given function to each element in
an RDD.
    val pairs = words.map(word => (word, 1))

    //Further we will aggregate the value of each key by using/
applying the given function.
    val wordCounts = pairs.reduceByKey(_ + _)

    printValues(wordCounts,streamCtx)
    //Most important statement which will initiate the Streaming
Context
    streamCtx.start();
```

```
        //Wait till the execution is completed.
        streamCtx.awaitTermination();

      }

      /**
       * Simple Print function, for printing all elements of RDD
       */
      def printValues(stream:DStream[(String,Int)],streamCtx:
    StreamingContext){
        stream.foreachRDD(foreachFunc)
        def foreachFunc = (rdd: RDD[(String,Int)]) => {
          val array = rdd.collect()
          println("---------Start Printing Results----------")
          for(res<-array){
            println(res)
          }
          println("---------Finished Printing Results--------")
        }
      }

    }
```

And we're done with the coding of our first Spark Streaming job. Our job is again pretty simple and straightforward. It receives some random text from our stream producer and simply counts the occurrence of unique words and finally prints the same on the driver console. We will soon execute our job but before that let's move to the next section where we will code the same job in Java too.

Follow the comments provided in the code to understand the business logic and other operations. The same style is used further in the chapter and book.

Writing our Spark Streaming job in Java

Perform the following steps for writing our first Spark Streaming job in Java:

1. Create a new Java class in our `Spark-Examples` project named `chapter.nine.JavaFirstSparkStreamingJob.java`.
2. Next, edit `JavaFirstSparkStreamingJob.java` and add the following piece of code:

```
package chapter.nine;
```

```
import java.util.Arrays;

import org.apache.spark.*;
import org.apache.spark.api.java.function.*;
import org.apache.spark.storage.StorageLevel;
import org.apache.spark.streaming.*;
import org.apache.spark.streaming.api.java.*;

import scala.Tuple2;

public class JavaFirstSparkStreamingJob {

public static void main(String[] args) {

System.out.println("Creating Spark Configuration");
  // Create an Object of Spark Configuration
    SparkConf conf = new SparkConf();
// Set the logical and user defined Name of this //Application
conf.setAppName("Our First Spark Streaming Application in Java");
System.out.println("Retrieving Streaming Context from Spark
Conf");
// Retrieving Streaming Context from SparkConf Object.
// Second parameter is the time interval at which streaming //data
will be divided into batches
    JavaStreamingContext streamCtx = new
JavaStreamingContext(conf,
        Durations.seconds(2));

// Define the type of Stream. Here we are using TCP Socket //as
text stream,
// It will keep watching for the incoming data from a //specific
machine
// (localhost) and port (provided as argument)
// Once the data is retrieved it will be saved in the //memory and
in case memory
// is not sufficient, then it will store it on the Disk.
// It will further read the Data and convert it into //DStream
    JavaReceiverInputDStream<String> lines = streamCtx.
socketTextStream(
        "localhost", Integer.parseInt(args[0]),
        StorageLevel.MEMORY_AND_DISK_SER_2());

  // Apply the x.split() function to all elements of
    // JavaReceiverInputDStream
// which will further generate multiple new records from
```

```
// each record in Source Stream
// And then use flatmap to consolidate all records and //create a
new
// JavaDStream
JavaDStream<String> words = lines
        .flatMap(new FlatMapFunction<String, String>() {
          @Override
          public Iterable<String> call(String x) {
            return Arrays.asList(x.split(" "));
          }
        });

    // Now, we will count these words by applying a using
mapToPair()
    // mapToPair() helps in applying a given function to each
element in an
    // RDD
    // And further will return the Scala Tuple with //"word" as
key and value
    // as "count".
    JavaPairDStream<String, Integer> pairs = words
        .mapToPair(new PairFunction<String, String, Integer>() {
@Override
public Tuple2<String, Integer> call(String s)
            throws Exception {
            return new Tuple2<String, Integer>(s, 1);
          }
        });

// Further we will aggregate the value of each key by //using/
applying the given function.
    JavaPairDStream<String, Integer> wordCounts = pairs
        .reduceByKey(new Function2<Integer, Integer, Integer>() {
  @Override
  public Integer call(Integer i1, Integer i2)
            throws Exception {
            return i1 + i2;
          }
        });

    // Lastly we will print First 10 Words.
    // We can also implement custom print method for printing all
values,
    // as we did in Scala example.
    wordCounts.print(10);
```

```
        // Most important statement which will initiate the Streaming
    Context
        streamCtx.start();
        // Wait till the execution is completed.
        streamCtx.awaitTermination();

      }
    }
```

And we are done with our first Spark Streaming job in Java. It also performs the same function as our Scala job, where it receives some random text from our Stream producer, simply counts the occurrence of unique words, and finally print the same on the driver console. Let's move forward and see some action by executing our first streaming job.

Follow the comments provided in the code to understand the business logic and other operations. The same style is used further in the chapter and book.

Executing our Spark Streaming job

In this section, we will execute/launch our first streaming job and will analyze the output on the console. Perform the following steps for launching our first Spark Streaming job:

1. Compile the Eclipse project `Spark-Examples` and export it as a JAR file named `spark-examples.jar` from Eclipse itself.
2. Next, open your console and execute the following command from the location where we exported our `Spark-Examples` project:

   ```
   java -classpath spark-examples.jar chapter.nine.StreamProducer
   9047
   ```

   Our stream producer is up and running and waiting for clients to connect at port `9047`.

3. Assuming our Spark cluster is up and running, open a new console and execute the following command for launching our Spark Streaming Scala job:

   ```
   $SPARK_HOME/bin/spark-submit --class chapter.nine.
   ScalaFirstSparkStreamingJob --master spark://ip-10-155-38-161:7077
   spark-examples.jar 9047
   ```

4. For executing a Spark Streaming Java job, execute this command:

```
$SPARK_HOME/bin/spark-submit --class chapter.nine.
JavaFirstSparkStreamingJob --master spark://ip-10-155-38-161:7077
spark-examples.jar 9047
```

And we are done! Isn't it interesting, simple, and straightforward?

Now whatever we type on the console of our stream producer, it will be sent to our Spark Streaming job and our job will further count the words and will print the same on the driver console itself. The following screenshot shows the output produced by our stream producer:

```
sumit@localhost $ java -classpath spark-examples.jar chapter. nine .StreamProducer 9047
Defining new Socket on 9047
Waiting for Incoming Connection on - 9047
Hello from our First Spark Streaming Job in ScalaConnection Received
Waiting for user to input some data

Data received and now writing it to Socket
Waiting for user to input some data
```

The following screenshot shows the output produced by our streaming job that receives the input from our stream producer and then counts and prints the distinct words on the console itself:

```
sumit@localhost $ $SPARK_HOME/bin/spark-submit --class chapter. nine .ScalaFirstSparkStreamingJob --master spark://ip-10-155-38-161:7077 spark-examples.jar 9047
Creating Spark Configuration
Retreiving Streaming Context from Spark Conf
15/12/06 10:41:27 WARN NativeCodeLoader: Unable to load native-hadoop library for your platform... using builtin-java classes where applicable
15/12/06 10:41:29 WARN MetricsSystem: Using default name DAGScheduler for source because spark.app.id is not set.
---------Start Printing Results----------
(Hello,1)
(First,1)
(our,1)
(Scala,1)
(Streaming,1)
(from,1)
(Spark,1)
(in,1)
(Job,1)
---------Finished Printing Results----------
---------Start Printing Results----------
---------Finished Printing Results----------
---------Start Printing Results----------
---------Finished Printing Results----------
---------Start Printing Results----------
---------Finished Printing Results----------
```

In this section, we coded and executed our first Spark Streaming job in Scala and Java. Let's move forward where we will extend our Chicago crime example and will perform some real-time analysis by integrating Spark Streaming and Spark SQL.

Querying streaming data in real time

In this section, we will extend our Chicago crime example and will perform some real-time analysis using Spark SQL on the streaming crime data.

All Spark extensions extend a core architecture component of Spark: RDD. Now whether it is DStreams in Spark Streaming or DataFrame in Spark SQL, they are interoperable with each other. We can easily convert DStreams into DataFrames and vice versa. Let's move ahead and understand the integration architecture of Spark Streaming and Spark SQL. We will also materialize the same and develop an application for querying streaming data in real time. Let's refer to this job as *SQL Streaming Crime Analyzer*.

The high-level architecture of our job

The high-level architecture of our *SQL Streaming Crime Analyzer* will essentially consist of the following three components:

- **Crime producer**: This is a producer that will randomly read the crime records from the file and push the data to a socket. This is same crime record file which we downloaded and configured in the *Creating Kinesis stream producers* section in *Chapter 5, Getting Acquainted with Kinesis*.
- **Stream consumer**: This reads the data from the socket and converts it into RDD.
- **Stream to DataFrame transformer**: This consumes the RDD provided by the stream consumer and further transforms it into a DataFrame using dynamic schema mapping.

Once we have the DataFrame, we can execute our regular Spark SQL operations. The following diagram represents the interaction between all three components in realization of the overall use case:

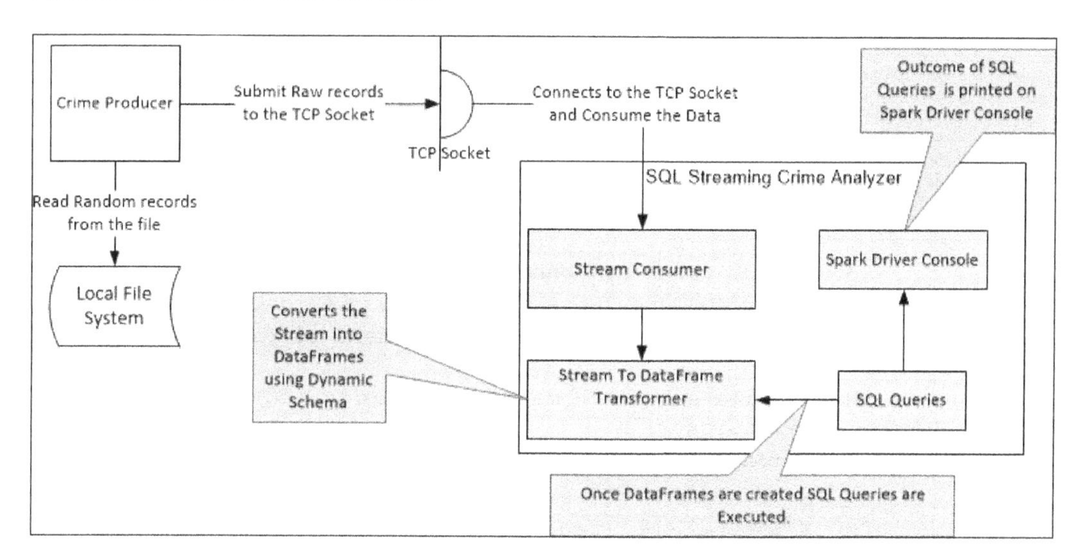

Let's move forward towards the next section and code our *SQL Streaming Crime Analyzer*.

Coding the crime producer

Perform the following steps to code our crime producer that will read the crimes from a predefined file and submit the data to a socket:

1. Open and edit the `Spark-Examples` project and add a new Java file named `chapter.nine.CrimeProducer.java`.
2. Edit `CrimeProducer.java` and add the following code in it:

```
package chapter.nine;
import java.io.*;
import java.net.*;
import java.util.Random;

public class CrimeProducer {

  public static void main(String[] args) {

    if (args == null || args.length < 1) {
      System.out
          .println("Usage - java chapter.nine.StreamProducer
<port#>");
      System.exit(0);
    }
    System.out.println("Defining new Socket on " + args[0]);
    try (ServerSocket soc = new ServerSocket(Integer.
parseInt(args[0]))) {

      System.out.println("Waiting for Incoming Connection on - "
          + args[0]);
      Socket clientSocket = soc.accept();

      System.out.println("Connection Received");
      OutputStream outputStream = clientSocket.getOutputStream();
      // Path of the file from where we need to read crime
records.
      String filePath = "/home/ec2-user/softwares/crime-data/
Crimes_-Aug-2015.csv";
      PrintWriter out = new PrintWriter(outputStream, true);
      BufferedReader brReader = new BufferedReader(new FileReader(
          filePath));
```

```
        // Defining Random number to read different number of
records each
        // time.
        Random number = new Random();
        // Keep Reading the data in a Infinite loop and send it over
to the
        // Socket.
        while (true) {
          System.out.println("Reading Crime Records");
          StringBuilder dataBuilder = new StringBuilder();
          // Getting new Random Integer between 0 and 60
          int recordsToRead = number.nextInt(60);

          System.out.println("Records to Read = " + recordsToRead);
          for (int i = 0; i < recordsToRead; i++) {
            String dataLine = brReader.readLine() + "\n";
            dataBuilder.append(dataLine);
          }
          System.out
              .println("Data received and now writing it to
Socket");
          out.println(dataBuilder);
          out.flush();
          // Sleep for 6 Seconds before reading again
          Thread.sleep(6000);

        }

      } catch (Exception e) {
        e.printStackTrace();
      }

    }
  }
```

And we are done with our crime producer. Let's develop our stream consumer and transformer, and then we will deploy and execute all components and analyze the results on the Spark driver console.

Coding the stream consumer and transformer

Perform the following steps for coding the stream consumer and transformer in Scala:

1. Open and edit the `Spark-Examples` project and add a new Scala object named `chapter.nine.SQLStreamingCrimeAnalyzer.scala`.
2. Edit `SQLStreamingCrimeAnalyzer.scala` and add the following code:

```
package chapter.nine

import org.apache.spark._
import org.apache.spark.streaming._
import org.apache.spark.sql._
import org.apache.spark.storage.StorageLevel._
import org.apache.spark.rdd._
import org.apache.spark.streaming.dstream._

object SQLStreamingCrimeAnalyzer {

  def main(args: Array[String]) {
    val conf = new SparkConf()
    conf.setAppName("Our SQL Streaming Crime Analyzer in Scala")
    val streamCtx = new StreamingContext(conf, Seconds(6))
val lines = streamCtx.socketTextStream("localhost", args(0).toInt,
MEMORY_AND_DISK_SER_2)

    lines.foreachRDD {
      x =>
//Splitting, flattening and finally filtering to exclude any Empty
Rows
      val rawCrimeRDD = x.map(_.split("\n")).flatMap { x => x
}.filter { x => x.length()>2 }
      println("Data Received = "+rawCrimeRDD.collect().length)
      //Splitting again for each Distinct value in the Row
      val splitCrimeRDD = rawCrimeRDD.map { x => x.split(",") }
      //Finally mapping/ creating/ populating the Crime Object
with the values
      val crimeRDD = splitCrimeRDD.map(c => Crime(c(0),
c(1),c(2),c(3),c(4),c(5),c(6)))
      //Getting instance of SQLContext and also importing
implicits for dynamically creating Data Frames
      val sqlCtx = getInstance(streamCtx.sparkContext)
      import sqlCtx.implicits._
      //Converting RDD to DataFrame
```

```
        val dataFrame = crimeRDD.toDF()
        //Perform few operations on DataFrames
        println("Number of Rows in Table = "+dataFrame.count())
        println("Printing All Rows")
        dataFrame.show(dataFrame.count().toInt)
        //Now Printing Crimes Grouped by "Primary Type"
        println("Printing Crimes, Grouped by Primary Type")
        dataFrame.groupBy("primaryType").count().sort($"count".
desc).show(5)
 //Now registering it as Table and Invoking few SQL Operations
         val tableName ="ChicagoCrimeData"+System.nanoTime()
        dataFrame.registerTempTable(tableName)
        invokeSQLOperation(streamCtx.sparkContext,tableName)
      }
      streamCtx.start();
      streamCtx.awaitTermination();
    }

    def invokeSQLOperation(sparkCtx:SparkContext,tableName:String){
      println("Now executing SQL Queries.....")
      val sqlCtx = getInstance(sparkCtx)
      println("Printing the Schema...")
      sqlCtx.sql("describe "+tableName).collect().foreach { println
}
      println("Printing Total Number of records.....")
      sqlCtx.sql("select count(1) from "+tableName).collect().
foreach { println }

    }

    //Defining Singleton SQLContext variable
    @transient private var instance: SQLContext = null
    //Lazy initialization of SQL Context
    def getInstance(sparkContext: SparkContext): SQLContext =
      synchronized {
        if (instance == null) {
          instance = new SQLContext(sparkContext)
        }
        instance
      }
}

 // Define the schema using a case class.
   case class Crime(id: String, caseNumber:String, date:String,
block:String, IUCR:String, primaryType:String, desc:String)
```

And we are done with our stream consumer and transformer. Let's move forward and execute our producers, consumers, and transformers and analyze the results.

Executing the SQL Streaming Crime Analyzer

Perform the following steps to execute the *SQL Streaming Crime Analyzer*:

1. Assuming that your Spark cluster is up and running, export your Eclipse project as `spark-examples.jar`.
2. The first task is to bring up our crime producer, so open a new Linux console and execute the following command from the same location where we exported `spark-examples.jar`:

   ```
   java -classpath spark-examples.jar chapter.nine.CrimeProducer 9047
   ```

   The argument to `CrimeProducer` is the port number on which our producer will open a new TCP socket (which is `9047` in our case) for listening to the clients that want to receive the data. As soon as we execute the command, the producer will wait for an incoming connection before it starts reading and submitting the crime data.

3. Next, we will open a new Linux console and execute the following command from the same location where we exported `spark-examples.jar`:

   ```
   $SPARK_HOME/bin/spark-submit --class chapter.nine.
   SQLStreamingCrimeAnalyzer --master spark://ip-10-234-208-221:7077
   spark-examples.jar 9047
   ```

   We also provided the port number in the last argument of our `spark-submit` command. This port number should be same as the one we provided while executing `CrimeProducer` (in our case, it is `9047`). Our job will connect to the provided port and start receiving the data available and submitted by our producer.

And we are done! Awesome, isn't it ?

The outcome of this execution would be similar to what's shown in the following screenshot:

```
sumit@localhost $ java -classpath spark-examples.jar chapter. nine .CrimeProducer 9047
Defining new Socket on 9047
Waiting for Incoming Connection on - 9047
Connection Received
Reading Crime Records
Records to Read = 7
Data received and now writing it to Socket
Reading Crime Records
Records to Read = 18
Data received and now writing it to Socket
```

The preceding screenshot shows the output produced on the console. It shows the number of records read and submitted by the crime producer.

The following screenshot shows the output produced by the consumer and transformer on the Spark driver console. It shows the results of the analysis performed by Spark SQL:

```
sumit@localhost $ $SPARK_HOME/bin/spark-submit --class chapter.nine.SQLStreamingCrimeAnalyzer --master spark://ip-10-234-208-221:7077 spark-examples.jar 9047
Creating Spark Configuration
Retreiving Streaming Context from Spark Conf
15/12/09 10:43:42 WARN NativeCodeLoader: Unable to load native-hadoop library for your platform... using builtin-java classes where applicable
15/12/09 10:43:44 WARN MetricsSystem: Using default name DAGScheduler for source because spark.app.id is not set.
Data Received = 7
Number of Rows in Table = 7
Printing All Rows
+--------+----------+--------------------+--------------------+----+-----------------+--------------------+
|      id|caseNumber|                date|               block|IUCR|      primaryType|                desc|
+--------+----------+--------------------+--------------------+----+-----------------+--------------------+
|      ID|Case Number|               Date|               Block|IUCR|     Primary Type|         Description|
|10217189|  HY404004|08/31/2015 12:00:...|  051XX W ADDISON ST|1320|  CRIMINAL DAMAGE|          TO VEHICLE|
|10217252|  HY403984|08/31/2015 12:00:...|083XX S MARYLAND AVE|041A|          BATTERY| AGGRAVATED: HANDGUN|
|10217276|  HY403985|08/31/2015 12:00:...|093XX S LAFAYETTE...|031A|          ROBBERY|      ARMED: HANDGUN|
|10218505|  HY404795|08/31/2015 12:00:...|078XX S CONSTANCE...|1310|  CRIMINAL DAMAGE|         TO PROPERTY|
|10218642|  HY405268|08/31/2015 12:00:...|   014XX W OLIVE AVE|1360|CRIMINAL TRESPASS|          TO VEHICLE|
|10217212|  HY404049|08/30/2015 11:52:...| 060XX S ASHLAND AVE|1811|        NARCOTICS|POSS: CANNABIS 30...|
+--------+----------+--------------------+--------------------+----+-----------------+--------------------+

Printing Crimes, Grouped by Primary Type
+---------------+-----+
|    primaryType|count|
+---------------+-----+
|CRIMINAL DAMAGE|    2|
|        BATTERY|    1|
|   Primary Type|    1|
|        ROBBERY|    1|
|      NARCOTICS|    1|
+---------------+-----+
only showing top 5 rows

Now executing SQL Queries.....
Printing the Schema...
[id,string,]
[caseNumber,string,]
[date,string,]
[block,string,]
[IUCR,string,]
[primaryType,string,]
[desc,string,]
Printing Total Number of records.....
[7]
```

In this section, we discussed the integration of two different Spark extensions: Spark Streaming and Spark SQL. We also developed/executed a Spark Streaming job that receives the data in near real-time and then further leverages Spark SQL for performing analysis over streaming data.

Let's move forward and look at the deployment and monitoring aspects of Spark Streaming.

Deployment and monitoring

In this section, we will discuss the various methodologies for deploying and monitoring Spark Streaming applications. Deployment and monitoring is a vast topic and it becomes complex when we talk about distributed deployments and monitoring. Discussing all aspects of Spark deployment is out of the scope of this book, but we will touch upon the various aspects of deployments and monitoring which will help us to understand the various features and flexibility provided by Spark and Spark Streaming.

Cluster managers for Spark Streaming

Spark is a framework that does not enforce any app servers or deployment stack. Spark provides the integration and deployment of Spark and Spark-based applications on various distributed cluster managers such as Standalone, Yarn, or Mesos. We saw the deployments on Standalone in the *Configuring the Spark cluster* section in *Chapter 6, Getting Acquainted with Spark*. Let's move forward and deploy our streaming application on Yarn and Apache Mesos.

Executing Spark Streaming applications on Yarn

YARN or Hadoop 2.0 is a generic purpose cluster computing framework, entrusted with the responsibility of allocating and managing the resources required to execute the various applications. It introduced three new daemon services: **ResourceManager** (**RM**), **NodeManager** (**NM**), and **ApplicationMaster** (**AM**). All these new services collectively are responsible for managing cluster resources, individual nodes, and applications.

For more information on the architecture of YARN, please refer to `http://hadoop.apache.org/docs/current/hadoop-yarn/hadoop-yarn-site/YARN.html`.

Perform the following steps for deploying our Spark Streaming application on Yarn:

1. The first step is to set up and configure Yarn. Yarn can be set up in two different modes:
    - **Single node setup**: Follow the steps/instructions provided at `http://tinyurl.com/zpz45vw` for configuring all Yarn services on a single node.
    - **Cluster setup**: Follow the steps/instructions provided at `http://tinyurl.com/zejnjtb` for setting up Yarn in the clustered mode.
2. Once our Yarn setup is up and running in any of the specified modes, we will submit or execute any of our Spark Streaming applications by executing the following command on the Linux console:

    ```
    $SPARK_HOME/bin/spark-submit --class chapter.nine.
    SQLStreamingCrimeAnalyzer --master yarn-client spark-examples.jar
    9047
    ```

    Or we can also use this command:

    ```
    $SPARK_HOME/bin/spark-submit --class chapter.nine.
    SQLStreamingCrimeAnalyzer --master yarn-cluster spark-examples.jar
    9047
    ```

And we are done!

The only difference between the preceding commands is that the former leverages `yarn-client` that will enable the Spark driver to execute on the same machine which is used to execute the `spark-submit` command and the latter leverages `yarn-cluster` that will execute the Spark driver within the Yarn cluster, providing HA, failover, and reliability of the Spark driver. Refer to `https://spark.apache.org/docs/1.5.1/running-on-yarn.html` for more information on deploying Spark Streaming applications on Yarn.

Ensure that your `HADOOP_CONF_DIR` variable is configured as an environment variable and is pointing to the directory containing Hadoop configurations files, which is usually at `HADOOP_HOME/etc/hadoop`.

Executing Spark Streaming applications on Apache Mesos

Apache Mesos (`http://mesos.apache.org/`) is a cluster manager that provides efficient resource isolation and sharing, across distributed applications or frameworks. It can run Hadoop, MPI, Hypertable, Spark, and other frameworks on a dynamically shared pool of nodes. Spark and Mesos are related to each other but they are not the same. The story started back in 2009 when in Berkeley Lab, discussions and thoughts were going on about the ideas/frameworks that can be developed on top of Mesos, and that's exactly how Spark was born. The objective was to showcase the ease of development and deployment in Mesos and, at the same time, the target was to support interactive and iterative computations like machine learning and also provide ad hoc querying.

Mesos provides the fault tolerant and elastic distribution of the compute resources by abstracting out physical and virtual resources such as CPU or memory and maintaining a pool. Now further, as per the demand/request of the application, the appropriate resources are allocated. Let's move forward and deploy our Spark Streaming application on Apache Mesos.

Perform the following steps for deploying your Spark Streaming application on Apache Mesos:

1. Follow the instructions provided at `http://mesos.apache.org/documentation/latest/getting-started/` for setting up and configuring Apache Mesos.

2. Once your cluster is up and running and you are able to browse the Mesos UI at http://<hostnname>:5050, configure a few environment variables. Execute the following commands on your Linux console:

```
export MESOS_HOME =<Path of mesos installation dir >
export MESOS_NATIVE_JAVA_LIBRARY=<Path of ibmesos.so >
```

By default, libmesos.so can be found at /usr/local/lib/libmesos.so, but if it is not found at the default location, you can find it at <MESOS_HOME>/build/src/.libs/libmesos.so.

3. The final step is to configure a new environment variable spark.executor.uri. The value of this variable will be the location of the Spark binaries, accessed via http://, hdfs:// (Hadoop), or s3:// (Amazon S3 at http://aws.amazon.com/s3/). This variable is required by the Mesos slave nodes for fetching Spark binaries required for executing Spark jobs. For the sake of simplicity, we can use http:// and mention the URL of the Spark website. Edit your <SPARK_HOME>/conf/spark-defaults.conf file and add the following variable:

```
spark.executor.uri= http://d3kbcqa49mib13.cloudfront.net/spark-1.5.1-bin-hadoop2.4.tgz
```

In production systems, it is recommended to upload Spark binaries on HDFS, which should be in same network/subnet as of Mesos slave nodes.

And we are done! Now our Mesos cluster is configured to execute our Spark jobs. We can open a new Linux console and execute the following commands for submitting our Spark Streaming jobs to a Mesos cluster:

```
$SPARK_HOME/bin/spark-submit --class chapter.nine.SQLStreamingCrimeAnalyzer --master mesos://<master-host>:5050 spark-examples.jar 9047
```

As soon as we execute the preceding command, we will see the logs coming on the console, and at the same time, the Mesos master UI will also show us the status of our job.

Refer to https://spark.apache.org/docs/1.5.1/running-on-mesos.html for more information on deploying Spark Streaming applications on Mesos.

In this section, we discussed the steps involved in deploying our Spark Streaming applications in various cluster computing frameworks such as Yarn and Apache Mesos. Let's move to the next section where we will discuss the monitoring of Spark Streaming applications.

Monitoring Spark Streaming applications

Monitoring distributed and streaming applications is a vast and complex task. Again, discussing all aspects of monitoring is out of scope of this book, but we will look at the various methodologies for monitoring Spark and Spark Streaming applications.

There is no single framework which can meet all the monitoring requirements of enterprise systems and that's the reason enterprises deploy multiple monitoring systems leveraging the best features of each of the available and deployed monitoring tools.

Spark exposes various metrics around jobs running or completed that can be very well captured and exposed to the user. Spark leverages the Coda Hale metrics library (`https://github.com/dropwizard/metrics`) and provides a flexible, extendable, and configurable metrics system. This library also helps in integrating with other monitoring tools such as Nagios, Graphite, Ganglia, JMX, and many more. Spark also exposes REST APIs for monitoring the various running and completed jobs.

The JSON for both running applications and completed applications is accessible at `http://<server-url>:18080/api/v1` for completed jobs and `http://<server-url>:4040/api/v1` for running applications.

Refer to `http://spark.apache.org/docs/1.5.1/monitoring.html` for more information on monitoring Spark and Spark Streaming applications.

In this section, we discussed the various aspects of deploying and monitoring our Spark Streaming applications.

Spark Streaming is a vast topic and we have just scratched the surface. If you are interested or working or plan to work with Spark Streaming, then it is recommended to learn the nitty-gritty and intrinsic details of Spark Streaming. It is covered in *Learning Real-time Processing with Spark Streaming, Sumit Gupta, Packt Publishing* (`https://www.packtpub.com/big-data-and-business-intelligence/learning-real-time-processing-spark-streaming`).

Summary

In this chapter, we discussed various aspects of Spark Streaming. We discussed the architecture, components, and the packaging structure of Spark Streaming. We also coded and executed our first Spark Streaming application and we also performed real-time analysis on our Chicago crime data using Spark Streaming and Spark SQL.

In the next chapter, we will discuss the Lambda Architecture that provides a unified framework for batch and real-time processing.

10
Introducing Lambda Architecture

Enterprises have come a long way where there's a demand for a unified system that meets both batch and real-time data processing needs. To extend it further, the need is for a distributed, scalable, highly-available, and fault-tolerant Big Data enterprise system, which is capable of presenting unified views/insights from the batch as well as real-time data systems. Though architects/developers have been working on discrete systems where batch and real-time use cases were developed and deployed separately, presenting this as a single view to the users was a real challenge. Perceiving the objective of a unified view has its own challenges. In some places where it was realized using leveraged traditional architectural patterns, it made the whole system too complex and, in some cases, made the whole system almost unmanageable.

In order to meet the needs and challenges of enterprises for presenting a unified view, which is combination of batch and real-time data, a new architecture paradigm was introduced by Nathan Marz in late 2012 called the **Lambda Architecture** (`http://lambda-architecture.net/`).

In this chapter, we will discuss the Lambda Architecture and its various components. We will also talk about its various features and the technologies involved in coming up with Lambda Architecture.

This chapter will cover the following topics:

- What is Lambda Architecture
- The technology matrix for Lambda Architecture
- The realization of Lambda Architecture

What is Lambda Architecture

In this section, we will talk about the various features and components of Lambda Architecture. Let's move forward and first look at the need for Lambda Architecture, then, we will dive deep into the various other aspects of it.

The need for Lambda Architecture

The driving force behind Lambda was the latency introduced by the MapReduce paradigm. Hadoop or MapReduce solved the purpose of a distributed and scalable batch processing system, but, at the same time, it was also true that batch views were created on stale and outdated data (by at least 3-4 hours). Though it was acceptable in a few cases where data arrived once or twice in a day, but it was not acceptable to use cases where real-time updates could make a significant difference to the overall computations.

The next evident question is as to why we can't compute and recompute everything on the fly.

We can only do this if our systems have unlimited CPU, memory, and network speed, which obviously is not the case. So, we need to perform trade-offs and choose the amount of data required to be processed in real-time versus batches.

Lambda Architecture completely solves the same paradigm where it introduces a new architectural paradigm, which enables end users to view the analysis or computations on historical data and data arriving in near real-time as a single view or entity. Lambda Architecture is developed on the principle of Unified Architecture to solve both batch and near real-time data processing needs.

It leverages the batch processing layer to provide accurate and comprehensive views while maintaining the balance between varied non-functional requirements, such as latency, throughput, and fault tolerance. At the same time, it also utilizes the real-time or stream capabilities for consuming near real-time updates, finally combining/joining batch and real-time views to produce a single view for the end users.

Lambda Architecture is more of a specification that provides a general-purpose approach for implementing an arbitrary function on an arbitrary dataset, finally returning its results with low latency. It is important to note that, *as Lambda Architecture is a specification*, it does not mandate any specific technology for implementing batch or real-time views. It defines the architecture paradigm and a consistent approach for choosing technologies to wire them together to meet our requirements.

We will shortly discuss the architecture/layers/components of Lambda Architecture, but, before this, let's quickly discuss the various features of Lambda Architecture:

- **Scalable**: Scalability is one of the prime requirements/mandates of Lambda Architecture. Scalability means to serve the growing number of users of the system without any modifications to the underlying architecture or code. This can be achieved by adding more resources, such as CPU, memory, disk, and more, to the existing boxes; this is popularly known as vertical scalability (scale up). This can also be achieved by adding a higher number of machines to the existing cluster, which is popularly known as horizontal scalability (scale out). Lambda Architecture should support vertical as well as horizontal scalability, but the latter is always preferred. Each layer in the Lambda Architecture, whether it is a real-time or batch layer, should be capable of processing an additional amount of data just by adding more nodes to the existing cluster without stopping or halting the existing cluster.

Refer to `https://en.wikipedia.org/wiki/Scalability` for more information on scalability.

- **Resilient to failures**: Fault tolerance or resilience to system failures is another intrinsic feature of Lambda Architecture. Though the state and behavior of the system depends upon the type of failure, it is necessary for the system to gracefully handle failures and continue responding to the best of its abilities with a reduced or decreased quality. A fault-tolerant design or architecture ensures that in the case of failure in some of the system components, the complete system is not brought down. The system still responds, but with either reduced capacity or degraded quality for a few affected components and not the complete system. For example, in a cluster of 20-30 nodes, in a case where 4-5 nodes went down for some reason (such as faulty hardware) it should not bring down the whole cluster. The system response may be slower as it works at the reduced capacity, which may impact overall SLAs too, but the system would still be responsive. Fault tolerance is a much sought after feature in systems that mandate High Availability, which further mandates the inclusion or development of features such as redundancy and replication in the overall system design so that the system does not have any **single point of failure** (**SPOF**).

Refer to `https://en.wikipedia.org/wiki/Fault_tolerance` for more information on fault tolerance.

- **Low latency**: Latency is the time required by any system to consume new events, process them, and finally produce the results. Though it varies from system to system and use case to use case, any variations (increase or decrease) in latency does impact the speed layer because it is responsible for consuming and processing the event in real time. A delay of a few milliseconds or seconds may not be acceptable and would require serious consideration. The objective of Lambda Architecture is to provide a low-latency, near real-time layer, which can consume and process the input in a few milliseconds.
- **Extensible**: Software systems need to be flexible enough to incorporate new or modified requirements without re-architecting or changing the overall software system. Lambda Architecture has also been developed on a similar principle where batch and real-time layers are segregated so that any enhancement in either of the layers cannot impact or bring down the whole system.

Refer to `https://en.wikipedia.org/wiki/Extensibility` for more information on extensibility.

- **Maintenance**: The cost and effort required for maintaining a software system is another major area of concern. Architects/developers have always preferred to work and deploy a software system which is less complex and provides easy maintenance. Lambda Architecture has also focused on this aspect where it separates the complexities of batch and real-time processing into separate layers, which not only helps in adding new requirements in either of the layers (batch or real-time) but, at the same time, also provides a minimum or no impact of changes in one layer to the other one.

Let's move forward and discuss the architecture/components/layers of Lambda Architecture.

Layers/components of Lambda Architecture

In this section, we will discuss the various layers/components of Lambda Architecture.

The specifications of Lambda Architecture define the series of interconnected or loosely coupled layers/components where each layer is entrusted with a specific responsibility. Lambda Architecture is focused on handling a variety of Big Data problem statements, which may involve all of the three Vs—**Volume**, **Velocity**, and **Variety** (`https://en.wikipedia.org/wiki/Big_data#Definition`).

At a high level, Lambda specifications define the following major layers/components and the integration between each of the components:

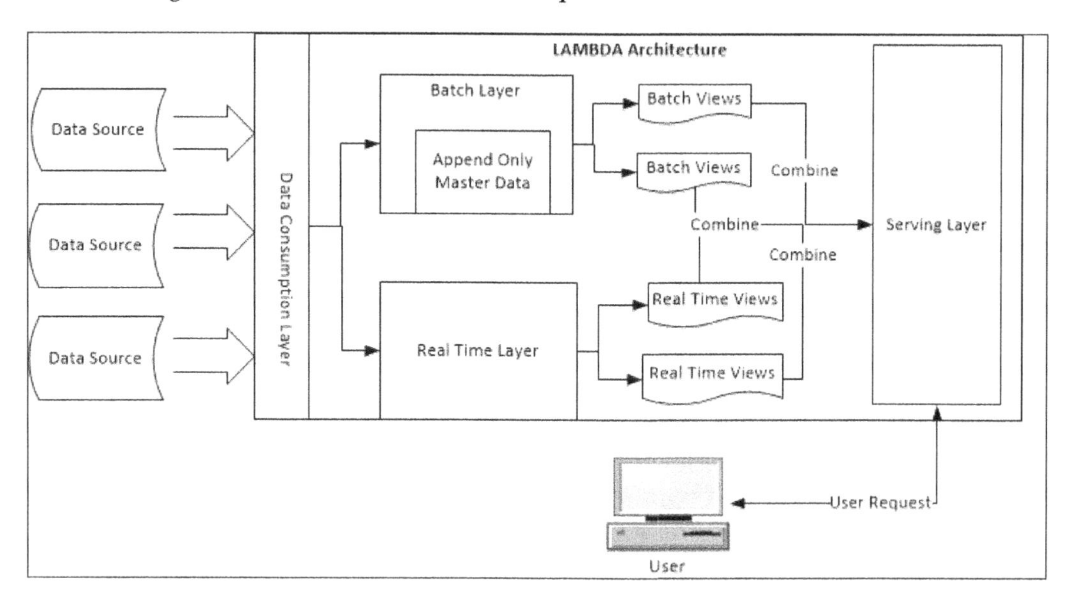

The preceding illustration defines the high-level architecture/layers/components specified by Lambda Architecture.

Let's move forward and discuss the roles and responsibilities of each of the components defined by Lambda Architecture:

- **Data sources**: Data sources are external data sources that are entrusted to deliver the data as and when it arrives. Data sources can follow various models to deliver data. It can leverage MQ, web services, directory/file (which is polled at a regular interval for new data), direct database, or maybe even a raw socket-based data delivery mechanism. In most of the scenarios, data delivery mechanisms are not in our control as they are defined by the vendor who delivers and provides access to the data. So, not much can be done in this layer, but we can develop our data consumption layer to hide all the complexities of accessing data from varied sources and only consume data in a specific format.
- **Data consumption layer**: This layer is entrusted with the responsibility for encapsulating the complexity of fetching data from varied data sources and then converting it into the standard format that can be further consumed by the batch or real-time layer. Once the data is converted into the standard consumable format, it can be pushed to the batch and real-time data layers for further processing.

- **Batch layer**: This is one of the most important components of Lambda Architecture. Batch layers receive/fetch the data from the data consumption layer and further persist it into the user-defined data structure, which is immutable and ever growing. In short, the batch layer maintains *Append Only Master Data*, which is never changed. Systems such as Hadoop/HDFS are a classic example of creating the master data, which is immutable and never changing. The batch layer is also responsible for creating and maintaining batch views. Batch views are the data structures/views that are computed or refreshed at regular intervals over the master data. Batch views can be seen as aggregated views or transformed views, which can be directly consumed by the serving layer. Let's take an example where we want to process weblogs and calculate the number of distinct URLs. In this scenario, the *Append Only Master Data* will contain the raw records of all the user hits. Next, there will be a MapReduce job or a Hive query, which is executed over the master data, finds the count of each distinct URL, and finally persists it into another Hive table, HDFS, or some NoSQL. This MapReduce job or Hive query is executed at regular intervals and refreshes the aggregated view. These aggregated views are known as batch views:

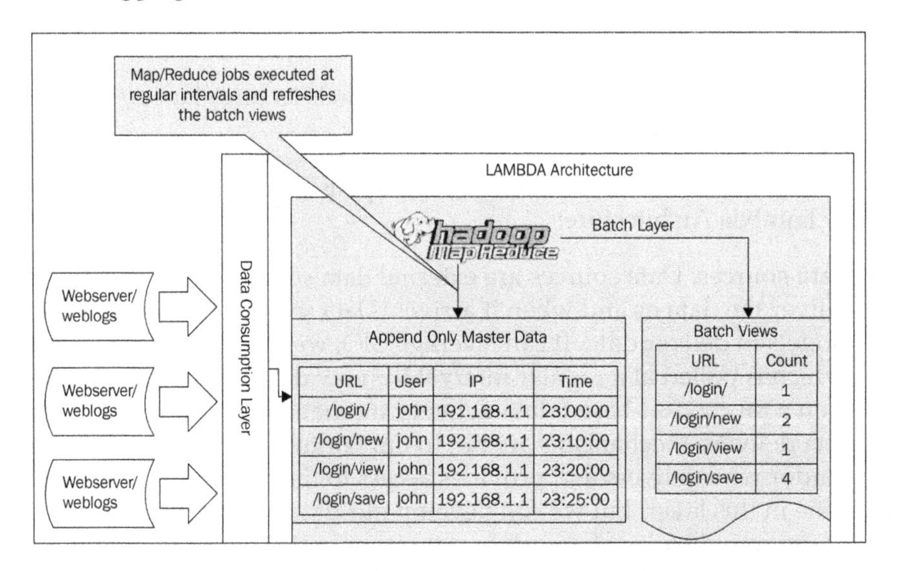

The preceding illustration shows a high-level design for the batch layer, with the help of an example where weblogs are captured and URLs are aggregated to find the popularity of each webpage.

* **Real-time layers**: This is another important and critical layer in Lambda Architecture. Batch layers mostly satisfy all the needs, but they serve stale data for a certain period of time (until the system refreshes the batch views). The amount of latency introduced by the batch views may not be acceptable because of the requirements specified by the use case where it may need the data to be available in real-time or near real-time format. We can argue that we can reduce the refresh interval of batch views, but this may aggravate the problem. The amount of data to be processed will be in TBs/PBs, which definitely takes a couple of hours no matter how much hardware we provide for computations. Real-time layers, also known as **speed layers**, solve the same problem where they store only a chunk of data or subset of data and make it available instantly to users. Now, the amount of data that it can capture will depend upon the hardware (especially memory) provided to the layer and the refresh interval of the batch views. The way it works is that the real-time layers will consume and persist the incremental dataset only for the duration when our batch views present stale data. Once our batch views are refreshed, the real-time layer will drop the old data and start afresh. Let's extend our weblogs example and assume that the batch views are regenerated every 15 minutes. So, our real-time layer will store and process the data only for the last 15 minutes. The real-time layer will essentially process the last 15 minutes of the data and generate real-time views, which are refreshed within a few milliseconds, or as and when the data is received. The real-time layer is generally designed and developed using in-memory systems such as Storm or Spark:

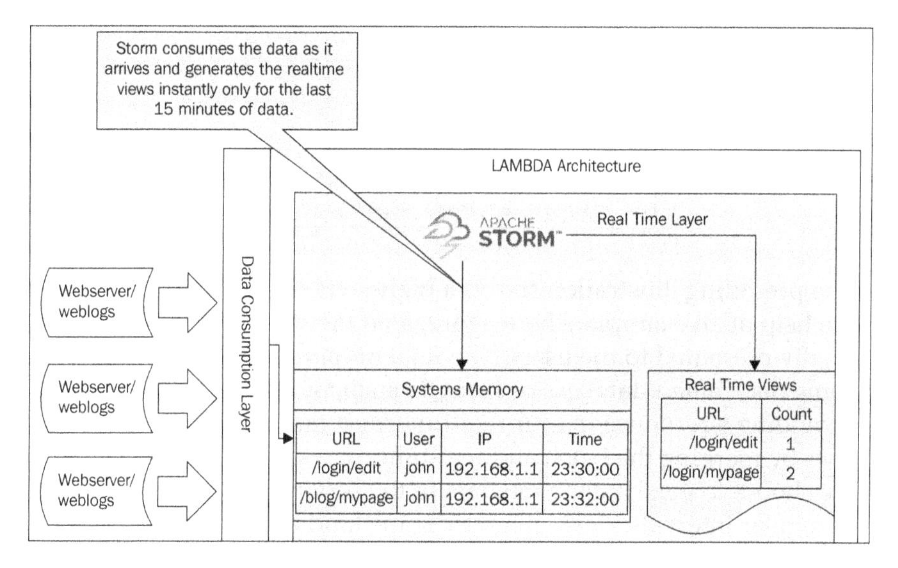

The preceding illustration shows a high-level design for real-time layers with the help of an example where weblogs are captured and URLs are aggregated to find the popularity of each webpage. The data is captured within the systems/cluster memory and views are generated instantly, but only for the data received in the last 15 minutes.

- **Serving layers**: This is the final layer in the complete Lambda Architecture. The responsibility of serving layers is to fetch and combine the data from the batch and real-time layer, and provide the combined view to the user. Extending the same example, our serving layer will combine the aggregated views of weblogs from the batch and real-time layer, persist them into a distributed database for further querying, and present them as a single view to the users.

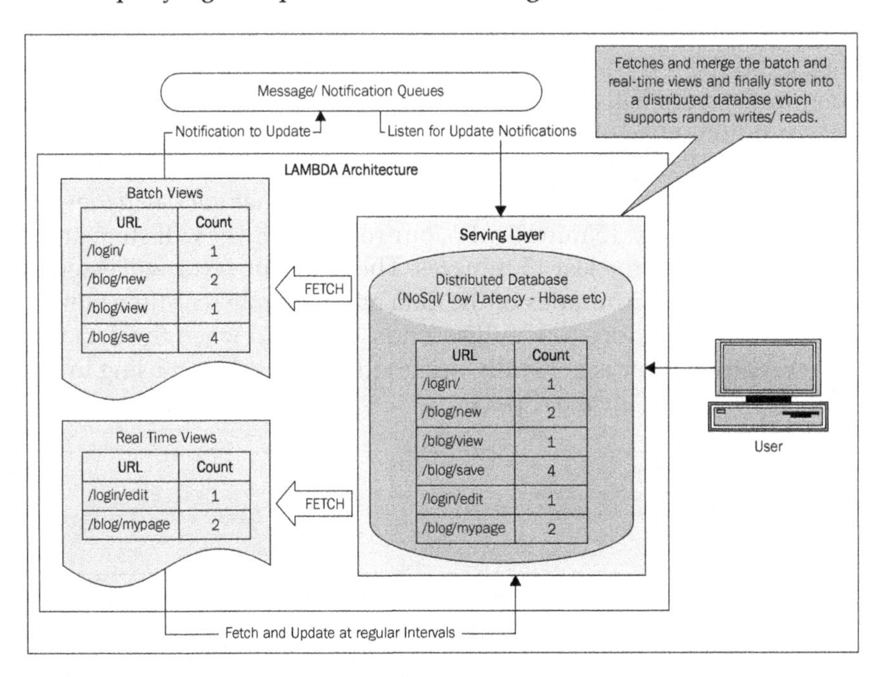

The preceding illustration shows a high-level design of serving layers with the help of an example where aggregated views are fetched, merged, and finally presented to the users. The final or merged views can be stored in some distributed database or NoSQL, such as, HBase, which is capable of providing a response in near real-time, or it may be directly presented to the user by merging the batch and real-time views on the fly. In a case where we choose to persist, then the data in the serving layer needs to be refreshed at regular intervals, or we may use some kind of notification mechanism to inform the serving layer.

The real benefit of Lambda Architecture is that it is capable of presenting some real-time data merged with historical data, and it presents it as a single view to the user. Now, the overall latency has reduced and the usability of the system has increased to a much larger extent.

In this section, we have discussed the various aspects of Lambda Architecture. We have talked about the needs of such architecture and, at the same time, we have also discussed the various layers of Lambda Architecture with appropriate examples.

Let's move forward to the next section where we will talk about the various technology options available for developing Lambda Architecture.

The technology matrix for Lambda Architecture

In this section, we will discuss various technology options available for developing the various layers of Lambda Architecture.

Lambda Architecture talks about four different layers, and each layer has its own function and purpose. Let's look at the variety of technologies available that can be leveraged for developing these layers of Lambda Architecture:

The data consumption layer is the first layer in the overall architecture. Going by the name, it seems to be the simplest layer, but, in reality, it needs to deal with a lot of complexities. Here are a few challenges that we need to keep in mind before developing or choosing any technology for the data consumption layer:

- **Highly available**: It should be highly available and it should be ensured that it works either in master, slave, or peer architecture. There should be no single point of failure that can stop the consumption of messages.
- **Fault tolerant**: It is extremely important that it is fault tolerant. Once a message is consumed, it should not be lost under any circumstances. It may leverage various methods to achieve fault tolerance, such as replication, persisting to some database, **Write Ahead Logs** (**WAL**), and more.
- **Reliability**: Once a message is consumed, the system has to be reliable in delivering the message. For example, it may choose to leverage a transactional approach for guaranteed message delivery. No matter what, the approach is followed, but it should clearly state and be consistent in its delivery semantics, which can be any of the following:
    - **At most once**: Process/deliver messages either once or do not process them at all.

    - **At least once**: Process/deliver messages once or more than once.
    - **Exactly once**: Process/deliver messages only once; not less than once and not more than once.

- **Performance-efficient**: It should be capable of handling millions of messages within a few minutes or even seconds. It will work in distributed mode and will be scalable for handling additional loads without any changes to the existing software.
- **Extendable and flexible**: The system should be flexible enough to be extendable so that new data sources can be added or the default functionality can be modified to accommodate the business needs.

Considering all the previous aspects, there are various technologies that can be leveraged for data consumption, such as Apache Flume (`https://flume.apache.org`), Apache Sqoop (`http://sqoop.apache.org/`), Logstash (`https://www.elastic.co/products/logstash`), or messaging technologies such as Apache Kafka (`http://kafka.apache.org/`) or RabbitMQ (`https://www.rabbitmq.com/`).

Batch layers are entrusted with the processing of large data. Large data is large enough not to be able to be consumed and processed by a single machine, so we need to consider technologies/frameworks that implement the paradigm of distributed computing (`https://en.wikipedia.org/wiki/Distributed_computing`). Apache Hadoop and MapReduce are the most popular batch processing frameworks and our obvious choice, but there a few more choices, such as Apache Spark, Hive, Apache Pig, and Cascading, that can be leveraged to create our batch layer. Refer to `http://tinyurl.com/z63dpv5` for a quick comparison between all the available batch processing technologies.

The speed layer or real-time layer is entrusted with consuming and processing events in near real-time , which can be in milliseconds or seconds. It is imperative for the speed layer to process and consume the data as it arrives and to do that within the system memory itself, without dumping the data to the local disks. So, we need to consider the technologies/frameworks that implement the paradigm of distributed, in-memory data processing. We talked about Storm in *Chapter 3, Processing Data with Storm*, and Spark Streaming in *Chapter 9, Analysis of Streaming Data Using Spark Streaming*, which follow the paradigm of distributed, in-memory data processing, but there are a few more choices such as Apache Samza, Apache S4, and Spring XD that can be leveraged to create our speed layer. Refer to `http://tinyurl.com/o46tfsr` for a quick comparison between all the available near real-time frameworks/ technologies.

The serving layer is entrusted with fetching, consolidating, and persisting batch and real-time views into a distributed and performance-efficient database, which is capable of handling random reads and writes at a very fast pace. There are various NoSQL databases that can be leveraged to handle random reads and writes, such as HBase and many more. Refer to `http://tinyurl.com/znlblfo` for a quick comparison between the various low-latency NoSQL databases available for persisting data merged by the serving layer.

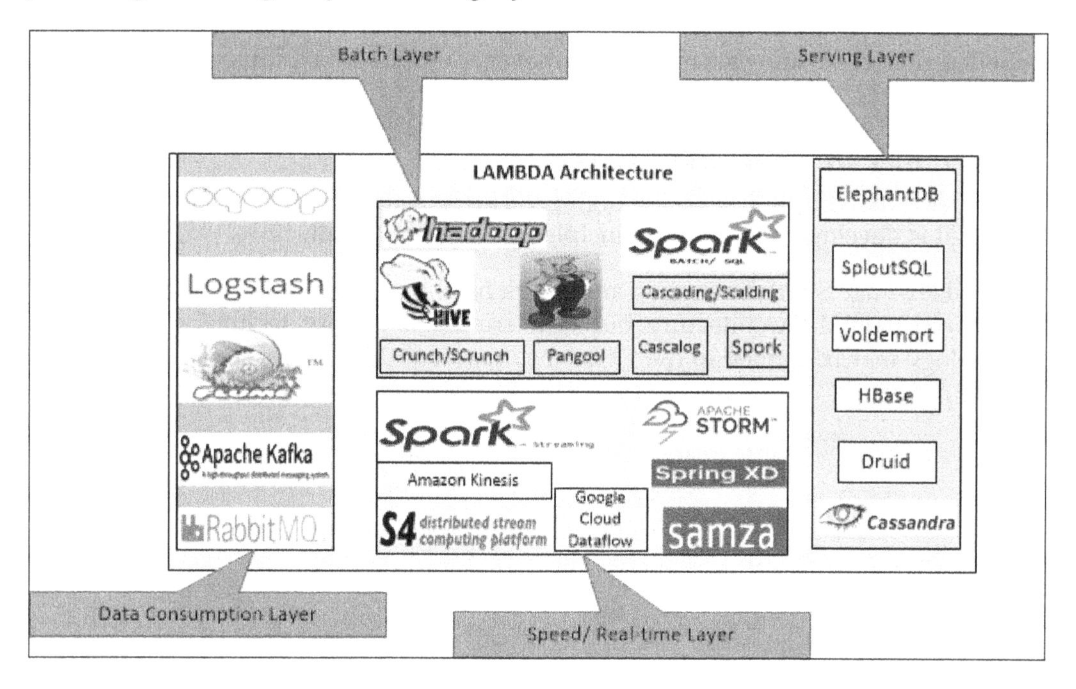

The preceding illustration shows a complete ecosystem for Lambda Architecture along with the various technology options available for each layer.

In this section, we discussed the various technology options available for developing the various layers of Lambda Architecture. Let's move forward and realize the Lambda Architecture using our Chicago crime dataset.

Realization of Lambda Architecture

In this section, we will extend our Chicago crime use case to design and code the different layers of Lambda Architecture in Spark.

Let's extend our Chicago crime dataset and assume that the Chicago crime data is delivered in near real-time. Next, our custom consumers will consume the data and will need to find out the number of crimes for each crime category. Though, in most cases, users will require the grouping of data only for the chunk of data received in near real-time, but, in a few use cases, aggregations need to be done on historical data.

Seems like a Lambda use case, doesn't it?

Let's first analyze the complete architecture with all of its components, and then we will describe, code, and execute each and every component of Lambda Architecture.

high-level architecture

In this section, we will discuss the high-level architecture of our Chicago crime use case that is developed using the principles of Lambda Architecture.

We will leverage Spark Streaming and Spark batches along with Cassandra to realize our Lambda Architecture, but users are free to use any technology as per the technology matrix defined in the *Technology matrix for Lambda Architecture* section.

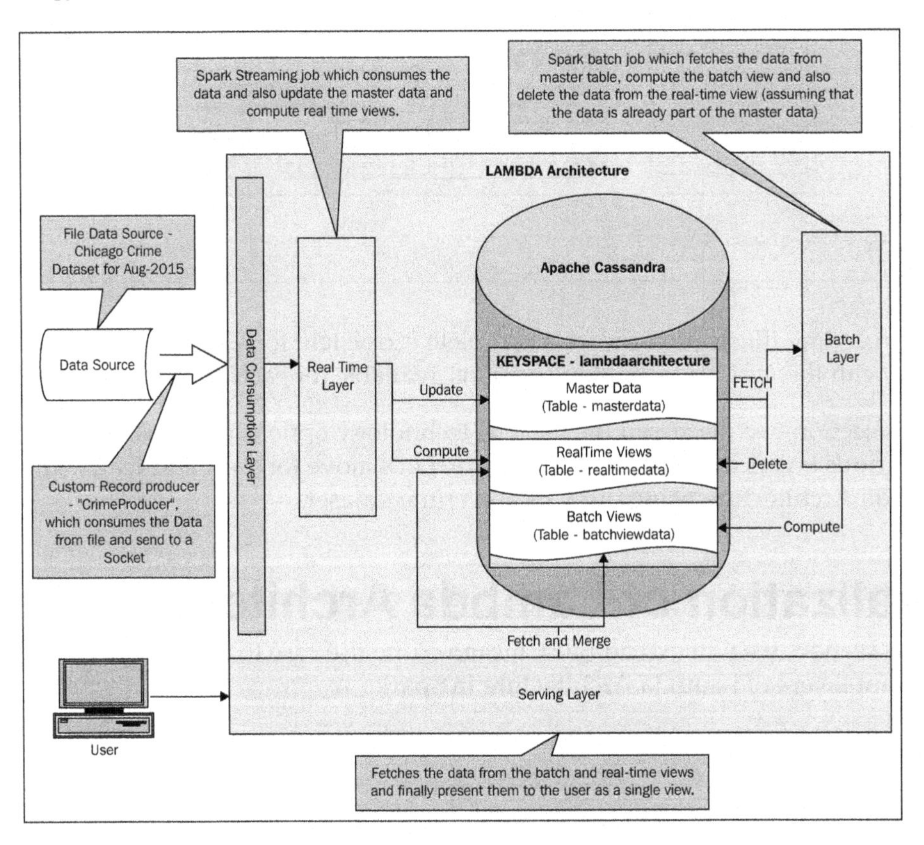

The preceding illustration shows a high-level architecture and its various components, which are used to develop the Lambda Architecture for the Chicago crime dataset.

Let's move forward and discuss the role of each of the components:

- **Data source and custom producer**: The data source is again the same Chicago crime dataset that we used in the *Creating Kinesis stream producers* section in *Chapter 5, Getting Acquainted with Kinesis*. We will place this dataset in a specific location on the file system. Our custom producer will read the few records from this file at regular intervals and will send them to a socket for further consumption.
- **Real-time layer**: The real-time layer is a Spark Streaming job, which listens to the socket opened by our custom producer and performs two functions:
    - Submits/persists the raw records into the database, which, in our case, is Cassandra with keyspace `lambdaarchitecture` and table `masterdata`.
    - Performs the grouping operation and finds the count of each distinct crime type only in the chunk of records received, and finally persists it into the database, which is, Cassandra with keyspace `lambdaarchitecture` and table `realtimedata`. This table will contain the aggregated data for each batch received by our socket streams.
- **Batch layers**: Batch layers are Spark batches that can be executed either manually or scheduled to be executed every hour, two hours, or even once a day. They basically perform the following functions:
    - They fetch the complete data from the Cassandra table `masterdata` and perform the grouping operation to find out the count of each distinct crime type.
    - Finally, they persist the same data into Cassandra with keyspace `lambdaarchitecture` and table `batchviewdata`.
    - They also truncate the data from the table `realtimedata`, assuming that the records in this table are already updated in `masterdata`.
- **Serving layers**: Finally, our serving layer is a Spark batch job that combines both the views: `batchviewdata` and `realtimedata`. It performs the grouping on the data for each distinct crime type and prints it on the console.

Now, let's move to the next section where we will code each of these components.

Configuring Apache Cassandra and Spark

Perform the following steps to configure Apache Cassandra and integrate our Spark cluster with Cassandra:

1. Download and extract Apache Cassandra 2.1.7 from `http://www.apache.org/dyn/closer.lua/cassandra/2.1.7/apache-cassandra-2.1.7-bin.tar.gz` on the same machine where we installed our Spark binaries.
2. Execute the following command on your Linux console and define the environment variable called `CASSANDRA_HOME`, which will point to the directory where we have extracted the downloaded archive file:

   ```
   export CASSANDRA_HOME = <location of the extracted Archive>
   ```

3. Next, on the same console, execute the following command to bring up your Cassandra database with the default configuration:

   ```
   $CASSANDRA_HOME/bin/cassandra
   ```

   The preceding command will bring up our Cassandra database, which is now ready to serve the user request, but, before this, let's create the keyspace and tables to store our data.

4. Open a new Linux console and execute the following command to open the **Cassandra Query Language** (CQL) console:

   ```
   $CASSANDRA_HOME/bin/cqlsh
   ```

   CQLSH is the command-line utility that provides SQL-like syntax to perform CRUD operations on Cassandra databases.

5. Next, execute the following CQL commands on your CQLSH to create the keyspace and required tables in your Cassandra database:

   ```
   CREATE KEYSPACE lambdaarchitecture WITH replication = {'class':
   'SimpleStrategy', 'replication_factor': 1 };

   CREATE TABLE lambdaarchitecture.masterdata (
     id varchar,
     casenumber varchar,
     date varchar,
     block varchar,
     iucr varchar,
     primarytype varchar,
     description varchar,
     PRIMARY KEY (id)
   ```

```
);
CREATE TABLE lambdaarchitecture.realtimedata (
  id bigint,
  primaryType varchar,
  count int,
  PRIMARY KEY (id)
  );

CREATE TABLE lambdaarchitecture.batchviewdata (
  primarytype varchar,
  count int,
  PRIMARY KEY (primarytype)
  );
```

Next, we will configure and integrate our Spark cluster to leverage the Spark-Cassandra APIs for performing CRUD operations:

1. Download Spark 1.4.0 from `http://archive.apache.org/dist/spark/spark-1.4.0/spark-1.4.0-bin-hadoop2.4.tgz`.

The Spark-Cassandra connector is still in the development stages for Spark 1.5.0, so we will use the stable versions of the driver and connector that are available for Spark 1.4.0.

2. Extract the Spark binaries and point your `$SPARK_HOME` environment variable to the folder we extracted the binaries to:

   ```
   export SPARK_HOME = <location of the Spark extracted Archive>
   ```

3. Download the following JAR files and persist them into your `$CASSANDRA_HOME/lib` directory:
   - The Spark-Cassandra connector (`http://repo1.maven.org/maven2/com/datastax/spark/spark-cassandra-connector_2.10/1.4.0/spark-cassandra-connector_2.10-1.4.0.jar`)
   - The Cassandra Core driver (`http://repo1.maven.org/maven2/com/datastax/cassandra/cassandra-driver-core/2.1.9/cassandra-driver-core-2.1.9.jar`)
   - The Spark-Cassandra Java library (`http://repo1.maven.org/maven2/com/datastax/spark/spark-cassandra-connector-java_2.10/1.4.0/spark-cassandra-connector-java_2.10-1.4.0.jar`)

- Other dependent JAR files (`http://central.maven.org/maven2/org/joda/joda-convert/1.2/joda-convert-1.2.jar`)
- Other dependent JAR files (`http://central.maven.org/maven2/joda-time/joda-time/2.3/joda-time-2.3.jar`)
- Other dependent JAR files (`http://central.maven.org/maven2/com/twitter/jsr166e/1.1.0/jsr166e-1.1.0.jar`)

4. Next, open and edit the `$SPARK_HOME/conf/spark-default.conf` file and define the following environment variables:

```
spark.driver.extraClassPath=$CASSANDRA_HOME/lib/apache-cassandra-2.1.7.jar:$CASSANDRA_HOME/lib/apache-cassandra-clientutil-2.1.7.jar:$CASSANDRA_HOME/lib/apache-cassandra-thrift-2.1.7.jar:$CASSANDRA_HOME/lib/cassandra-driver-internal-only-2.5.1.zip:$CASSANDRA_HOME/lib/thrift-server-0.3.7.jar:$CASSANDRA_HOME/lib/guava-16.0.jar:$CASSANDRA_HOME/lib/joda-convert-1.2.jar:$CASSANDRA_HOME/lib/joda-time-2.3.jar:$CASSANDRA_HOME/lib/jsr166e-1.1.0.jar:$CASSANDRA_HOME/lib/spark-cassandra-connector_2.10-1.4.0.jar;$CASSANDRA_HOME/lib/spark-cassandra-connector-java_2.10-1.4.0.jar;$CASSANDRA_HOME/lib/cassandra-driver-core-2.1.9.jar
spark.executor.extraClassPath=$CASSANDRA_HOME/lib/apache-cassandra-2.1.7.jar:$CASSANDRA_HOME/lib/apache-cassandra-clientutil-2.1.7.jar:$CASSANDRA_HOME/lib/apache-cassandra-thrift-2.1.7.jar:$CASSANDRA_HOME/lib/cassandra-driver-internal-only-2.5.1.zip:$CASSANDRA_HOME/lib/thrift-server-0.3.7.jar:$CASSANDRA_HOME/lib/guava-16.0.jar:$CASSANDRA_HOME/lib/joda-convert-1.2.jar:$CASSANDRA_HOME/lib/joda-time-2.3.jar:$CASSANDRA_HOME/lib/jsr166e-1.1.0.jar:$CASSANDRA_HOME/lib/spark-cassandra-connector_2.10-1.4.0.jar;$CASSANDRA_HOME/lib/spark-cassandra-connector-java_2.10-1.4.0.jar;$CASSANDRA_HOME/lib/cassandra-driver-core-2.1.9.jar
spark.cassandra.connection.host=localhost
```

   Replace `$CASSANDRA_HOME` with the actual location on the filesystem and save the file.

5. Next, bring down your Spark cluster and bring up the master and worker process with Spark 1.4.0 binaries.

Refer to `https://github.com/datastax/spark-cassandra-connector` for more information on the Spark-Cassandra connector.

We are done with the configuration and integration of Spark with Cassandra. Now, we will move to the next section where we will code the producer and other layers/jobs.

Coding the custom producer

Perform the following steps to code a custom producer in Java:

1. Open the `Spark-Examples` project in Eclipse, and add a new package and class called `chapter.ten.producer.CrimeProducer.java`.
2. Edit `CrimeProducer.java` and add the following piece of code in it:

```
package chapter.ten.producer;

import java.io.BufferedReader;
import java.io.FileReader;
import java.io.OutputStream;
import java.io.PrintWriter;
import java.net.ServerSocket;
import java.net.Socket;
import java.util.Random;

public class CrimeProducer {

  public static void main(String[] args) {

    if (args == null || args.length < 1) {
System.out.println("Usage - java chapter.ten.CrimeProducer
<port#>");
      System.exit(0);
    }
System.out.println("Defining new Socket on " + args[0]);
try (ServerSocket soc = new ServerSocket(Integer.
parseInt(args[0]))) {

System.out.println("Waiting for Incoming Connection on - "
          + args[0]);
    Socket clientSocket = soc.accept();
  System.out.println("Connection Received");
OutputStream outputStream = clientSocket.getOutputStream();
// Path of the file from where we need to read crime //records.
String filePath = "/home/ec2-user/softwares/crime-data/Crimes_-
Aug-2015.csv";
PrintWriter out = new PrintWriter(outputStream, true);
BufferedReader brReader = new BufferedReader(new
FileReader(filePath));
// Defining Random number to read different number of //records
each time.
```

```
        Random number = new Random();
      // Keep Reading the data in a Infinite loop and send it //over to
      the Socket.
          while (true) {
          System.out.println("Reading Crime Records");
          StringBuilder dataBuilder = new StringBuilder();
        // Getting new Random Integer between 0 and 20
        int recordsToRead = number.nextInt(20);
      System.out.println("Records to Read = " + recordsToRead);
          for (int i = 0; i < recordsToRead; i++) {
        String dataLine = brReader.readLine() + "\n";
                dataBuilder.append(dataLine);
              }
      System.out.println("Data received and now writing it to Socket");
          out.println(dataBuilder);
          out.flush();
      // Sleep for 20 Seconds before reading again
          Thread.sleep(20000);
            }
          } catch (Exception e) {
            e.printStackTrace();
          }}
      }
```

We are done with our crime producer!

Follow the comments provided in the code to understand the flow of code. The same style will be used further in the chapter.

Coding the real-time layer

Perform the following steps to code real-time layer in Scala:

1. Open the `Spark-Examples` project in Eclipse, and add a new Scala package and object to it named `chapter.ten.dataConsumption.LADataConsumptionJob.scala`.

2. `LADataConsumptionJob` will be our Spark Streaming job that will listen to the socket and consume data as it arrives. So, apart from creating `StreamingContext` and leveraging `socketTextStream` for consuming data, we will also define two functions: one for persisting/appending data in the master table (`masterdata`) in Cassandra, and another for grouping the same data to find out the count of distinct crime types and finally persisting it into the real-time view table (`realtimedata`) in Cassandra. So, as the first step, define `persistInMaster(...)` for persisting the raw data into the master table:

```
def persistInMaster(streamCtx:StreamingContext,lines:DStream[Stri
ng]){

    //Define Keyspace
    val keyspaceName ="lambdaarchitecture"
    //Define Table for persisting Master records
    val csMasterTableName="masterdata"

    lines.foreachRDD {
      x =>
      //Splitting, flattening and finally filtering to exclude any
Empty Rows
      val rawCrimeRDD = x.map(_.split("\n")).flatMap { x => x
}.filter { x => x.length()>2 }
      println("Master Data Received = "+rawCrimeRDD.collect().
length)

      //Splitting again for each Distinct value in the Row and
creating Scala SEQ
      val splitCrimeRDD = rawCrimeRDD.map { x => x.split(",")
}.map(c => createSeq(c))
      println("Now creating Sequence Persisting")
      //Finally Flattening the results and persisting in the
table.
      val crimeRDD = splitCrimeRDD.flatMap(f=>f)
      crimeRDD.saveToCassandra(keyspaceName, csMasterTableName, So
meColumns("id","casenumber","date","block","iucr", "primarytype",
"description"))
    }
  }
```

3. The preceding function accepts an RDD of strings and persists the same into the master table (`masterdata`) in Cassandra. Now, define `generateRealTimeView(...)`, which will aggregate the raw crime data (RDD of strings) and persist it into the real-time table (`realtimedata`) in Cassandra:

```
def generateRealTimeView(streamCtx:StreamingContext,lines:DStream[
String]){
      //Define Keyspace
     val keyspaceName ="lambdaarchitecture"
     //Define table to persisting process records
     val csRealTimeTableName="realtimedata"

     lines.foreachRDD {
       x =>
       //Splitting, flattening and finally filtering to exclude any
Empty Rows
       val rawCrimeRDD = x.map(_.split("\n")).flatMap { x => x
}.filter { x => x.length()>2 }
       println("Real Time Data Received = "+rawCrimeRDD.collect().
length)
       //Splitting again for each Distinct value in the Row
       val splitCrimeRDD = rawCrimeRDD.map { x => x.split(",") }
       //Converting RDD of String to Objects [Crime]
       val crimeRDD = splitCrimeRDD.map(c => Crime(c(0),
c(1),c(2),c(3),c(4),c(5),c(6)))
        val sqlCtx = getInstance(streamCtx.sparkContext)
        //Using Dynamic Mapping for creating DF
       import sqlCtx.implicits._
       //Converting RDD to DataFrame
       val dataFrame = crimeRDD.toDF()
       //Perform few operations on DataFrames
       println("Number of Rows in Data Frame = "+dataFrame.count())

// Perform Group By Operation using Raw SQL
       val rtViewFrame = dataFrame.groupBy("primarytype").count()
       //Adding a new column to DF for PK
       val finalRTViewFrame = rtViewFrame.withColumn("id", new
Column("count")+System.nanoTime)
       //Printing the records which will be persisted in Cassandra
       println("showing records which will be persisted into the
realtime view")
       finalRTViewFrame.show(10)
```

```
      //Leveraging the DF.save for persisting/ Appending the
complete DataFrame.
      finalRTViewFrame.write.format("org.apache.spark.sql.
cassandra").
      options(Map( "table" -> "realtimedata", "keyspace" ->
"lambdaarchitecture" )).
      mode(SaveMode.Append).save()
    }
  }

  //Defining Singleton SQLContext variable
  @transient private var instance: SQLContext = null
  //Lazy initialization of SQL Context
  def getInstance(sparkContext: SparkContext): SQLContext =
    synchronized {
      if (instance == null) {
        instance = new SQLContext(sparkContext)
      }
      instance
    }
```

Refer to the code bundle provided with the book for a complete implementation.

Coding the batch layer

Perform the following steps to code the batch layer in Scala:

1. Open the `Spark-Examples` project in Eclipse, and add a new Scala package and object named `chapter.ten.batch.LAGenerateBatchViewJob.scala`.
2. `LAGenerateBatchViewJob` will be our Spark batch job, which will simply get the data from the master table, group the records based on the crime type, and persist the grouped records into the master view table (`batchviewdata`) in Cassandra. Apart from defining `SparkContext` and `SparkConf` in the `main` method, we will define and invoke one more function called `generateMasterView(SparkContext)`:

```
def generateMasterView(sparkCtx:SparkContext){
    //Define Keyspace
    val keyspaceName ="lambdaarchitecture"
    //Define Master (Append Only) Table
    val csMasterTableName="masterdata"
    //Define Real Time Table
```

```
    val csRealTimeTableName="realtimedata"
    //Define Table for persisting Batch View Data
    val csBatchViewTableName = "batchviewdata"

    // Get Instance of Spark SQL
    val sqlCtx = getInstance(sparkCtx)
    //Load the data from "masterdata" Table
     val df  = sqlCtx.read.format("org.apache.spark.sql.
cassandra")
     .options(Map( "table" -> "masterdata", "keyspace" ->
"lambdaarchitecture" )).load()
     //Applying standard DataFrame function for
     //performing grouping of Crime Data by Primary Type.
     val batchView = df.groupBy("primarytype").count()
     //Persisting the grouped data into the Batch View Table
     batchView.write.format("org.apache.spark.sql.cassandra").
     options(Map( "table" -> "batchviewdata", "keyspace" ->
"lambdaarchitecture" )).mode(SaveMode.Overwrite).save()

     //Delete the Data from Real-Time Table as now it is
     //already part of grouping done in previous steps
     val csConnector = CassandraConnector.apply(sparkCtx.getConf)
     val csSession = csConnector.openSession()
     csSession.execute("TRUNCATE "+keyspaceName+"."+csRealTimeTabl
eName)
     csSession.close()
     println("Data Persisted in the Batch View Table -
lambdaarchitecture.batchviewdata")
  }


  //Defining Singleton SQLContext variable
  @transient private var instance: SQLContext = null
  //Lazy initialization of SQL Context
  def getInstance(sparkContext: SparkContext): SQLContext =
    synchronized {
      if (instance == null) {
        instance = new SQLContext(sparkContext)
      }
      instance
    }
```

Refer to the code bundle provided with the book for a complete implementation.

Coding the serving layer

Perform the following steps to code the serving layer in Scala:

1. Open the `Spark-Examples` project in Eclipse, and add a new Scala package and object called `chapter.ten.serving.LAServingJob.scala`.
2. `LAServingJob` again is a batch job, which gets the data from both the Cassandra tables, `batchviewdata` and `realtimedata`, and groups them to present final records to the consumer. Apart from defining `SparkContext` and `SparkConf` in the `main` method, we will define and invoke one more function called `generatefinalView(SparkContext)`:

```
def generatefinalView(sparkCtx:SparkContext){
    //Define Keyspace
    val keyspaceName ="lambdaarchitecture"
    //Define Master (Append Only) Table
    val csRealTimeTableName="realtimedata"
    //Define Table for persisting Batch View Data
    val csBatchViewTableName = "batchviewdata"

    // Get Instance of Spark SQL
    val sqlCtx = getInstance(sparkCtx)
    //Load the data from "batchviewdata" Table
    val batchDf  = sqlCtx.read.format("org.apache.spark.sql.
cassandra")
     .options(Map( "table" -> "batchviewdata", "keyspace" ->
"lambdaarchitecture" )).load()

    //Load the data from "realtimedata" Table
    val realtimeDF  = sqlCtx.read.format("org.apache.spark.sql.
cassandra")
     .options(Map( "table" -> "realtimedata", "keyspace" ->
"lambdaarchitecture" )).load()

//Select only Primary Type and Count from Real Time View
     val seRealtimeDF = realtimeDF.select("primarytype", "count")

     //Merge/ Union both ("batchviewdata" and "realtimedata") and
     //produce/ print the final Output on Console
     println("Final View after merging Batch and Real-Time Views")
     val finalView = batchDf.unionAll(seRealtimeDF).
groupBy("primarytype").sum("count")
     finalView.show(20)
  }
```

We are done with all the layers of our Lambda Architecture! Now, let's move to the next section, where we will execute all the layers one by one and see the results.

[Ensure that you provide the required dependencies for Cassandra and the Spark-Cassandra driver to your Eclipse project for compilation.]

Executing all the layers

Let's perform the following steps and bring up all our services:

1. As a first step, export your `Spark-Examples` project as `spark-examples.jar` and save it in a directory. Refer to this directory as `<LA-HOME>`.
2. Next, bring up your crime producer. Open a new Linux console and execute the following command from `<LA-HOME>`:

   ```
   java -classpath spark-examples.jar  chapter.ten.producer.
   CrimeProducer 9047
   ```

3. Next, we will bring up our real-time job so that the master table is populated, and, at the same time, real-time views are also populated. So, open a new console, browse to `<LA-HOME>`, and execute the following command to bring up your real-time job:

   ```
   $SPARK_HOME/bin/spark-submit --class chapter.ten.dataConsumption.
   LADataConsumptionJob --master spark://ip-10-149-132-99:7077 spark-
   examples.jar 9047
   ```

4. As soon as we execute the preceding command, our two Cassandra tables—`masterdata` and `realtimedata`—will be populated. Now, in order to browse the data, we can open a new Linux console and execute the following commands:

   ```
   $CASSANDRA_HOME/bin/cqlsh
   Select * from lambdaarchitecture.masterdata;
   ```

The output is shown in the following screenshot:

```
cqlsh> Select * from lambdaarchitecture.masterdata;

 id       | block                  | casenumber  | date                   | description                         | iucr | primarytype
----------+------------------------+-------------+------------------------+-------------------------------------+------+---------------------
 10217827 |   067XX S EAST END AVE |    HY404420 | 08/30/2015 11:00:00 PM |                              SIMPLE | 0560 |             ASSAULT
 10218590 |   011XX W RANDOLPH ST  |    HY405013 | 08/30/2015 11:30:00 PM |                     PURSE-SNATCHING | 0880 |               THEFT
 10217156 |      001XX W 104TH PL  |    HY403966 | 08/30/2015 11:27:00 PM |                              SIMPLE | 0560 |             ASSAULT
 10217140 |   052XX W CHICAGO AVE  |    HY403976 | 08/30/2015 11:45:00 PM |             STRONGARM - NO WEAPON   | 0320 |             ROBBERY
 10217196 |      004XX W 100TH ST  |    HY403969 | 08/30/2015 11:22:00 PM |                              SIMPLE | 0560 |             ASSAULT
 10217128 |     009XX N MOZART ST  |    HY403951 | 08/30/2015 11:17:00 PM |       VIOLATE ORDER OF PROTECTION   | 4387 |       OTHER OFFENSE
 10217121 |     071XX S DAMEN AVE  |    HY403983 | 08/30/2015 11:45:00 PM |   POSS: CANNABIS MORE THAN 30GMS    | 1812 |           NARCOTICS
 10217119 |      122XX S GREEN ST  |    HY403967 | 08/30/2015 11:28:00 PM |             AGGRAVATED: HANDGUN     | 051A |             ASSAULT
 10217169 |      074XX N CLARK ST  |    HY404009 | 08/30/2015 11:13:00 PM |   POSS: CANNABIS MORE THAN 30GMS    | 1812 |           NARCOTICS
 10217095 |       040XX W 26TH ST  |    HY403960 | 08/30/2015 11:20:00 PM |                        RETAIL THEFT | 0860 |               THEFT
 10218454 |     090XX S MORGAN ST  |    HY404717 | 08/30/2015 11:00:00 PM |                         TO PROPERTY | 1310 |     CRIMINAL DAMAGE
 10218505 | 078XX S CONSTANCE AVE  |    HY404795 | 08/31/2015 12:00:00 AM |                         TO PROPERTY | 1310 |     CRIMINAL DAMAGE
 10217186 |   014XX N SEDGWICK ST  |    HY403964 | 08/30/2015 11:33:00 PM |          DOMESTIC BATTERY SIMPLE    | 0486 |             BATTERY
 10218392 | 044XX S MARSHFIELD AVE |    HY404654 | 08/30/2015 11:00:00 PM |          DOMESTIC BATTERY SIMPLE    | 0486 |             BATTERY
 10217252 |  083XX S MARYLAND AVE  |    HY403984 | 08/31/2015 12:00:00 AM |             AGGRAVATED: HANDGUN     | 041A |             BATTERY
 10217120 |       064XX W 60TH ST  |    HY403952 | 08/30/2015 11:12:00 PM |                        TO RESIDENCE | 1365 |   CRIMINAL TRESPASS
 10217101 | 048XX N MILWAUKEE AVE  |    HY403965 | 08/30/2015 11:30:00 PM |                             TO LAND | 1330 |   CRIMINAL TRESPASS
 10217159 | 055XX W FULLERTON AVE  |    HY403979 | 08/30/2015 11:28:00 PM |         FALSE/STOLEN/ALTERED TRP    | 502P |       OTHER OFFENSE
 10217276 | 093XX S LAFAYETTE AVE  |    HY403985 | 08/31/2015 12:00:00 AM |                 ARMED: HANDGUN      | 031A |             ROBBERY
 10217162 |    044XX W ALTGELD ST  |    HY403990 | 08/30/2015 11:42:00 PM |        UNLAWFUL POSS OF HANDGUN     | 143A |   WEAPONS VIOLATION
 10217259 |    049XX W MADISON ST  |    HY403961 | 08/30/2015 11:23:00 PM |   ARMED: OTHER DANGEROUS WEAPON     | 0313 |             ROBBERY
 10217212 |   060XX S ASHLAND AVE  |    HY404049 | 08/30/2015 11:52:00 PM |    POSS: CANNABIS 30GMS OR LESS     | 1811 |           NARCOTICS
 10217969 |      005XX N PINE AVE  |    HY404453 | 08/30/2015 11:00:00 PM |                              SIMPLE | 0460 |             BATTERY
 10217189 |    051XX W ADDISON ST  |    HY404004 | 08/31/2015 12:00:00 AM |                          TO VEHICLE | 1320 |     CRIMINAL DAMAGE
 10217596 |  058XX W AUGUSTA BLVD  |    HY404273 | 08/30/2015 11:30:00 PM |                          AUTOMOBILE | 0910 | MOTOR VEHICLE THEFT
 10217200 | 033XX W CONGRESS PKWY  |    HY404033 | 08/30/2015 11:35:00 PM |             AGGRAVATED: HANDGUN     | 0261 | CRIM SEXUAL ASSAULT
 10217198 |     029XX W NORTH AVE  |    HY403991 | 08/30/2015 11:30:00 PM |                              SIMPLE | 0560 |             ASSAULT
 10217125 |     007XX W WILSON DR  |    HY403958 | 08/30/2015 11:21:00 PM |                              SIMPLE | 0460 |             BATTERY
 10219005 |    038XX S WABASH AVE  |    HY405560 | 08/30/2015 11:00:00 PM |                     $500 AND UNDER  | 0820 |               THEFT
 10217117 |   062XX S LANGLEY AVE  |    HY403963 | 08/30/2015 11:15:00 PM |                         TO PROPERTY | 1310 |     CRIMINAL DAMAGE
 10217277 |   082XX S HALSTED ST   |    HY404002 | 08/30/2015 11:41:00 PM | AGGRAVATED:KNIFE/CUTTING INSTR      | 0420 |             BATTERY
 10217133 |    052XX S KEDZIE AVE  |    HY403981 | 08/30/2015 11:35:00 PM |                 ARMED: HANDGUN      | 031A |             ROBBERY
       ID |                  Block | Case Number |                   Date |                         Description | IUCR |        Primary Type
 10218642 |    014XX W OLIVE AVE   |    HY405268 | 08/31/2015 12:00:00 AM |                          TO VEHICLE | 1360 |   CRIMINAL TRESPASS
 10217148 |  028XX W ROOSEVELT RD  |    HY403954 | 08/30/2015 11:10:00 PM |                              SIMPLE | 0460 |             BATTERY

(35 rows)
```

The preceding screenshot shows the output of the master table in Cassandra. We can also execute `Select * from lambdaarchitecture.realtimedata;` on the same CQLSH window to see the data in the real-time table.

5. The next step will be to bring up our batch layer and execute our batch job—`LAGenerateBatchViewJob`. Our batch job is a manual job, which can be scheduled to be executed at regular intervals, but, for the sake of simplicity, we can execute the following command on a new Linux console:

```
$SPARK_HOME/bin/spark-submit --class chapter.ten.batch.
LAGenerateBatchViewJob --master spark://ip-10-149-132-99:7077
spark-examples.jar
```

As soon as we execute the preceding command, our `batchviewdata` table in Cassandra will be populated with the latest data. We can execute `Select * from lambdaarchitecture.batchviewdata;` on our CQLSH window to browse the data:

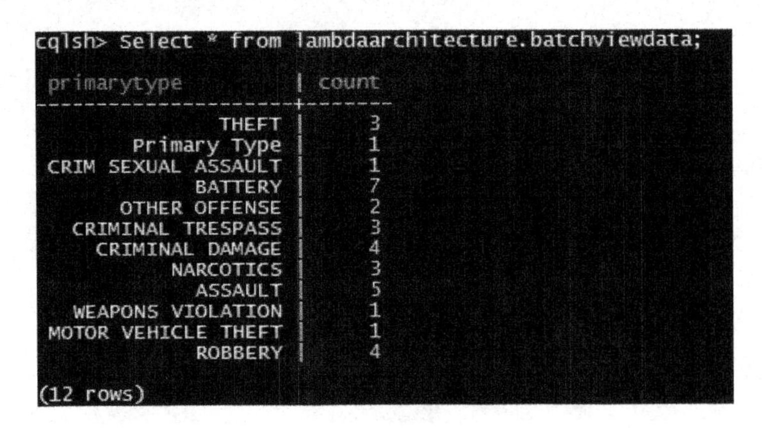

The preceding illustration shows the aggregated crime data in the `batchviewdata` table.

6. The final step is to bring up our serving layer, called `LAServingJob`, which is again executed on user request. This job will merge the batch and real-time views and present a single output. We can open a new Linux console and execute the following command:

   ```
   $SPARK_HOME/bin/spark-submit --class chapter.ten.serving.
   LAServingJob --master spark://ip-10-149-132-99:7077 spark-
   examples.jar
   ```

   As soon as we execute the preceding command, it will produce and print the merged views of data residing in `batchviewdata` and `realtimedata`, which will be similar to the following screenshot:

```
sumit@localhost-inst-1 $ $SPARK_HOME/bin/spark-submit --class chapter.twelve.serving.LAServingJob --master spark://ip-10-149-132-99:7077 spark-examples.jar
Creating Spark Configuration
Retreiving Spark Context from Spark Conf
15/12/28 10:28:04 WARN NativeCodeLoader: Unable to load native-hadoop library for your platform... using builtin-java classes where applicable
Final view after merging Batch and Real-Time views
+-------------------+----------+
|        primarytype|SUM(count)|
+-------------------+----------+
|      OTHER OFFENSE|         2|
|  WEAPONS VIOLATION|         1|
|            BATTERY|         7|
|            ROBBERY|         4|
|MOTOR VEHICLE THEFT|         1|
|    CRIMINAL DAMAGE|         4|
|       Primary Type|         1|
|CRIM SEXUAL ASSAULT|         1|
|            ASSAULT|         5|
|          NARCOTICS|         3|
|  CRIMINAL TRESPASS|         3|
|              THEFT|         3|
+-------------------+----------+
```

We are done with all the layers of our Lambda Architecture!

We have just touched the tip of the iceberg where we have discussed the overall concept and objective of Lambda Architecture. Architectures developed on the principles of Lambda can be much more complex and thought provoking, which is interesting to discuss and solve, but that will not be in the scope or context of this book or chapter.

In this section, we have realized the Lambda Architecture using Spark and Cassandra. We have developed all the layers of Lambda Architecture using Spark Streaming and Spark batches, and also leveraged and integrated Apache Cassandra with Spark for persisting the data.

Do write back or e-mail me at `sumit1001@gmail.com` with any queries or use cases regarding Lambda Architecture, and I will work with you to solve or implement your queries or use cases.

Summary

In this chapter, we have discussed the various aspects of Lambda Architecture. We have discussed the roles performed by the various layers/components of Lambda Architecture. We have also leveraged Spark and Cassandra, and designed, developed, and executed all the layers of Lambda Architecture.

Index

A

B

C

Q

R

S

T

U

W

Y

Z

Thank you for buying

Real-Time Big Data Analytics

About Packt Publishing

Packt, pronounced 'packed', published its first book, *Mastering phpMyAdmin for Effective MySQL Management*, in April 2004, and subsequently continued to specialize in publishing highly focused books on specific technologies and solutions.

Our books and publications share the experiences of your fellow IT professionals in adapting and customizing today's systems, applications, and frameworks. Our solution-based books give you the knowledge and power to customize the software and technologies you're using to get the job done. Packt books are more specific and less general than the IT books you have seen in the past. Our unique business model allows us to bring you more focused information, giving you more of what you need to know, and less of what you don't.

Packt is a modern yet unique publishing company that focuses on producing quality, cutting-edge books for communities of developers, administrators, and newbies alike. For more information, please visit our website at `www.packtpub.com`.

About Packt Open Source

In 2010, Packt launched two new brands, Packt Open Source and Packt Enterprise, in order to continue its focus on specialization. This book is part of the Packt Open Source brand, home to books published on software built around open source licenses, and offering information to anybody from advanced developers to budding web designers. The Open Source brand also runs Packt's Open Source Royalty Scheme, by which Packt gives a royalty to each open source project about whose software a book is sold.

Writing for Packt

We welcome all inquiries from people who are interested in authoring. Book proposals should be sent to `author@packtpub.com`. If your book idea is still at an early stage and you would like to discuss it first before writing a formal book proposal, then please contact us; one of our commissioning editors will get in touch with you.

We're not just looking for published authors; if you have strong technical skills but no writing experience, our experienced editors can help you develop a writing career, or simply get some additional reward for your expertise.

Building Web Applications with Python and Neo4j

ISBN: 978-1-78398-398-8 Paperback: 184 pages

Develop exciting real-world Python-based web applications with Neo4j using frameworks such as Flask, Py2neo, and Django

1. Develop a set of common applications and solutions with Neo4j and Python.
2. Secure and deploy the Neo4j database in production.
3. A step-by-step guide on implementing and deploying interactive Python-based web applications on graph data model.

Learning Real-time Processing with Spark Streaming

ISBN: 978-1-78398-766-5 Paperback: 202 pages

Building scalable and fault-tolerant streaming applications made easy with Spark Streaming

1. Process live data streams more efficiently with better fault recovery using Spark Streaming.
2. Implement and deploy real-time log file analysis.
3. Learn about integration with Advance Spark Libraries - GraphX, Spark SQL, and MLib.

Please check **www.PacktPub.com** for information on our titles

Lightning Source UK Ltd.
Milton Keynes UK
UKOW07f1040221217
314734UK00005BA/603/P

9 781784 391409